Brilliant
DEDUCTION

Brilliant
DEDUCTION

The Story of Real-Life
Great Detectives

MATT KUHNS

LYON
■HALL■

Lyon Hall Press
Lakewood, Ohio

Published in the United States by Lyon Hall Press, Lakewood, Ohio

www.brilliantdeduction.info

Every reasonable effort has been made to respect the owners of material reproduced in this book, but if any rights have been overlooked, the author and publisher welcome notification of the error.

Library of Congress Control Number: 2012919747

ISBN-13: 978-0-9882505-1-2

Printed on acid-free paper

Designed and typeset by Modern Alchemy LLC

For my first, best, and
favorite English teacher—thank you for
everything Mom.

CONTENTS

CONTENTS

HERCULE POIROT
AND
H.H. HOLMES

THE DISCOVERY of a counterfeit $100 James Monroe silver certificate, in 1897, presented a genuine mystery. The U.S. Treasury had printed the notes, featuring the fifth president's likeness, for 19 years with only one slight modification to the design, in 1891. In that time they had never encountered anything as dismaying or confounding as the bill that appeared in Philadelphia in the autumn of 1897. The reproduction was absolutely perfect. No one would have suspected the bill at all if not for the red seal that had been smeared by a chance drop of moisture. Even then, Treasury staff who investigated suspected that only the seal was a fake, added to an otherwise genuine note; though no one could guess at a means or motive for such an act, it seemed more plausible than an entirely flawless counterfeit. Until, that is, someone soaked the entire bill and peeled it apart to expose a two-ply laminated sheet. At that point, the unpleasant fact was no longer possible to deny. Someone was counterfeiting U.S. currency with unimaginable perfection.

But who? And even more puzzling, how? Within the known limits of the day's printing technology, the fake Monroe note was inexplicable. A technique called photo etching could produce an engraved metal printing plate that perfectly duplicated the image of a real Treasury bill. But photo etching only worked with relatively soft metals, which would wear down far too quickly for a practical counterfeiting operation. The technology for photo etching on something like steel, by contrast, simply didn't exist. The resulting paradox was a mysterious crime of uncommon quality. If the standard for mysteries is the classic "whodunit," and "where have they gone" comprises a simpler version, "how can this be explained at all" represents the detective's greatest challenge. The Monroe note mystery, incorporating all three questions, was tailor made for a real-life great detective to step forward and prove himself.

One operative of the Treasury's Secret Service was more than ready to volunteer. Thirty-six-year-old William J. Burns, in his eighth year as a Secret Service agent, had already proven himself an unusually able investigator in other counterfeiting cases. Yet his proposed answer seemed nearly as unbelievable as the Monroe note mystery itself. Burns declared that someone, somewhere, must have secretly discovered a method for photoengraved steel. The Secret Service, in Operative Burns's view, needed to immediately begin not only investigations in Philadelphia but also a nationwide project of identifying every engraver whose background and ability might permit such a breakthrough. It was a tall order, but the threat posed by this suspected innovation seemed to demand boldness in both thought and action.

Eventually the Secret Service agreed, though only after months of delay, and a new chief to replace the skeptical William Hazen, who had ordered Burns to pursue other, less imaginative angles. With the full backing of Hazen's replacement, however, Burns got his chance. The labyrinthine investigation that followed ultimately revealed puzzles within puzzles. Solving them all required a degree of observation, inventiveness and initiative worthy of the liveliest detective fiction. When the entire story with its locked rooms, red herrings and dramatic discoveries was finally complete, Edward Marshall of *The New York Times* noted without irony that it "Sounds like Sherlock Holmes's work."

Burns delighted in recognition, and judging from some of his later enterprises, he may well have noted Marshall's comparison and thought he liked the sound of it. Which is both a curious and, perhaps, telling reaction, given the subsequent history of detectives and celebrity. The Monroe note mystery was by no means the last time William Burns made headlines. Through his even more spectacular subsequent exploits, he became very likely the most famous detective who ever lived. Yet he is almost completely forgotten today, along with nearly all of the men who achieved similar heights in his profession.

History is full of such figures, of course. Entertainers, athletes, explorers, eccentrics; for every celebrity remembered by later generations there are vastly more who were household names once, but barely even constitute trivia today. The transient fame of the great detectives, however, stands in remarkable contrast to the enduring public fascination with their fictional counterparts. The once famous sleuths of real life have not vanished from history's record entirely, but they have undeniably faded into obscurity. The *Oxford Dictionary of National Biography* features far more detective novelists than actual detectives, despite Britain's nurturing of more than one specimen of note. Of the several thousand profiles in the bio network's online archive precisely one describes a famous detective, and even he is lumped under "Police Officer" for an occupational category. Detectives have fared slightly better in printed media, where most of the field's luminaries have inspired at least one biography; in a few cases a handful. All the same, the name of Burns, or Pollaky, or Vidocq will draw little more than a blank look from the great majority of people who could, by contrast, name detectives of fiction with ease.

The real detectives can boast no public monuments or statues, while the best known of their imaginary auxiliary is the model for at least four. And not only does the latter group account for vastly more space at a typical library— where works of mystery fiction number enough to merit their own separate section almost invariably—more than one of its number has even challenged his historic counterparts with a full-length biography as well.

Meanwhile in the most popular of all modern media, film and television, decade after decade of audiences have shown dependable enthusiasm for made-up cops and private eyes and, significantly, for real criminals and crimes. The long memory of certain infamous crimes and the individuals who committed them, when known, offers a further pointed contrast with general amnesia toward eminent detectives. Films or documentaries about historic crimes provide most of the rare occasions when a great detective can enjoy once more the attention of a general audience—yet their very nature as great detectives remains obscured by the fact that crimes and criminals are invariably the featured attraction. A century later, interest remains far higher in both Holmes the fictional crime solver *and* Holmes the real-life criminal, with almost as many works about the notorious Chicago World's Fair murderer as all of history's greatest detectives combined.

This waning of detection's once celebrated names, even as those of detective fiction and real-world crime still flourish, is itself something of an interesting mystery worth examining more closely. This book is an attempt at just such an inquiry, an attempt to recall the names and lives of those figures who once upon a time were every bit as familiar as the invented characters who have succeeded them. A quote from one of the most prominent among those characters summarizes the grounds for the inquiry, as well as the interest it might offer readers. In Agatha Christie's 1928 novel, *The Mystery of the Blue Train*, the author's hero delivers this exceptionally confident introduction: "'My name is Hercule Poirot,' he said quietly, 'and I am probably the greatest detective in the world.'" Devotees of the most famous of all detectives, fictional or otherwise, might take some small offense at this declaration. But Poirot's boast also invites a second, arguably more legitimate question that has nothing to do with the boundaries of literary universes.

Who are, or were, the indisputably valid, real person candidates for "the greatest detective in the world?"

The question seems obvious once considered, even if the answers are not. Any profession must have its select few who stand out from the ranks. Detectives should be no different, even if most of those elite are now little known. If nothing else, the name of Allan Pinkerton likely prompts some dim recognition from many people even if his life and achievements are a blank. One name suggests the possibility of others, and that the history of detection could include a few more individuals worth remembering, as well. *Brilliant Deduction* represents a humble, but hopefully rewarding attempt to discover some of them. It is certainly not exhaustive, even to the extent that any finite selection may ever be, even in theory. The detectives featured herein are not an especially diverse lot demographically, though neither was the field of detection in general, for much of its history.

It's worth noting, too, that the notion of a "great detective" offers diverse potential interpretations, and perhaps some of these are left unrepresented as well. Every detective considered in these pages was a smart, capable investigator, but their selection over others who might claim equal or even greater skill is largely a product of fame. This, largely, is simply necessity. The very nature of detection is inherently bound up with discretion, at least within the private detective's sphere. Some detectives found ways to achieve celebrity, both in government and in private practice, but it is more than plausible that a few of the most talented among their peers accomplished equal feats but left little or no record. Their number, inevitably, must remain obscure.

William Burns and other once renowned detectives offer quite enough marvels of deductive reasoning, and even variety, within the limitations noted above. From a Napoleonic-era French polymath, to lawmen of the American West, to a small-town detective who nearly rewrote the history of one of the 20th century's most notorious crimes, the great detectives varied widely in manners and method. They varied in their approach to the fame that accompanied greatness, with some actively seeking it, others shunning it, and more than one ultimately destroyed by it. The differing types of fame they met and ways in which they responded are worth examining, as well. The result should entertain, and perhaps offer a little insight into the mystery of why real-life great detectives dazzled society for more than a century and then vanished, leaving scarcely a trace.

CHAPTER ONE
VIDOCQ

"Observation is the first rule of investigation."

I T WILL GIVE OFFICER LEES rank with Vidocq and Macé," the *Marin County Journal* boasted in 1880. Isaiah Lees, a San Francisco detective, had solved a mysterious disappearance that had stymied the local sheriff, and in lauding his accomplishment this was the highest praise the writer could offer. The comment itself is an interesting artifact of the field's history. Within less than a decade, *A Study in Scarlet* would establish Sherlock Holmes as the ultimate company for detectives to seek. But with that convention still in the future, the northern California *Journal* was proposing its man as a peer of two real-life detectives instead.

Both were French. Gustave Macé was director of the French Sûreté in that year, so he would have been in the news for his roles in one or two high profile cases. But why was the other man, a predecessor of Macé who had departed life in 1857, still named as a standard for other detectives a generation later and a quarter of the way around the world? And why has the name of Vidocq since been so completely forgotten outside of his native France?

An explanation of the second question may reveal itself, eventually, through examination of Vidocq and his varied successors. The most direct answer to the first question is, simply, that Vidocq was first.

*

Again and again, in nearly every serious examination of detective history, Vidocq's name turns up first. Jurgen Thorwald's *The Century of the Detective*. Angus Hall's *The Crime Busters*. Katherine Ramsland's *History of Forensic Science and Criminal Investigation*. Even biographies of the field's other luminaries often acknowledge Vidocq, at least briefly. Such consistency implies a good reason, and much of it may be found in the 1825 episode of a Monsieur Matthieu.

The Parisian Matthieu was *un millionaire*. One of his countrymen had invented the very term, a century earlier, and despite economic and political upheaval its essential meaning still held: he was a very rich man, indeed. When police found the wealthy gentleman dead in the grand house he had called home, they had no difficulty establishing a robbery as the likeliest explanation. In addition to Matthieu's well-known wealth, the crime scene suggested a violent struggle; though old, the late Matthieu had been a strong man, and many pieces of his furniture were smashed and broken. Unfortunately, an explanation of robbery offered no help in coming up with suspects. Tracing stolen objects offered little promise, either. As Matthieu had lived by himself in a house stuffed with curiosities and bric-a-brac, it was difficult even to establish what items were missing.

The police's ally and rival Vidocq, founder of the dozen-year-old metropolitan detective department, took all of this in at a glance. Vidocq also took note of blood stains on the door latches and study floor, as well as the staircase. He insisted the stains be preserved, which, though a curious order at the time, now seems an obvious enough action. Vidocq's next moves, however, were just the sort that made him both a legend in his time and a challenge to the credulity of later generations. The relatively respectable detective exchanged his own identity for that of a Monsieur Jules, war veteran, burglar and general purpose thug, who was quite familiar among the outlaws of Paris despite the fact that "Jules" did not exist except as a creation of Vidocq. In this disguise, Vidocq then began trawling the dens and hangouts of Jules's tribe, i.e. criminal society.

After hours of searching grimy bars and cafés, he found a man matching exactly what the crime scene had suggested to his detective's mind: a strong man, keeping disreputable company and, most importantly, very recently injured in a bloody brawl. Vidocq then casually picked a fight with this man, Richard, and applied his own considerable strength to pummeling him, until finally the owner of the bar summoned the gendarmes. Just as officers arrived to pull them apart, Vidocq reached into his pocket for a clean cloth he had brought and dabbed at a bloody wound that the fight had reopened above the astonished Richard's eye.

Throughout his career, Vidocq studied and experimented with new methods for combating crime, whether organizational, procedural or technical. He had no formal advanced education or scientific training, but Vidocq still kept abreast of discoveries that might prove useful. By 1825, he knew how experiments had shown that an individual person's dried blood, if exposed to certain chemicals, predictably turned different colors: crimson, pink, etc. So he obtained the appropriate materials and conducted tests on the cloth with Richard's blood and on the blood stains leading away from M. Matthieu's study. The results were identical.

This was crude evidence, and at the same time too sophisticated; such testing would not be admissible in a court room for many years. But what a detective can prove is never as important as what he can convince a suspect that he can prove, and Vidocq was as effective in applying this principle as anyone in history. His suspect in the case at hand, Richard, had been taken to jail following the barroom brawl. (The police had to release Vidocq, though many of them longed to throw him in a cell, too.) Vidocq confronted Richard with the blood test results and his reasoning in the case. In combination with the seeming wizardry performed on Richard's blood, Vidocq's confidence and reputation were enough to demolish the thief's hopes of bluffing it out. Richard confessed. The press soon celebrated another coup for Vidocq, and blood analysis in detection, which in lesser hands might have fizzled and set back the cause of innovation, instead got an early start which encouraged further research.

Innovation is hardly unique to Vidocq. The champions of many great detectives of the 19th century always claim some "first" for their subject. Some innovations are claimed more than once; the photographic "rogues' gallery" is probably the most widely assigned first of them all. Ironically, Vidocq is one of the very few pioneers of detection who has absolutely no claim to the rogues' gallery (the dry plate photography that made it practical arrived only in the last few years of his life). It's a modest enough concession to subsequent colleagues, as the list of methods and systems of detection owed to Vidocq is still remarkable.

Vidocq was the first modern detective in nearly every major sense. He was the first full-time specialist detective. He organized the first public force of such detectives, and the first private detective agency. Arguably, as the author or inspiration of volume after volume of adventure stories, he was even the first fictional detective. Vidocq did not remain alone in the field, but he had a good lead on everyone who followed him and might well have missed more of them entirely, but for his own longevity. Scotland Yard introduced detectives 30 years after Vidocq's Sûreté, while Allan Pinkerton's very first accidental, amateur detective work began the same year Vidocq closed his own private detective agency to retire.

In fact Vidocq, though celebrated in his own time, may present an even more remarkable figure today than his contemporaries could have appreciated. Vidocq's many, mostly successful, experiments were novel and interesting to the public in the 1820s. But nearly a century would pass before anyone could examine those clever tricks in the context of established scientific detection. In many ways the epitome of the brilliant lone reasoner since relegated to fictional detective work, Vidocq was at the same time conducting early trials in methodical, scientific approaches: forensic chemistry, ballistics, handwriting analysis, criminology theory. Yet no one could have guessed this at the time.

Even Vidocq himself probably could not imagine the full extent of the extraordinary changes to police work of which he was at the forefront. But until he was nearly 35 years old, Vidocq probably never even imagined that he would make a living from police work, to say nothing of his name and fortune. The career of "detective" did not even exist until he created it. In light of which it seems entirely natural that, like many great detectives who followed, Vidocq arrived at his life's calling only after some unlikely detours along the way.

*

Eugène Vidocq's eccentric path through life began in humble and ordinary circumstances in the northern French town of Arras. Ordinary, that is, unless one counts the likely embellished accounts setting his nativity against the backdrop of a raging storm, and in the same house where Robespierre was born 17 years before. Or approximately 17 years before. Between exaggeration for dramatic effect by Vidocq and his admirers, exaggeration for less flattering purposes by his detractors, and two centuries of sometimes casually researched histories, the specifics of Vidocq's life are often contested, literally from his first day to his last. It may be that the deliberate man of mystery, who employed a range of disguises and assumed identities even before his career as a detective, would have liked it this way.

In any event, Vidocq was probably born on July 23, 1775, in Arras, where his father baked bread. As a child, little Eugène soon displayed the same energy, curiosity, and aptitude for trouble that would last him his entire life. During the modest formal education offered him, Vidocq was a gifted student and demonstrated great promise. Yet he was one of those children who would never be satisfied being at the front of the pack when his abilities permitted him to dash out far ahead of the pack and explore. Stories that Vidocq was a troublemaker or even something of a bully are certainly plausible. Nearly anything is plausible with Vidocq, except fitting in and conforming to others' expectations. Fortunately for the ambitious baker's son, he was born to a society that was to present him with far greater opportunities than anyone might have expected.

As a young man, Vidocq seriously considered emigrating to America on at least one occasion. Instead, he did not even venture beyond France's borders until much later in life, and the possibilities of an American Vidocq must be left to the imagination. But in one sense the young New World republic did provide opportunity to Vidocq. The American colonists' revolution (and more importantly the enormous debt resulting from the French government's costly role in it) led directly to the first in a series of revolutions and restorations that would regularly convulse France throughout Vidocq's long life. For a man like Vidocq, bored by a structured and predictable existence, it was just the place to be.

And as the *ancien régime* began to give way to experimentation and a dangerous but exciting new France, Vidocq began his own trials of life beyond schoolwork and bread ovens. The results were no doubt much more appealing to a mischievous boy's tastes. Even allowing for some embellishment, the adventures of the adolescent and young adult Vidocq could serve as the very definition of "picaresque." At one point Vidocq ran off with a traveling theatre company. From them he learned the arts of acting and costume, which he would practice long after his brief stage career officially ended. The pugnacious youth also graduated from fist fights to fencing and pistols; he learned the former well enough to kill a fencing master in a duel fought over a shared romantic interest.

Though only 15 years old, Vidocq faced prison for that mischance. Instead he was sentenced to army service, as the new republican France found its troubles compounded by war with much of Europe and wanted every able man available in uniform. Records of the period show Vidocq's army career marked by acts of skill and valor, but frequent indiscipline as well. Even in a war of revolution, the army was no more a place for Vidocq than the classroom. Vidocq remained with the army anyway, for a few years; when brawling or insubordination, e.g., led to imprisonment, he escaped only to re-enlist elsewhere under an assumed identity. At one point he married, but walked away when it didn't work as hoped. In 1795, he managed to leave his regiment with permission, for once, then set himself up in Brussels as a gambler named Rousseau and decided to extend his presence at the card tables beyond his allotted leave. As he had also taken the liberty of promoting himself to the rank of captain, he was faced with a lengthy prison sentence once again upon being arrested for desertion.

Following his inevitable escape, Vidocq did not re-enlist as he had before. Precisely what he did occupy himself with the next few years, other than evading the law, is open to question. Whatever it was, leaving a clear trail was very likely the last thing he wanted. Vidocq's life in his early twenties seems to have involved these events or something like them: He regularly eluded or escaped police custody, including two escapes from the inescapable Brest prison "the galleys." He may have adopted the identity of a sailor and spent a year as a "privateer," or simply a pirate. He also, certainly, became closer and more familiar with the criminal underworld back on land, where his record as an escape artist gave him status.

Along with whatever other lawbreaking Vidocq took a hand in, himself, he also committed forgery, and this charge would prove more difficult to slough off. He alleged the best of excuses, forging a pardon during a prison stint for a poor man whose only crime, in turn, was stealing grain to feed his family. The story seems suspiciously exculpatory, as well as maudlin. Yet it is not entirely implausible. In his later actions and words, Vidocq demonstrated a strong personal sense of justice. When the goal was merely his personal liberty, moreover, he had never found it necessary to employ forgery before.

One way or the other, Vidocq arrived in Lyons around 1799, where the fugitive criminal would first turn criminal catcher. Either voluntarily, or following yet another arrest, in Lyons Vidocq met with fate in the form of an unusually open-minded police commisaire, Jean-Pierre Dubois. Examining the young vagabond's record, Dubois decided that Vidocq had not actually committed any serious crimes and could serve society far more usefully than by filling a prison cell. Dubois elected instead to "turn" Vidocq, in the language of spies, and employ him as an informer on the underworld in which he had achieved status and familiarity. A busy and effective period of undercover work followed. Vidocq was not yet a detective, but he was on his way.

That way remained winding and indirect. After several months, Vidocq the police spy was unmade by his own success: in order to secure an important conviction he had to appear personally in court, and subsequently Lyons became too hot for informing, even with Vidocq's facility with disguise. Dubois did his best for his compromised agent. He provided Vidocq with papers identifying him as an itinerant peddler, and thus with some security against being arrested simply for vagrancy. But Dubois could do nothing to efface the forgery charge. So Vidocq returned to an uncertain life, traveling the underworld of criminals and other outcasts evading the notice of authority.

Vidocq's travels brought him to Paris, eventually—perhaps inevitably, for at the turn of the 19th century the Parisian underworld was nearly as large and as shadowy as any has ever been. Compared with the City of Light that greets modern tourists, even the nicer parts of Paris were often dark and dangerous, 200 years ago. In very real ways the French capital in which a fugitive Vidocq at last found redemption was still a medieval city. Alistair Horne declares in *Seven Ages of Paris* that as Napoleon was rising to power, "Paris now smelt more of filthy mud and sewage than she had at the worst moments of the Middle Ages," and was more poorly lit than in the time of Louis XIV. At night the darkness was broken only by flickering candles or lamps, or, given the constant unrest in the city, torches. Years of fires, mobs, unruly soldiers and unstable government had done the great city no favors. Streets were mud, buildings vandalized and defaced, inflation spiraling. Despite all this, Paris continued to expand with new arrivals, though like Vidocq many were at the far fringes of what remained of law abiding, respectable society. In this was both a peril and an opportunity, and Vidocq was about to seize it firmly.

By 1809, Vidocq was settled into a modestly prosperous and comfortable niche. He kept a small shop selling dry goods, and had a home with a woman named Annette, which they shared with his widowed mother. It was, in many ways, improbably like the life back home in Arras that he had turned away from 20 years before. Just like life in Arras, it was not for Vidocq, but it was about to change again.

And just like any significant event in Vidocq's life, there are multiple versions to choose among, any or all of which may be true in part or in whole. All the different stories imply that Vidocq was still keeping up some measure of association with the criminal underworld. The dramatic version involves Vidocq discovering, through those connections, the name behind a jewelry heist committed against the Empress Josephine, upon which Vidocq gallantly recovered the Empress's necklace and brought the thief to justice, winning Napoleon's personal commendation and assignment to continued efforts against crime. A more likely explanation for Vidocq's second try at police work is that he was under direct or implied threat of blackmail by other denizens of the underworld who knew his history. (Or, perhaps, he was simply bored and tired of a life structured around avoiding attention, so wholly contrary to his nature.) He had endured the confinement of a fugitive's life for years and must have longed to dispense with it for good. With that in mind, Vidocq probably brought himself to the attention of authorities before someone else could do so, and offered to resume the informing efforts that had impressed the authorities in Lyons.

The result: Vidocq sent back behind prison walls. Vidocq remained in prison this time, probably longer than all of his previous stays combined. He spent the greater part of two years among Paris's convicts, but not because he had lost his touch or found La Forre prison to be even more secure than the dreaded "galleys." Instead he chose to remain there. Vidocq's second effort at informing started within the prison system, which, like much of America's prison system today, was itself an active part of criminal networks.

Vidocq had found an interested audience for his offer of assistance, once again. The Parisian authorities' existing resources and methods were simply overwhelmed by a burgeoning population and disrupted social order. With so many able young men pressed into Napoleon's huge conscript armies, and the remaining police resources stretched even further by demands to contain antigovernment activity, offers of subverting the criminal ranks from within could not be easily dismissed. And so the divisional chief, "Papa" Henry, sent Vidocq to prison, and Vidocq (perhaps giving weight to the suggestion that other volunteer informants were threatening to return him there anyway) went along with the plan.

Eventually Vidocq was re-assigned back "outside" to spy on Paris's *demi-monde*, a long prison spell having burnished his relevant credentials, except as an escape artist. Henry and the police were still struggling and continued to find their undercover agent's reports a welcome assistance. But Vidocq had been through all this already, once before. Though he had so far avoided the fate of his earlier employment in Lyons, the career of an informer was always vulnerable. Perhaps it was with this in mind that he began lobbying for larger (and more durable) roles on a regular basis.

The freelance police spy had no shortage of ideas to offer. Central to all of them was a citywide, "at large" police force, which would elevate his informing work from a sideline to a dedicated independent organization, commensurate with surveillance of the entire underworld membership. The need was plainly there. Traditional police forces were still too small, and too Balkanized, while the criminal underworld was an expansive and fluid society whose members were as yet unchecked by any sort of effective system of identification or records. Vidocq himself had exploited these deficiencies as a fugitive, and now believed he was the best man to solve them. If the old ways were inadequate, it seemed obvious that the problems of policing called for new ways, and a new kind of policeman.

One episode from 1810, shortly after Vidocq left La Forre prison and began operating out on the streets, indicates how his thinking was already working along the lines of a detective's. Checking in on a sometimes thief named Hotot whom he had befriended, Vidocq made a mental note of the man's very wet clothes and muddy boots. As heavy rains had soaked Paris earlier that day, Vidocq thought it worth investigating what business had drawn Hotot outdoors in such bad weather. Learning of a burglary at a count's house in the midst of a remodeling, Vidocq visited the scene along with some of the gendarmes. There, in the garden mud, he found the clear prints of hobnailed boots, which could have been those of Hotot.

In later years, perhaps with this case in mind, Vidocq made plaster casts a standard item in the detective's toolkit. Lacking convenient access to that option in this instance, he improvised instead. Persuading a couple of the gendarmes to keep watch over the boot prints, he paid another call on Hotot's billet to share a few bottles of strong wine. After drinking Hotot under the table, Vidocq helped himself to the man's boots and returned to the crime scene for a direct comparison with the garden prints. Hotot shortly found himself under arrest, and, confronted with the evidence Vidocq had outlined for the police, he confessed to the burglary and gave up the loot. They were early days, still, but Vidocq clearly had ideas to transform the old approaches to policing on his mind.

He had to be patient with them; even under an ambitious emperor actively transforming all of French society, police authorities remained slow and reactive by nature. But they were open-minded, or simply desperate, enough to continue giving Vidocq chances, and he continued making the most of them. Vidocq gradually managed to recruit other agents and employ them under his own supervision, training them in the rules and techniques for observation that he had developed through long experience. Within a few years of his first approach to "Papa" Henry, Vidocq had nearly all of the pieces for a new kind of city-wide specialist police, except formal recognition.

The methods employed by Vidocq in his informing work, and later in establishing the first detective police force, were at their core simple and even obvious. Most of Vidocq's theories about how to combat crime proceeded from *observation*; his truly important contributions to policing and detection were to be found not so much in theory, but in practice. As Vidocq phrased it, "the detective who won convictions saw and listened, then utilized anything he learned that was out of the ordinary and aroused his suspicions." From this common sense beginning follow certain basic challenges: being in a position to see and listen, and knowing what to look and listen for. To address both of these problems, Vidocq firmly believed that it was essential to employ the kind of person who could mingle with criminals and understand their ways naturally. In other words, those who were themselves criminals, or at least former criminals. This was Vidocq's own background, after all, and it succeeded for him. He never believed that any true outsider to the underworld could be as effective as someone with a criminal record, and he considered the latter a basic qualification when selecting his agents. The authorities never entirely accepted this part of Vidocq's system, unsurprisingly. One Vidocq was acceptable but a whole such squad seemed too risky, even with Vidocq's shrewd judgment of character, and simply inappropriate as well. But Vidocq was insistent on the old aphorism: to catch a thief, set a thief.

His approach to infiltrating criminal enterprises had a further important dimension, however: disguise. Given Vidocq's enthusiasm for assumed identities and even the larger habit of personal reinvention throughout his life, this tactic may have been as much a product of his own nature as a solution arrived at through need. Still, his ready use of disguise fed into, and on, his emphasis on observation. A disguise aided the act of observation, of course. And, though Vidocq would have learned some of his technique from his brief sojourn with the players' company, as a youth, he noted that the real key to making an adopted identity convincing was, itself, observation: watching how different types of people move, noting their clothing and gestures, listening to their way of speech, until one could reproduce these small details convincingly.

Vidocq's effectiveness in disguising his identity was, all the same, one technique he could never really teach to another, which only helped make it a lasting part of his personal legend. By nature, he was hardly a naturally anonymous figure. Of modest height, around five feet six inches, he was broad and solid as a stone wall, with massive shoulders and a large, leonine head. Yet he could create an array of distinct, convincing identities from this template because his approach to disguise was holistic, rather than dependent on costume: a roughneck sailor; a scarred, sullen gypsy; on occasion even a (very sturdy) old peasant woman. One famous legend had Vidocq so well established in an assumed identity that he was approached for his help in carrying out an ambush—on Vidocq.

As has been noted, Vidocq's own mastery of shifting identities made him acutely aware of the problem represented by his criminal quarries' adroitness at the same game. Before photography, fingerprinting, or coordinated national law enforcement, the small scale but habitual criminal needed no great skill with disguise to thwart identification; regular movement and adoption of false names were often enough. Vidocq attacked this problem, too, first and foremost from the principle of observation. Gifted with a prodigious memory, Vidocq kept mental "profiles" of a large network of thieves, vagabonds, con artists, etc., which he was constantly expanding through his undercover roles. He also continued visiting the prisons after his stay in La Forre, to study the faces of inmates so reoffenders might be recognized even under an assumed name.

But Vidocq also worked to develop systems that were not dependent on one man or extraordinary powers of recall. A written, searchable record of the information in his own head was the first step. Names, ages, aliases; physical characteristics and sometimes drawings; even histories and habits, for Vidocq believed that career criminals often gave themselves away just through their methods and routines. Compared with modern, networked digital resources, mere drawers of indexed file cards seem practically Neolithic. But guided by

Vidocq's insistence on accuracy and detail, his files quickly became a resource trusted and envied by the established police, even those who distrusted Vidocq himself.

These varied ideas finally won a measure of official imprimatur, along with an office to house the file card database, and a staff to make use of it. By late 1812, the ministry of police was ready to overrule the protests of local commissaires and approve Vidocq's plans for a formal, city-wide plain clothes police force. The Brigade de la Sûreté was officially established by the government of Napoleon Bonaparte, just returning from his catastrophic invasion of Russia; fortunately the Sûreté would prove a much more sound initiative.

Setting up offices on Petite rue Sainte-Anne near the main police headquarters, Vidocq's Brigade began modestly, as little more than formalization of the network of agents he was already managing by that point. The first eight employees were, per Vidocq's policy, all men with criminal records. But the Brigade's numbers soon began to grow, and the additions included a few men transferred from the uniformed police, as well as clerks to manage the expanding file system.

Even with these resources, Vidocq remained personally active in tackling crimes that came under the Brigade's purview. Like his Emperor, in this regard, Vidocq was determined to manage affairs from the top and play a direct role on the front lines as well. With actual authority rather than an off-the-books, officially deniable auxiliary role, he was at last ready to commence his own career; he was no longer a mere informer, but something entirely new: a detective. He must have relished each opportunity to compete directly with the older uniformed force and show off the effectiveness of his Brigade, his methods, and himself. He certainly loved to promote his successes, particularly in cases where the regular police had been at a loss.

One such case was that of a "notorious" thief, named Fossard. His larceny had reached such a scale as to project above the fog of anonymity that Vidocq was just beginning to dispel. Police knew who Fossard was and even what he looked like, and wanted him badly, but had nonetheless failed to find him. Vidocq took up Fossard's trail, in not one, but two of his trademark disguises;

exactly the sort of unprofessional theatrics that made critics roll their eyes and frown. Vidocq's methods, however, had the merit of producing results. Thus, one should hesitate at least before dismissing as outlandish Vidocq's decision to dress up as an old "eccentric" (perhaps part of the role was not exactly acting) with pigtail, three-cornered hat, and cane. Or his insistence on wandering the streets in this outfit for a time, simply to establish the role. For, once Vidocq had done so to his satisfaction, he began making roundabout inquiries after Fossard, which quickly led to information the police had sought for months.

Visiting a seamstress, Vidocq claimed to be a forsaken husband seeking his runaway wife. Then, in case it helped, he gave a description of the companion who had led her astray. Regarding this curious, pitiful old figure, the seamstress freely confirmed that she had seen such a man; when her visitor broke into tears the seamstress even shared an address the man had left. Drying his eyes and thanking her profusely, the old fellow shuffled away, not breaking character until much later. Perhaps it was excessive, but Vidocq had the address of Fossard's house all the same.

Exchanging his wardrobe, Vidocq then adopted the role of a humble coal man in order to observe the house without drawing attention. In this guise he was able to see Fossard return home. Once convinced that the wanted thief was not going back out again, Vidocq arranged a squad of gendarmes to join him in raiding the upstairs apartment after nightfall. Catching Fossard with his pants down—literally if the story is unembellished—Vidocq succeeded in bringing in both a much wanted man and a small treasure in cash and stolen jewels.

Dramatic episodes like the capture of Fossard made for fine stories, then as now. But even as Vidocq's promotion allowed him more opportunities for personal accomplishment than had his subordinate role as an informer, it placed more responsibility on him as well. Vidocq was directing his own department and was expected to produce more than amusing tales of his exploits. The Brigade de la Sûreté was approved and funded, against the doubts and objections of many in the established police forces, to make a real difference in a citywide crime problem. And the doubters were more than ready to belittle anything less than a complete triumph.

Eugène François Vidocq, engraving by Marie-Gabriel Coignet
Public domain; retrieved from Wikimedia Commons.

The doubters were to be disappointed. The Brigade de la Sûreté was not an overnight success. But its modest early achievements, led by Vidocq's tireless personal efforts, kept it going long enough for this new type of police force to prove its value. In 1817, Vidocq and the dozen agents by then in his employ arrested more than 800 thieves, swindlers and murderers. Faced with this relentless assault, the enemy in this war on crime soon appeared to be not only losing, but losing the will to fight. For *The Vidocq Dossier*, Samuel Edwards examined the records of the period and concluded that "by 1820, eight years after the founding of the Brigade de la Sûreté, the crime rate of Paris had been reduced by an astonishing 40 percent, and the Sûreté was responsible for most of the credit."

This type of success brought a variety of rewards, not the least of which was continued employment as governments rose and fell. In 1813, Vidocq's achievements were already enough for Napoleon to recognize him with a letter of commendation, medal, and cash bonus, as well as an expansion of the Brigade's authority to a national scale, with branch offices soon following in Brest, Toulon, Lyons and, perhaps a particularly proud moment for Vidocq, his home town of Arras. Within a year, however, Napoleon's victorious foes had exiled him to Elba. Suddenly, the former emperor's glowing support was no longer such an enviable asset.

But Vidocq could point to his record as evidence of earning his position with the Sûreté through merit, rather than through imperial patronage of a crony whom the new government could replace with no consequence. He did exactly that, without much care for modesty; according to Edwards "the returning Bourbons were greeted by a flood of pamphlets enumerating the triumphs of the Sûreté National." The new government was apparently satisfied with Vidocq just as the old government had been, and further reward followed. In May 1817, Vidocq received an official pardon for the forgery committed years before, thanks to his continued successes and some lobbying by his growing circle of friends

Vidocq handled relations with France's politicians and power brokers nearly as deftly as his work at the opposite end of the social continuum, on the whole, despite lacking the traditional background, and perhaps even the typical motivations, of a courtier. Vidocq had many interests but personal involvement in political intrigues was simply not among them. He had found work that was interesting and meaningful to him and that satisfied his taste for adventure and drama, and his main interest in governments was that as his employer they allowed him to keep doing his job. Vidocq was not entirely detached from the nobility and other men of affairs. As his reputation grew, some of them turned to him for discreet help with awkward problems, such as extricating them from a potential scandal they had foolishly gotten into. In solving such matters, usually trivial to him, Vidocq made friends who helped secure his pardon and keep him in office as government succeeded government. By earning the respect of France's elite while leaving politics to them, Vidocq remained on the job through Napoleon, Louis XVIII, Charles X, and Louis Philippe, a relatively rare accomplishment that even the master political survivor Talleyrand might have regarded with approval.

By the middle of the 1820s Vidocq's force, with branch offices extending its activity across much of France, had expanded to 120. The uniformed police chafed at this upstart and grumbled that the former criminals of the Sûreté were still working both sides of the law, their chief included. A few of his hires did betray Vidocq's trust, over the years. But far more often he proved an effective judge of men, both as a detective and as an employer.

The 1820s were a high point of Vidocq's detective career, when he solved most of the cases that would be studied and celebrated in subsequent accounts of his work. In addition to his experiment with blood evidence in 1825, he also won admirers in the 1823 Sénart Forest Affair. Learning of a planned stage-coach robbery, Vidocq turned the expected ambush inside-out. The coach set off packed with police, who then captured a very surprised band of highwaymen. In his biography of the detective, Philip John Stead remarks that the scene "became famous in the print-shops, the great coach drawn up, the police firing, sabers flashing too, and Vidocq amid the throng at the coach door in his caped overcoat." Vidocq's 1821 search for another team of roadway brigands, who had robbed a butcher named Fontaine and only left the man alive through carelessness, was another classic. The case featured a cryptic fragment of writing, Vidocq calling on his extensive knowledge of criminal affairs to spin a web around his suspects, and a reappearance of Vidocq's alter ego Jules. The story ended with the sort of flourish Vidocq savored; one of the suspects, despairing of hope that he could deceive the seemingly omniscient detective, confessed to an entirely unrelated murder before his interrogator explained that Fontaine's murder was the crime under discussion. (The chagrined outlaw then gave up his role in that, as well.)

The untangling of the murder of the Comtesse d'Arcy was perhaps the most impressive detective work of Vidocq's 1820s triumphs, or else a close second to the case of M. Matthieu. When the young Isabelle d'Arcy was found in bed, killed by a bullet to the forehead, police immediately arrested her much older husband. Though he vigorously protested his innocence, they kept the Comte in jail, yet they could find no real proof to proceed with charges against him. Finding themselves at a stalemate, police reluctantly turned the case over to Vidocq's Sûreté.

Vidocq had little use for the police's theory. He believed the Comte's character made him an unrealistic murder suspect and considered the Comtesse's Italian lover, a man named Deloro, a more promising lead. Beneath his showmanship, however, Vidocq was generally very methodical in pursuing a case. So he started his investigation with the official prime suspect. Police had seized a set of dueling pistols, the Comte's only known firearms, and Vidocq examined these. Neither showed any sign of recent firing, though, as he noted in his report, the killer might have cleaned the murder weapon after use. Therefore Vidocq pursued this lead even further. In fact, he pursued it beyond the strict boundaries of the law by quietly recruiting a physician friend to dig the bullet out of the late Comtesse's skull. Autopsies remained officially taboo in France—even decades after the Revolution—but Vidocq was by no means the last detective to bend the rules. In this case he found the risk justified. Though somewhat deformed by impact, the bullet was clearly too large for the barrels of the Comte's pistols.

Satisfied of the prime suspect's innocence, the Sûreté chief then turned his mind to Deloro. By this point, Vidocq had officially employed a number of women for a few years. The practice provided material for a number of salacious rumors, unsurprisingly. His first move in the investigation of Deloro did nothing to dispel these. He hired an actress—a profession still considered disreputable, just by itself, at the time—to "get close to" Deloro. Tall, slim and redheaded, Vidocq's agent was much the same type as the Italian's late mistress and, within days, was set up in the same role.

Unfortunately for Deloro, when next he went out his new friend promptly opened his apartment to her employer. He proceeded with a thorough search of the lodgings despite having no warrant—this was another detail of the law that Vidocq sometimes overlooked. He therefore concluded this unofficial search with all possible dispatch upon discovering a large pistol and a concealed stash of jewelry. Racing to the jail, he showed the jewelry to the Comte, who identified the pieces as gifts to his wife. Then it was back to his office, where Vidocq found the pistol from Deloro's apartment a much better match for the fatal bullet.

Vidocq, more sure of his case than ever, was still on very shaky ground when it came to proving that case. Deloro was no poorly educated brigand, and at least one piece of more legitimate evidence would be reassuring before Vidocq tried to frighten his suspect into confessing. From one source or another, Vidocq had discovered that Deloro had been fencing jewelry for some time, and indeed had no other visible source of income. Enter Jean-Louis, another of Vidocq's long running alter egos, in this case an old Breton and sometime fence. Visiting another member of that essential underworld trade, who was well known for purchasing unconventionally obtained jewelry, Jean-Louis claimed to be seeking Deloro to collect on money he had borrowed. The other fence allowed that Signor Deloro had been in a few days earlier and sold a diamond ring. Obviously, no questions had been asked, but selling jewelry to a known receiver of stolen goods was hardly a badge of innocence.

With this last piece of information, Vidocq discarded his disguise and returned to the apartment to confront his suspect. Deloro, probably not a particularly brave man, quickly crumbled like so many others when barraged by this confident detective who seemed to know everything. Yes, Deloro confessed, he did it. He murdered the Comtesse and stole her jewelry to keep himself in funds.

Charged with the murder, Deloro was eventually convicted and sent to the guillotine. The Comte d'Arcy, promptly released following Deloro's confession, became another well-placed proponent of Vidocq and the Sûreté. And ballistics science, from rough beginnings like these, gradually received more attention from science and law enforcement following its role in one of Vidocq's celebrated adventures.

As the Sûreté approached its 15th birthday, its larger record of achievements, as well as Vidocq's personal accomplishments and his gift for public relations, had won many friends and admirers. But two significant exceptions remained unappreciative of the poacher-turned-gamekeeper's work. The first, naturally enough, was the criminal society whose trade Vidocq had done so much to disrupt. The second, in an unlikely concord, was the traditional police forces. And, as Edwards notes in *The Vidocq Dossier*, the latter's resentment was not so much in spite of Vidocq's effective campaigns as it was *because of* them:

> His success, however, caused problems that would haunt him throughout his career. He had triumphed where the uniformed police of the Prefecture had failed, and they were jealous of him. Their hatred grew as he expanded his activities and they never forgave him for accomplishing what they could not do.

So when Vidocq abruptly resigned on June 20, 1827, no one believed it was an entirely voluntary act. Particularly in view of its closely following the arrival of a new chief at the Police Prefecture, who had assailed the Sûreté with criticism and interference constantly since taking office. To the extent that Vidocq's resignation was, in some sense, by choice, it was almost certainly a choice made in response to the new administration's hostility.

Not quite 52 years old, Vidocq's somewhat early "retirement" failed to slow him down in any appreciable way. Even while busily building up and directing the Sûreté as well as personally pursuing cases himself, Vidocq had maintained a full life outside of police work. Especially when it came to romantic life. Just as he kept up with the activities of seemingly every thug, thief and con man in Paris, Vidocq also seemed to maintain a comprehensive mental directory of every attractive single woman in the city. His biographers make no pretense of denying that Vidocq was intimately acquainted with a great many of those women, too, despite spending most of his adult life married.

Vidocq's first, abandoned marriage was eventually ended officially with a divorce. Annette, for a number of years his mistress and occasionally a partner in clandestine surveillance, disappeared too from his life at some point. In 1820 Vidocq wed for a second time, to Jeanne-Victoire Guerin. Sadly, his young bride became sick with rheumatic fever just two years into their marriage and died aged 24. Just one month later, his mother followed his wife in death, and friends urged Vidocq to rest, but he rebuffed their advice. Insisting that "the underworld never rests, so I cannot afford a holiday," Vidocq dealt with his grief by plunging into work instead. After a few years, however, he married once more, and for Vidocq the third try proved to be the charm. Around age 50, Vidocq returned to Arras and married his young cousin Fleuride Maniez. Vidocq was never entirely faithful, but he and Fleuride seemed to have a genuine bond. Vidocq did change his habits, too, at least in some ways, becoming more of an administrator around this time and reducing the front line role played in his best known adventures as a detective.

He collected many of those adventures, after his resignation from the Sûreté, into his influential *Memoirs*. The exact relationship between Vidocq and the *Memoirs* is uncertain. Most modern authorities believe its tales to be significantly fictionalized and probably in part written by one of Vidocq's friends among the literati, possibly Honoré de Balzac. One account suggests that Vidocq himself "utterly repudiated" the book, afterward, as a fabrication. Whether themselves fictional or not, though, the *Memoirs* of Vidocq enormously influenced the subsequent genre of detective fiction. They were the beginning of years of popular novels, stories and plays about or inspired by Vidocq. They were a considerable influence on the work of later authors including Edgar Allan Poe and Arthur Conan Doyle, also, whose works in turn laid the foundation of the detective story in English language literature.

Meanwhile, even as Vidocq purchased and settled into an estate in Saint-Mandé with his new bride, his mind was never far from real-world crime, either. He had always considered a proactive approach to crime at least as important as effective detection, going so far as to declare that "a repressive police that is never preventive is a monstrosity." Now he had time to devote more energies to preventive tactics, and, as with detection, he saw much promise in technological innovation. Vidocq, or perhaps specialists working at his direction, experimented with ways to create a more secure lock, as well as secure paper and ink to deter fraud; patent royalties for the latter eventually produced significant income for the one-time forger. Having struggled for years to free himself of that forgery charge, Vidocq also retained much sympathy for the ex-convict who faced harsh discrimination if he or she aspired to go straight. To provide some job opportunities for ex-cons, Vidocq spent some of his retirement and a great deal of money trying to start a box factory, although in the end he had to write off the venture as a loss.

Throughout the years following Vidocq's departure from the Sûreté, he also remained in contact with many of the underworld sources he had cultivated, and passed occasional information along to the authorities. Vidocq still had friends at the Sûreté, and probably even one or two in the uniformed police. In any event, his tips were not turned away. Law enforcement had found itself hard pressed to make up for the absence of Vidocq, and as the latest revolution stirred up social unrest once more in 1830, authorities found increasingly frequent uses for the semi-retired detective. After the office of police prefect changed hands again, the new man, Gigquet, made Vidocq's return to work official. Vidocq returned to his old job directing the Brigade de la Sûreté, with the additional status of a deputy prefect.

Yet for various reasons Vidocq did not last as the Orléans government's troubleshooter; he would have a second act as a detective, but it did not play out at the Sûreté. He retired from the department he had founded a second and final time, November 15, 1833. Rumors suggested a return to crime by one or more of the ex-convicts Vidocq employed as having played a part, and Prefect Gigquet did ordain a clean record policy for the Sûreté and all police agencies the same year. Vidocq, by contrast, never wavered in his insistence on the value of firsthand knowledge of crime, believing that without it a detective force was neutered. His second retirement was nonetheless much more his own choice, per most accounts, and relatively amicable on both sides. Samuel Edwards suggests that Vidocq may have been less motivated by a disagreement with his employer and, instead, more motivated by opportunities elsewhere. The always ambitious Vidocq could see tremendous possibilities in rapidly industrializing France's growing prosperity, and craved greater participation than his demanding government job would allow. So Vidocq, who had built the prototype public detective force, now established another pattern followed by many of his successors: parlaying a successful government career into a more lucrative private practice.

Vidocq had never considered his modest government salary as sufficient for a comfortable living. His taste in clothing, constant entertaining of society friends and lady acquaintances, as well as his estate in Saint-Mandé were all beyond what his official income from the Sûreté could possibly afford. His critics always insisted that here was plain evidence the old criminal had never really changed his ways. They charged that Vidocq was billing many wealthy citizens for "protection" from thieves, blackmailers, et al., most of whom were in turn on Vidocq's payroll, officially or otherwise. Vidocq forever denied this, and no one ever offered proof to the contrary. On the other hand, the detective did, as noted, assist many well-off and well-connected clients, and remarked that he felt it inconsiderate to refuse non-cash gestures of thanks. In the absence of specifics, the difference between these versions of events, if any, most likely depends on the observer's perspective on Vidocq's character in general.

Vidocq did acknowledge, late in life, another of his critics' speculations regarding his income. He did, apparently, conduct a small money lending business for many years. France's Catholicism-influenced culture still had a very negative view of "usury," though Vidocq was by no means alone in finding that official strictures differed from practical market demand. So he conducted his lending trade quietly, and in general very fairly, although a client who reneged on a debt even though able to repay it might, sadly, have found his home suddenly the target of burglars. Rumors also accused Vidocq of a busy trade in arranging substitutes for those desiring to avoid serving in the often warring nation's conscript armies; this, too, is certainly plausible. It should be remembered, however, that Vidocq also had entirely above board and very successful sidelines to explain his finances. The royalties from his secure-paper and -ink patents, for example, and his best selling *Memoirs*.

One way or another, at all events, Vidocq probably could very easily have stayed retired from detective work following either of his first two leavings (to the extent that his mélange of schemes and activities could really even be called retirement). But detective work had clearly become more than a means to a living long ago, for Vidocq—not exactly a crusade, or a mission, but certainly a lasting fascination. So the entrepreneurial-minded detective fused together his two skill sets, and on January 3, 1834, opened the first private detective agency, *Le Bureau de Renseignements*: the Information Office.

It was, as Vidocq had suspected, a propitious moment for relocating his services to the commercial economy. The urban Paris was still, largely, a medieval warren decades before Baron Haussmann's massive redevelopment works, and sanitation remained poor with a terrible cholera outbreak only two years before Vidocq started business. But France was fast closing the distance between its traditional agrarian economy and that of its industrialized neighbor and victorious rival, Britain. Gas lighting had arrived in Paris, and major rail connections would be up and running by 1840. The sluggish, medieval economy of pre-Revolutionary France on the way to joining its discarded system of government.

As later detectives would also discover—in one or two cases reaping a fortune in the process—this generated growing new demand for their skills. Increasingly industrial and urban societies needed detectives on the police force to solve robberies, violent crimes, and such problems. But those same societies also produced a market for detective work outside of the police force. In some instances clients simply wanted more discretion than an official investigation. Often what they wanted was a proactive investigation before a crime had been committed. The inhabitants of growing cities found themselves mingling among great numbers of strangers every day, and this, along with larger and more complex business networks, presented constant questions about whom to trust. What clients wanted, in a word, was information, and as another outcome of economic transformation not only the wealthy but a growing middle class could afford to pay for it.

Vidocq was the first to address this demand in any significant way, whether he actually went through this reasoning or simply responded instinctively to what was happening around him. Either way, he shaped his practice to those things the market wanted. Much, perhaps a majority, of his business was actually providing credit reports rather than solving robberies or murders. Much in demand, this service still capitalized on his past experience: who better than Vidocq, with his extensive mental directory of cheats and swindlers of every stripe, to advise a merchant on a prospective business partner's trustworthiness? If due diligence had proven inadequate, the Bureau also offered help with related problems, investigating employee theft and financial crimes. For these investigations, Vidocq returned to his earliest strategies and recruited convicted con men who knew firsthand what to look for. Meanwhile, the demand for information services was not completely exclusive to commercial clients. And so without really even seeking to, Vidocq also turned his hand to domestic problems such as missing persons cases, and the staple of hard working private investigators since, infidelity and adultery, i.e. "divorce work."

As a private detective, Vidocq was at least as enthusiastic an innovator as he had been at the Sûreté, and now he no longer had to go slow to accommodate traditionalist bosses. At the Bureau, he continued his trials of forensic investigative methods and augmented his filing system with a dedicated laboratory. He was also characteristically inventive and audacious in promoting his new enterprise. Though Vidocq's reputation was already well established, he placed newspaper ads touting the Bureau, and had flyers distributed on street corners, most often near financial offices. He also combined self-promotion with his belief in proactive deterrence by providing plaques, which clients could mount at their doors, to warn the ill intentioned that Vidocq's Bureau protected that place.

As a result of Vidocq's hard work, experimentation, and good timing, the Bureau de Renseignements prospered. So much so that a variety of imitators sought to join in this lucrative new market, though few of them lasted. Many, lacking Vidocq's long experience, fell afoul of the law and found themselves shut down by the authorities. The Paris police had the Bureau de Renseignements in their sights, as well, but it proved far more difficult to catch for sloppy or dishonest practices.

The Delessert family, at least, must have felt thankful for this, and at the same time painfully embarrassed. When a new client approached Vidocq for help recovering 75,000 francs stolen from him, the old detective recognized the banker Maurice Delessert immediately, in spite of the man's affectation of an alias. Portraits of Vidocq usually depict a confident looking man, with one eyebrow slightly raised and a hint of a smile, and this expression may well have been on display as he listened to his pseudonymous client. Vidocq was, under the circumstances, willing to overlook this small attempt at deception. He could well understand how seeking his assistance could be awkward for the brother of police prefect Paul Delessert.

Maurice had, indeed, only approached Vidocq at all after trying every other avenue. The Bureau accepted his case, which Vidocq pursued personally, no doubt with considerable relish. Recovering the funds was itself a routine matter; Vidocq made inquiries through his network of informants, and, after locating the thieves, made them a simple offer of handing over the money or else having Vidocq himself become their unrelenting nemesis. The thieves chose to cut their losses, Vidocq recovered the stolen francs, and, within 72 hours of taking the case, he returned them to their grateful owner and then refused to accept any fee for his services. Instead, Vidocq claimed a different kind of reward. He sent a complete report on the case to Prefect Paul Delessert, informing him of the resolution to his brother's complaint, as a courtesy of course. The prefect likely did not entirely appreciate this gesture, or the officially unexplained leak of the letter to Paris newspapers, which published the entire story with much praise for Vidocq and rather pointed Gallic scorn for the prefecture. If Vidocq, whatever his role in this "accidental" news leak, thought that his old bosses at the police would have a sense of humor about the episode, he had made a considerable misjudgment, however. The police had laid siege to Paris's other private detectives already, and Vidocq's continued one-upmanship was hardly earning his Bureau an exemption.

*

Paris's police never especially liked Vidocq, despite officially being allies for more than 30 years. As he became a more and more effective ally during that time, the old guard's dislike of him actually grew more and more intense. Not least because each advance Vidocq made against crime tended to coincide with an advance in his own independence from the Prefecture. When he was merely another informant, Vidocq drew little comment; once given his own force to direct, though, he became a regular target for complaint.

For the next couple of decades, disparaging Vidocq was enough for most critics, along with calling for some new check or restriction on the Sûreté once in a while. Vidocq showed up the gendarmerie on occasion, but he was still a government employee like themselves, and they could (and did) make free use of his files. This changed entirely when Vidocq opened his Bureau de Renseignements. Thereafter he became, in many ways, a more threatening enemy than the criminals whom he and the police both combated. At least burglars and highwaymen reinforced the need for the police; Vidocq's detective agency was a direct competitor. That the old guard had played a large role in inclining Vidocq to leave the public sector (twice) and eventually resume his work outside of it did little to curb police resentment, any more than did the fact that his Bureau was more a complement to public police than a real competitor. As far as the police of Paris were concerned, the famous Vidocq was and would always remain a scoundrel, a criminal and con man, who had been allowed to discredit honest policing for years. And the police, eventually, had enough.

The resultant war between Vidocq and the Paris police ultimately approached the scope and drama of an epic novel. It opened slowly and cautiously, with a few preliminary skirmishes. The police gradually escalated their complaints, then attempted to lend them some substance through one or another scheme of entrapment. But they had, by that point, given Vidocq more than ample warning of their animosity, and he easily avoided those first jabs.

In late 1839, the police intensified the conflict as well as the brazenness of their approach. That November, they arrested a few of Vidocq's employees and then raided the Bureau offices just days later, seizing thousands of files that they claimed were property of the Sûreté, unlawfully removed by its former chief. The police may have hoped by these assaults to put Vidocq in his place, though if so, they misjudged his resolve even worse than he had misjudged their appreciation of a joke. Harassment was not going to make Vidocq quietly lower his head and forfeit the field of detection. He had been resisting the will of the authorities for decades, and always, in the end, he had made them give ground rather than vice versa.

So the police arrested Vidocq himself, as many in their ranks had no doubt ached to do throughout their long association. They were the lawful authorities, after all, and their patience had entirely run out. Two days before Christmas, Vidocq was returned to prison; fate, it seemed, was determined that he spend his life among lawbreakers and law enforcers but indecisive as to which side was his. Officially Vidocq was charged with swindling, "deliberately corrupting government employees" and, perhaps most egregious of all from his captors' point of view, "usurping public functions." As Edwards notes, however, "the bill did not name the law that this alleged usurpation broke." And, unfortunately for the police, neither they nor the courts found such a law. In their eagerness for revenge, the police had overplayed their hand, and they paid a price for it. Vidocq was acquitted of all charges and, in late February, set free along with his employees. That was bad enough. The court went further, however, praising his record and commending Vidocq as a man of honor. Through their ill considered frontal assault on the Bureau and its chief, the police had only bolstered Vidocq's reputation while making themselves appear fumbling and petty. The result could scarcely have been worse.

Possibly the police saw it that way as well and decided that they had nothing more to lose by another attempt. In any event, within a couple of years they gave it a second try. It proved better planned than the earlier fiasco and much more difficult for Vidocq to brush aside. First, the police managed to place or recruit a spy of their own on the Bureau staff, a major coup against the longtime spymaster. Perhaps as a result, the charges leveled against Vidocq this time were more specific and much less easily dismissed. The police charged the private detective with taking money under false pretenses and with various abuses in a recently concluded debt recovery case, including false arrest and imprisonment, and kidnapping.

Given that Vidocq certainly did play fast and loose with legal niceties at times, even when he had the authority of the Sûreté behind his actions, a broader validity to these charges is impossible to refute entirely. The prosecution had to prove wrongdoing per the letter of the law, however. A first trial did convict Vidocq, though Edwards characterizes the proceedings as effectively vindicating Vidocq and then handing down a conviction anyway. Vidocq's critics would likely dispute that assessment, but when Vidocq appealed the verdict he was ultimately acquitted and released once again. Officially, Vidocq 2, prefecture o.

In a larger sense, this second duel's result was more mixed, for both participants. The police had invaded the Bureau and carted away its files twice, along with clients' confidence in the privacy that was for many the object of hiring a private detective agency. The Bureau had been effectively shut down entirely, moreover, while its chief was kept in prison for nearly a year. Throughout the months of legal wrangling, Vidocq spent most of his time behind the ancient stone walls of the Conciergerie, still in service as a prison 23 years after an official report had condemned it as unfit.

Here again, the hostility of the police may have led them to overreach and damage their own reputations while augmenting their foe's. Vidocq was an experienced hand at prison, but his patience had limits as well and conditions in the Conciergerie were genuinely awful, particularly at first. He eventually convinced his jailers to make things more tolerable by presenting them with a threat they dared not ignore: via his lawyer, Vidocq leaked word of a plan to send his wife abroad with their wealth, and then escape to join her. Capitulating to such a threat was certainly humiliating, particularly when the man issuing it was in his late 60s. But the prospect of its being made good was a disaster, and the prefect of police hadn't the nerve to see if the old escape artist was bluffing. Vidocq was made more comfortable and allowed visits from his wife. (Fleuride subsequently spent as much time as possible with Vidocq, and probably shared more of her husband's company during his months in jail than any other time during their marriage.)

The end result of the second trial of Vidocq might, for all this, have been considered no worse than a draw for his police opponents. They had drawn blood this time, undeniably. Yet they were intent on the full pound of flesh, and so kept fighting even after cooler heads would have let things alone. The last one or two efforts against Vidocq were a return to haste and even foolishness; some months after his release they ordered his exile from Paris on the grounds of his being an ex-convict, ignoring his official pardon. The procurator-general intervened to halt this nonsense. When the police made a third attempt to charge Vidocq in court, the judiciary did much the same, having lost its own patience with the police vendetta. One can imagine an exasperated judge angrily interrupting and telling the Paris police to quit fooling around and get back to work.

Vidocq at least did exactly that. In the last dozen years of his life, Vidocq seems to have mounted a personal challenge to the axiom that "old soldiers never die, they just fade away." Through his seventh decade and beyond, the one-time lieutenant in Napoleon's army resisted doing either one and very nearly succeeded. He worked hard to rebuild the Bureau de Renseignements, and though the repeated intrusions by the police had left clients concerned about their confidentiality, they had offset this somewhat by leaving Vidocq more popular than ever. Vidocq's ability to thumb his nose at the establishment, along with his flair for drama and roguish charm, had long proved endearing to the public. Once the Bureau was back up and running, he began spending more time at Saint-Mandé, where his relatively mortal wife had decided to settle full time, and there he penned more of the stories the public enjoyed so much. Amusingly, after all of Vidocq's battles with the police, it was these stories that led to his only defeat in court: a Paris restaurateur successfully protested his establishment's too thinly disguised appearance in one of Vidocq's tales, where it was depicted as a criminal hangout whose owner received stolen goods.

Vidocq could afford to take this minor loss in stride, as the popularity of his exploits had won him fans throughout France and beyond its shores, as well. In late 1843, Scotland Yard sent two of its inspectors to France to visit the Sûreté, which had inspired their own force. Apparently, however, they were mostly bored by Paris's official detective police. Instead they spent much of their stay discoursing with its founder and observing his Bureau. At some point in his life Vidocq had acquired a serviceable command of English, and he enjoyed a pleasant interview with the Scotland Yard men.

Two years later he paid his British admirers a return visit, venturing beyond France's shores for the first time at age 70. He had heard that London, much more than Paris or indeed most cities, had a sincere regard for its police and was curious to see this for himself. Vidocq embarked for London with various plans and schemes in mind, most of which met with only limited success; there was to be no London branch of the Bureau de Renseignements. While in London, though, Vidocq did track down a swindler who had cheated one of his clients. Like one of the fictional sleuths he would later inspire, he then turned the arrest and the credit over to Scotland Yard.

A very premature obituary announced Vidocq's death in May 1846, as well as a story of dying in poverty that persists to this day. Neither was true. Vidocq himself seemed immune to time's effects, though even he could not banish them from the world around him. It was, sadly, no fiction of newspapers when Fleuride died the following year, after a painful battle with cancer. And unlike when Jeanne-Victoire died, Vidocq himself seemed to slow down for a time and even prepare to withdraw from active life. He closed down the Bureau, from which he had been absent anyway throughout Fleuride's illness. He sold the estate in Saint-Mandé, then moved into modest quarters in Paris, like one more old pensioner living quietly in retirement.

Vidocq had always been adept at disguises, however, and this was no different. He was no more ready to settle down to a quiet existence than was France, and she was still disinclined to do anything of the sort. When revolution convulsed much of Europe in 1848, France was no exception, and Vidocq returned to the old game. *The Vidocq Dossier* describes this period in suitably dashing language:

Vidocq, who was approaching his seventy-third birthday, was recruited by Lamartine and Landrin to serve in the new Sûreté Générale. He responded with the enthusiasm of a man fifty years younger, donning various disguises and reporting on the plots and counterplots that were keeping politicians of all persuasions busy.

Rumors told as well of leading a defense of the police prefecture and Ile de la Cité during an uprising against Louis-Philippe, and later, Vidocq remaining as apolitical as ever, counter-espionage missions for Napoleon III.

The sands eventually began running out, though, even for Vidocq. He would have denied it, and continued doing so throughout his seventies. Old clients still approached him for help unraveling a swindle or fraud, and he readily responded, even though he was comfortably well off. Vidocq himself contributed to rumors of late life penury in campaigning for a larger state pension; most likely his efforts were driven less by need than by a desire for more recognition of his extraordinary service to the nation.

Meanwhile he remained an active and effective foe of crime as long as he had energy left to employ against it. What may have been his last case as a detective captured, one final time, the drama, humanity, and instinctive judgment that made his adventures endure. Approached by a wealthy, middle-aged merchant who had discovered 150,000 francs missing from his accounts, Vidocq sized up the situation directly: the man's wife was young and pretty, his cashier was 25, and never mind the "but." Vidocq would sort the affair out.

Advising his client to hide the detective, then feign his own departure, Vidocq was unsurprised when he heard the wife joined by the cashier, or when she mentioned her husband's suspicions and the two then began conspiring together. The pair were probably by contrast quite surprised when a broad, well-dressed old man casually appeared in front of them, and Vidocq's matter-of-fact explanation of what would happen next preempted any argument from either. Calmly, perhaps even a bit wearily, he reclaimed what was left of the missing funds, then advised the wife to "never mention anything." He personally escorted the cashier onboard a ship departing from Le Havre, and returned to inform his client that the cashier had taken the rest of the money to lavish on a dancer. Vidocq's client was left feeling grateful, with both bank balance and happiness intact. It was a modest day's work for a legendary detective and yet, combining pragmatism born of long experience, a streak of romance and just a bit of deception, it was a fitting last job all the same.

*

Eugène François Vidocq died, a few weeks after a debilitating stroke, in May 1857, although typically varying dates and even years are reported in some works. Likewise, one account places his remains at the Church of Saint-Denis in Paris, rather than beside those of Fleuride in Saint-Mandé. More certain is that his body was not yet in either resting place when the Paris police hastened to his apartment and seized his remaining records and files; having been defeated at every attempt while Vidocq yet lived, the prefecture could, as an institution, at least claim the victory of outlasting its mortal rival. It could also work to deprecate Vidocq's official legacy and minimize the significance of Vidocq in official histories of the Sûreté. By the middle of the 20th century the Sûreté Nationale itself effectively ceased to exist, following the sort of governmental reorganizations that Vidocq had been so unique in his ability to survive. Vidocq's private detective agency had, of course, been closed down by its founder long before.

Memory of Vidocq himself endured for a time, and still does if mostly in small ways. In addition to drawing inspiration from his career for fictional characters based on Vidocq, authors like Poe and Melville mentioned the great detective by name in some stories. And that name remained something of a byword for detection for decades, even in far corners of the world, until it was superseded by that of Vidocq's most successful of fictional protégés. In the 20th century Vidocq has been the subject and namesake of a few films, including a 2001 French production starring (inevitably) Gérard Depardieu. The fantasy tinged work received little notice outside of France, however. Otherwise the name of Vidocq is today largely unknown, outside of dedicated studies of detective history and one curious organization whose own low profile was given a bit of a boost in Michael Capuzzo's *The Murder Room*. The Vidocq Society, as described in his book, is "a private club of pro bono crime-fighting avengers," which meets to review and solve cold cases. It also honors its namesake with its membership of 82, one member for each year of Vidocq's life, as well as "in a shadowy corner a bronze bust, the visage wide and arrogant, of the 19th Century detective Eugène François."

Meanwhile the greater legacy of Vidocq is flourishing, well beyond a few books or a shadowy corner. As an innovator in detection and policing, his influence is much like that of the earliest pioneers of computing: their individual names are largely forgotten even as their ideas have become so ubiquitous that we take them for granted. Specialist detective forces, organized records of criminal histories, criminological study of behavior patterns; ballistics, laboratory examination of blood samples and other trace evidence; the private detective agency and security firm. As well as the popular detective story in both fiction and non-fiction realms; vexingly larger-than-life, Vidocq himself always seemed to operate in both categories at once. Which inevitably provokes some skepticism, as well as another problem even for those satisfied that Vidocq was genuinely extraordinary: after giving Vidocq his due the entire subsequent history of detection threatens to turn out anticlimactic.

In assessing man and career, Vidocq was arguably a genius and undeniably a remarkable success in a field that he practically invented. It is fair to suggest that as a detective his full catalog of achievements has never been surpassed. Vidocq was, nonetheless, not without his weaknesses. As a person, the most notable was simply a "weakness" for *filles jolies*, which seems never to have compromised him professionally; this may well be more a product of good fortune than of mastery of affairs, though. Considering Vidocq's well-known reluctance to pass up a pretty girl, it might be as remarkable as anything in his long life that none of his enemies ever turned this romantic profligacy against him. Even without attaching any virtue to monogamy, one can see in Vidocq's habits a man who could be cautious and meticulous, but in some ways consistently chose not to be, preferring passion and drama.

In this, Vidocq was hardly unique among great detectives and was, on the whole, far luckier than most. He enjoyed far less good fortune in his relations with the police, and it may be here more than anywhere else that Vidocq truly failed. He pioneered the roles of both police detective and private detective, and many of the techniques of both, yet Vidocq never managed to work out a way to coexist with police authorities. Even if the adventure-loving Vidocq, persecuted by the law long before he ever began competing with its authorities, enjoyed his jousts with resentful prefects, very likely he would have preferred amicable coexistence to 10 months in the Conciergerie.

It's also worth noting that, for all of Vidocq's talent and success as a detective, he had a few breaks. For one thing the quality of Vidocq's opponents seems a bit wanting when one looks at the whole. Vidocq typically made things look easy, but if this was partly a result of prodigious skill, it may also have been a result of never facing a foe who could come close to matching that skill. One might consider the notion of a sort of "arms race" between crime and crime fighting, here; Vidocq accomplished an enormous leap ahead for the latter but, in so doing, may have ended up missing out on any battles that would really test his wits. Later generations of detectives would be confronted with much more devious criminals and Byzantine crimes than the petty burglars and unassuming scams that generally opposed Vidocq. He might very well have triumphed if pitted against considerably more wily foes, but history would mostly reserve them for later detectives all the same.

The obstacles to Vidocq from the other side of the law were somewhat forgiving as well, compared to those that confronted his successors. Not only did he have the field effectively all to himself for many years but, in part as a result, he got to operate before society's rules and laws caught up to its demand for this new profession, the detective. Vidocq genuinely was breaking the rules at times, but got away with it in spite of the years of effort and resources expended by the Paris police. Detectives have continued elevating expediency over strict legality up to the present day, on occasion, but not all of those who followed Vidocq enjoyed his same happy results.

Throughout his long life, in fact, Vidocq seemed remarkably untroubled, whether by worry, infirmity or any sort of serious failure. Perhaps this, if a final assessment of the great detectives should ever be made, will prove to be his true claim to fame. By many measures Vidocq was the first detective, and he may well have been the greatest. Compared with the most remarkable of those who followed him, however, he was very likely the happiest.

CHAPTER TWO
JONATHAN WHICHER

"What I shall tell you will make you
very uncomfortable."

J ACK WHICHER must have felt more than uncomfortable as he awaited
the verdict in the case of Miss Constance Kent. If his interest in the
outcome was only professional, it was a profound interest, all the same.
And unfortunately that outcome didn't seem at all likely to turn out in the
Scotland Yard inspector's favor.

The signs were not reassuring. The defending barrister's scorching denunciation of Whicher's case had not troubled the inspector, by itself; that's what
a defense lawyer was hired to do and some of them were well practiced indeed.
The accompanying outbursts of applause from members of the public who had
packed the spellbinding inquest were another matter. Their reaction seemed a
strong hint to the magistrates' own leanings. And yet Whicher had done all he
could, surely, and had in fact found the answer to the dreadful murder mystery
that the nation had been demanding throughout most of the summer of 1860.
That Constance Kent had killed the infant Saville was as certain to Whicher
as the idea was appalling to those now judging his conclusion.

Judging it—and rejecting it. At the moment he heard their verdict,
Inspector Whicher may have felt pained, or ill, or simply numb, but he could
not have felt at all well. This was not just an ordinary, if disappointing, hazard

of the job. This case and his controversial solution had placed Whicher in the spotlight; his very competency as a detective had been judged along with his case against Constance and, now, rejected with it also. Whicher may well have thought, if only briefly, that his career was over. If so, that suspicion would very nearly prove correct, before turning out amazingly wrong.

One of first detectives on the London force, Jonathan Whicher receives particular notice in Douglas G. Browne's history of *The Rise of Scotland Yard*. "Of Whicher much was to be heard, as one of the most successful and most unlucky of detectives," Browne declares. Chance, if not fate, did indeed play curious roles in making Whicher a detective still worth recalling after 150 years.

The case for Whicher as a great detective rests heavily on the fact that he played key personal roles in solving great mysteries that achieved lasting infamy themselves. Whicher thus offers a distinct contrast with France's Vidocq—the two may well have met when the older sleuth visited London in 1845, although Whicher's own notoriety was at the time years away and would prove quite different. The most interesting feature in Vidocq's cases was almost always Vidocq, and with his limitless energy and inventiveness the Frenchman would likely have won fame in any era or setting. Whicher, on the other hand, was more ordinary fellow than genius. He was talented, and a shrewd detective who drew the notice of his peers well before the Kent case brought his name before the entire nation. But in another time and place, Whicher very likely would have gone no further than that: a very good detective, commended now and then on a local scale and given warm tributes at retirement, but relegated to complete obscurity as soon as those who knew him passed from the scene.

As Whicher's countryman Shakespeare could and did testify, however, "Some are born great, some achieve greatness, and some have greatness thrust upon 'em." Whicher had the mixed fortune to be a detective when the best man on the force could be called on to demonstrate greatness, whether he was genuinely great or merely very good. Put on the spot, Inspector Whicher had no alternatives except to rise to the occasion, or fall disastrously short.

This in spite of the fact that Whicher became a detective in 1842 and began the first of his real high profile cases in 1860. By that point, the concept of a detective force had been established in Paris and a number of other French cities for decades. Long after Whicher's time, even into the 20th century, detectives would continue to build reputations and fortunes in societies where official law enforcement lagged behind evolving needs. Yet the slow arrival of any professional detective force in Britain, even with a proven model right next door, is worth examining briefly.

It's a subtle paradox that, for all that British decisions and innovations have greatly influenced the shape of the modern world, much of the nation's own history depicts a deeply, stubbornly conservative people, holding tight to old ways in the face of change until mounting pressure simply forces an upheaval. At which point reform is at last sanctioned, usually in a grudging and limited fashion and in the face of general skepticism, only for the new practice to become absorbed into the familiar, "natural" order of things as a cherished tradition itself within a generation. Few things illustrate this pattern better than London's fitful and reluctant establishment of metropolitan police institutions.

Today, the friendly British Bobby is a popular icon and the guardian of an orderly society among the safest in the world. And as far back as 1845, when London lured Vidocq to investigate the curious idea of a major city whose police enjoyed real popularity, his impressions proved largely accurate. Yet a Metropolitan Police had been operating in London for scarcely 15 years, established in 1829 by Robert Peel; the nicknames "Bobbies" and "Peelers" are both legacies of the jeering reception that initially greeted the Met. If Londoners subsequently reconciled to these new patrolmen relatively quickly, likely it was because, as per usual, the need had long been acute. Parts of the city had law enforcement before the Metropolitan Police, but the creaking and fragmented forces of traditional watchmen and other groups were woefully inadequate to the challenges of a teeming imperial capital. The brutal and ambiguously resolved Ratcliffe Highway Murders had proven that in 1811, and it still took another generation to implement any significant reform.

In a small way, this may have been less in spite of having a model ready to hand in neighboring France as because of it. Anglophone skepticism of all things French is hardly a recent phenomenon; the fact that France had metropolitan police, then detectives and a national security agency, probably hardened the average Englishman's determination to persevere without them. Heavy-handed government enforcers patrolling the streets and a secret police with the whole nation under its watch were fine for *the French*, with their priesthood and emperors and horse meat. But the British people had *liberty*, and no small pride in it, and did not consider that at all compatible with intrusive foreign schemes of law enforcement. Until, of course, they eventually changed their minds following a very drawn out search for a murder suspect, two attempts on the Queen's life, and much controversy and argument.

London's response to another proposed reform around the same time may provide one more bit of context to the delayed arrival of policing and detection in the city. By the 1850s, the river Thames had become so polluted as to literally plague London with repulsive fumes. At one point Parliament itself fled from "The Great Stink." Even then, however, many voices including *The Economist* derided government plans for the modern sewer system and embankment that eventually restored basic sanitation. The project went forward and in time earned local and international respect, but only after proving itself in the face of skepticism and hostility—much like that which greeted the Metropolitan Police and the detective branch that followed it.

Under the circumstances, it's safe to say that few early recruits to either force could have signed on in hopes of celebrity or public acclaim.

Little information survives about the early years of Jonathan Whicher, including whatever reasons did motivate his application to Scotland Yard. Whicher was born in Camberwell on October 1, 1814, to working class parents Richard and Rebecca. Their son Jonathan may have become a policeman with some measure of eagerness, whatever his reasons, as he applied as soon as he was old enough in 1837. A desire to support a family of his own could have played a role. According to Kate Summerscale, author of *The Suspicions of Mister Whicher*, documents from 1838 note a child born to Jonathan and Elizabeth Whicher, though Mrs. Whicher and child make no further appearances in records. Much of London being a minefield of rot and contagion in those years, it's entirely possible that disease carried them both off during the child's infancy. One chronicler describes Whicher himself as "a reserved man, private about his past," and he might well have borne such an early tragedy entirely in private.

On the other hand, it's possible that Whicher simply needed a job and considered the police a better alternative than being press-ganged for the navy. The British Empire spanned much of the globe by the accession of Queen Victoria that same year of 1837, but its capital still offered limited options to the young man from an ordinary background such as Whicher's. Higher education remained the preserve of wealthier families, and any specialist training for the rest of Britain's working populace was likely to be on the job.

The police were no exception. If young constable Whicher were to become a capable policeman, let alone one day a detective, he would have to figure out how through his own initiative as he patrolled the slum of St. Giles. The very first arrest of Whicher's career showed promise though. The sight of a 17-year-old Cockney girl, drunk and showing off, wouldn't usually have merited special attention on Whicher's beat. But her feather boa and other implausibly expensive clothing made the patrolman pause, and then recall a robbery of a fortnight before, when items including a feather boa were taken from a Bloomsbury home from which the maid vanished at the same time. Whicher charged the young woman with theft, and was off to a good start; he had demonstrated observation, memory, and initiative, and just as important, he got a conviction.

As a result of work like this, and his single-handed pursuit and capture of three men attempting to rob Sir Roger Palmer in 1842, Whicher made a favorable impression on his superiors. When, that same year, police commissioners won permission to establish a formal, plain clothes detective division, Whicher made the very short list of eight names. The first squad of Scotland Yard detectives consisted of two detective-inspectors and six detective-sergeants. Commissioners selected two constables for inclusion in this new force, lifting them up to the rank of sergeant in the process. Whicher was one of these two.

Jonathan Whicher, photo by Powell of Charing Cross
The Tichborne Claimant archive, Hampshire Museums Service, Hampshire, UK.
Reproduced with permission. [HMCMS:FA2004.141.135]

*

Like the Metropolitan Police which had set up shop next to Great Scotland Yard a dozen years before, the detective branch proved its value, even if the process took time. Browne points to the 1849 affair of the "Bermondsey Murderess" as its first major challenge. The detectives measured up, winning the conviction of both Maria Manning and her husband after the pair fell out in custody and accused each other of every crime they were charged with and then some. Whicher did yeoman's work in what was, throughout, a team effort, but given the still modest size of the team the sergeant's contributions were valued. For their work in the case, the detectives, Whicher included, received an £8 reward and special commendation from the commissioners for "extraordinary exertions and skill in bringing to justice F.G. Manning and Maria Manning."

The reviews weren't always so positive for Whicher. A few years into his job as one of Scotland Yard's detectives, Whicher and another sergeant were reprimanded for "want of respect" to senior officers on the uniformed police. The public had its complaints, as well; even a well-established police force finds itself subject to some criticism and things were no different for the Yard and its detectives in the 1850s. In May 1851, after more than a decade observing London's criminal fraternity come and go, Sergeant Whicher immediately recognized two men stopping for a chat near the London & Westminster Bank. One was a familiar ex-con, returned from an involuntary sojourn in Australia; the fellow joining him on a bench facing the bank was "another old lag." Whicher and a colleague kept up observation of the pair, who spent the following weeks absorbed in their own surveillance of the bank's schedules and security. When the would-be bank robbers, confident of their preparation, finally moved on the bank on June 18, they were completely surprised by police lying in wait and their attempt to escape on foot was easily foiled. The result of Whicher's keen observation and patience: letters to *The Times* criticizing this reckless, inefficient and entirely unsporting approach.

The detectives of London had their fans as well, however. And the active support of a well-read author like Charles Dickens must be counted as worth scores of amateur busybodies. Dickens found Sergeant Whicher, along with

Charles Frederick Field, one of the two detective-inspectors, particularly fascinating subjects. With his journalist's attraction to a lively character, Dickens was naturally an eager audience for these men's stories from the job, like the following anecdote which his friend Field offered.

Once in 1850, according to Field, he, Whicher and a Mr. Tatt found themselves "rushed by four swell mobsmen." A scuffle ensued, and the "mobsmen" got the worst of it. They tried to flee, but were cut off by Sergeant Whicher. As Mr. Tatt got his bearings again, however, he discovered his diamond shirt pin had vanished, and Inspector Field began searching their detained attackers. He was interrupted by Sergeant Whicher, who astonished everyone else present by revealing the pin in his own possession, along with an amusing explanation: in the thick of the earlier struggle, he had seen the thief take the pin, and then managed to lightly tap the man's hand like a confederate might have done to signal a swap. The stolen pin was dropped right into Whicher's hand.

Though one photograph of the dexterous detective has survived, stories like these provide much of the sense of Whicher available to a modern reader. Dickens employed pseudonyms in his writing about the detectives, but there is little serious attempt to disguise his real subjects behind "Inspector Wield" and "Sergeant Witchem." The latter, Dickens observed, was a stout man, standing five feet eight inches, "shorter and thicker-set than his fellow officers." His face was pitted with small scars, from smallpox. He had pale skin and blue eyes, however, and a light, delicate manner. Further, "Sergeant Witchem… has something of a reserved and thoughtful air, as if he were engaged in deep arithmetical calculations. He is renowned for his acquaintance with the swell mob."

One member of that swell mob, and Whicher's chase for him, must be accounted as one of the first great English detective tales. According to Dickens's account, "Tally-ho Thompson was a famous horse-stealer, couper, and magsman." And, through Dickens's pen, Whicher (as "Witchem") recounted his search for this man in detail.

Thompson, in conjunction with a pal that occasionally worked with him, gammoned a countryman out of a good round sum of money, under pretense of getting him a situation — the regular old dodge — and was afterwards in the "Hue and Cry" for a horse — a horse that he stole down in Hertfordshire. I had to look after Thompson, and I applied myself, of course, in the first instance, to discovering where he was.

The colorful argot of 150 years ago may well produce a raised eyebrow or two, of course. And Dickens certainly took some license to emphasize novelty and suspense. Yet upon closer examination, the pursuit of Tally-ho Thompson seems worth consideration as an unusually detailed history of one of Whicher's cases and his methods in evaluating and pursuing leads. For all of the story's flourishes, it conveys a very credible sense of the waiting and genuine tedium which is inseparable from regular, workaday policing.

Whicher's search for the missing Thompson began with a stakeout, in hopes of observing some attempt at communication between the fugitive and his wife. He took up observation of the Thompson home in Chelsea, "especially at post-time in the morning, thinking Thompson was pretty likely to write to her." Right away, Whicher was left waiting, as days passed before any mail was delivered at all. When a letter was, at last, delivered, the sergeant tried chatting up the postman afterward, claiming to be anxious about money he had loaned Thompson. The letter carrier had taken no notice of the postmark, but was able to offer the fact that the letter had contained money, "I should say a sovereign." With this information, Whicher entertained hope that Mrs. Thompson would soon write her missing husband to confirm her receipt of the money. Upon observing the Thompsons' daughter purchase supplies from a stationer that same afternoon, the detective noted afterward, "I think to myself, 'that'll do!'"

Whicher's search was far from done, however. In fact his pursuit of Thompson, via the wanted man's mail, had scarcely begun. In Chelsea, Whicher managed to learn the letter's destination only through roundabout means; though unable to see the postmark during the daughter's trip to the post office, Whicher observed "what we call a kiss—a drop of wax by the side of the seal—and again, you understand, that was enough for me." That, and subsequently sifting through every piece of mail in the drop box, after identifying himself and his purpose to a cooperative postmaster.

The letter and the detective both made their way to an unnamed city, 120 miles from Chelsea, which proved to be merely a way station in a mail forwarding system arranged by Thompson. Whicher spent days waiting at the local bar, sipping brandy-and-water while the letter to Thompson sat in plain view, unmoving yet daring the detective to abandon the lead. The letter had, presumably as a further precaution, been addressed to "Mr. Thomas Pigeon," and finally Whicher, his investigation otherwise at a dead end, wrote a letter to John Pigeon at the same address "to see what THAT would do."

The somewhat desperate cast set the pursuit in motion once again. Whicher was back at the bar the next day, dividing his attention between the letter behind the bar and the pelting rain outside, when the postman came in and announced the letter to "John Pigeon." The barmaid checked the earlier letter to make sure, before replying "No, it's Thomas, and he is not staying here." And then added "Would you do me a favour, and post this for me, as it is so wet?" The letter moved from behind the bar at last and, sealed up inside a second envelope, left with the postman.

The redirected missive, however, only led to another way station in Northamptonshire, where Whicher was obliged to repeat much of what he had just been through at the first. Who had ever tested Vidocq's patience like this? Finally, after traversing much of England, Detective-Sergeant Whicher arrived at the New Inn, where his blue eyes must have widened at least a little in the midst of an attempt to chat up the landlady: from the front room, he spied three men in the adjoining parlor, "and one of those men, according to the description I had of him, was Tally-ho Thompson."

On his own against Thompson and two associates, all of them sturdy men, and far from any source of official help with night setting in for good measure, Whicher's next move seems entirely reasonable, if not technically police procedure. "I thought I couldn't do better than have a drop of brandy-and-water to keep my courage up." His courage fortified, Whicher was ready to bluff it out. After chasing his quarry so far, a more cautious decision very likely seemed unbearable. So the detective summoned up all the courage he and a drop of brandy could muster, backed it up with hints of colleagues in waiting, and arrested Thompson. Then, seizing the moment to lead Thompson away from the other men, Whicher pressed the landlady for someone he might deputize for a moment. Faced with Whicher's persistence, the woman admitted to employing an ostler, which "shaggy-headed young fellow" proved enough to prevent the arrest from being overturned by Thompson's companions.

All the effort apparently came to naught, after Whicher returned his prisoner to London. Dickens's account ends by noting that Tally-ho Thompson was acquitted on a technicality. The larger feature on the author's meeting with "The Detective Police" ends, moreover, with the information that "one of the sharpest among them, and the officer best acquainted with the swell mob, had his pocket picked going home!" Browne suggests that this latter mishap, at least, was "no doubt authorized with an eye to counter-propaganda," and either way these foibles probably seemed humorous enough in context. Charles Dickens was bound to offer his readers a laugh or two, after all. Particularly while he was on the whole praising Whicher and Scotland Yard's other detectives to the skies.

By the late 1850s, Dickens was by no means alone in his praise of Whicher. Inspector Field, who in "The Detective Police" decreed Whicher "better acquainted with the swell mob than any officer in London," left Scotland Yard in 1852, later opening a private practice. Whicher was subsequently promoted to Inspector. Police Commissioner Sir Richard Mayne had warmed considerably to Whicher since reprimanding him for "want of respect" a dozen years before. According to the memoirs of Tim Cavanagh, who served as the commissioner's clerk for a time during his own career at the Yard, "every important case was placed in [Whicher's] hands by Sir Richard." Cavanagh added that, in his own view, Whicher was "the best man the Detective Department ever possessed."

Such praise was the result of considerably more than congenial evenings sharing stories with a popular writer over brandy and cigars. Whicher had been busy, and showed no sign of slowing down after his promotion to inspector. In 1858, he solved the theft of Leonardo's *Virgin & Child* from the Earl of Suffolk, and tracked down would-be assassins who had chosen London to prepare bombs meant for Napoleon III. The recently deceased Vidocq would have been proud, then and two years later as well, when Whicher tracked down a gang that had fled Paris after a theft of £12,000.

When the brutal murder of a child at a bucolic country estate scandalized Victorian Britain later that same year, the press quickly grew impatient with the local investigation and demanded Scotland Yard's best. The *Somerset & Wilts Journal* cried "let the best detective talent in the country be engaged." The Yard responded to this clamor with Inspector Jonathan Whicher, and no one expressed particular surprise or disappointment with the man chosen for the task. Not, at least, quite yet.

The Road Child Murder, as many of the newspapers took to calling it, had all the elements for a legendary murder mystery. The murder took place at night on a relatively isolated estate, so the only obvious suspects were family members or servants, although an unseen intruder in the dark could be invoked to deflect the thought of a murderer inside the home. Upon investigation, multiple members of the household had a skeleton or two in the closet and locals were ready with gossip and suspicions. The nation followed every twist and turn, via Britain's highly competitive newspapers. And, of course, the story featured a ready-made hero, the infallible London detective dispatched to ride in like a white knight and save the investigation.

Whicher was not Sir Lancelot, however, and took the train at least to Trowbridge, before embarking from there for the tiny village of Road. During the journey, he probably reviewed once more the known facts of the case. Everything centered on the household of the relatively affluent Kents: Mr. and Mrs. Kent, four older children, a nurse, a cook, a housemaid, and two outdoor servants. And, of course, three-year-old Francis Saville Kent. The nursemaid, Elizabeth Gough, had reported Saville missing at a quarter past seven on the morning of June 29. A search of the estate, no doubt made with a growing sense of concern, eventually confirmed all of the worst possible fears and then some. Saville's body was found, wrapped in a torn section of flannel, in the outdoor privy. His throat had been cut, and later examination of the tiny body revealed that he had been stabbed in the chest also.

In the weeks that had followed, ample speculation had joined the facts and nearly threatened to crowd them out. Trowbridge Superintendent Foley, who rode out with Whicher upon the latter's arrival, suspected the nurse. Many locals, by contrast, were in no doubt that Saville's own father Samuel deserved the most suspicion, and if local attitudes were biased against Mr. Kent that was due in part to some genuinely fishy behavior. The present Mrs. Kent had originally joined the household as a governess, winning "promotion" to mistress of the house after an affair with her employer and the death of his wife. Claims that Mr. Kent had been slow in summoning the police the day Saville's body was discovered, and had then provided one or two pieces of information not officially discovered until hours later, did little to placate the village's distrust.

In his account of the Road murder, Browne notes that "So little is heard of his two eldest daughters that they seem scarcely to have been in the running as suspects, and the same is true of the cook and house maid and the two outdoor servants." The middle children, sixteen-year-old Constance and her brother William, were another matter. In terms of local suspicion, their father led the running, but one newspaper still noted "some uncomfortable feeling" toward the adolescent pair ever since they attempted to run away together a few years before.

In Road, Whicher and Foley stopped first at the local Temperance Hall, which the presiding magistrates commandeered for most of the official proceedings of the inquiry. On the day of Whicher's arrival, Mr. Kent, Elizabeth Gough, and a Reverend Peacock were being re-examined. Whicher, however, was very probably fastening his own suspicions on another suspect not among those at the Hall that day.

That Whicher should have formed a theory of the case so "early" is, in fact, reasonable enough given that the investigation was already weeks old by his arrival. His role was less to find clues or suspects, than to sift through the heap of them that had been piled up but so far obscured a solution rather than revealing one. Summerscale describes the challenge succinctly: "Whicher was joining the murder investigation two weeks late. The victim's body had been boxed up and buried, the testimony of the witnesses had been rehearsed, the evidence had been collected, or destroyed."

The inspector gamely made his way to the Kent estate, all the same, to learn what he might. The house, itself, still offered opportunities for observation and experiment after most of the portable evidence had been moved many times over. Whicher reviewed the layout of the rooms and noted that of all the home's inmates, only Constance and William had rooms of their own. Either could have moved around at night freely without the chance of a roommate observing them. The nursery where Saville had slept gave up a clue or two, as well. Whicher apparently borrowed a three-year-old, from some particularly helpful family, and attempted to recreate the theft of Saville from his cot. He found it could have been done without disturbing the child or anyone else's sleep. While examining the nursery, Whicher also learned that Saville's sheet had been found folded back very neatly when the child's absence was discovered. And in Whicher's mind, at least, "it can hardly be supposed a man would have done."

The exploration of the Kents' house also allowed Whicher to establish some clues as false or misleading, and thereby clear a bit of clutter out of the complicated affair. The Kents had naturally promoted the suggestion of an outsider behind the murder rather than a member of their own household. A drawing room window, found open the morning of Saville's disappearance after servants insisted it had been closed the night before, seemed to lend weight to this theory. But Whicher found that the window could only have been unfastened from inside, and that folding shutters found partially closed would have required someone inside as well. The drawing room window was an unlikely means of entry or exit. Its unaccounted-for opening the night of the murder was in fact quite suggestive of a guilty party within the household, trying to make the crime look like the work of an outsider.

A bloodstained scrap of newspaper, proposed as another indication of an outside culprit, proved to be from *The Times*, upon Whicher's examination; Samuel Kent was a *Times* subscriber, so this too could be discounted. Another document offered more interest to the inspector. In his search of the bedrooms, Whicher found a list of linen Constance had brought back from school, including three nightdresses. The local detectives' investigation had already taken confusing evidence from Constance and the maid suggesting that, while two such garments could be accounted for, a third had somehow disappeared. The full details of what may or may not have happened to one or more of Constance Kent's nightdresses are such as must baffle any but the most dedicated; it is otherwise best simply to note that, per an essay on the case by Roly Brown, "a missing nightdress provided something of a saga." Likewise the "breast flannel" found with Saville's body could have an array of significances or none at all. Whicher, under more strict obligations of thoroughness, gave these garments considerable attention during his investigation. But alongside the material evidence, he made a growing number of other discoveries relating to Constance, the significances of which are more readily communicated.

The story of Constance's and her brother William's runaway attempt of four years earlier drew Whicher to Bristol, their intended destination, to learn more of the incident. Every witness he spoke with described Constance as very bold and confident, and the episode itself indicated a person capable of making secret plans and seeing them through some considerable ways even at age 12. Whicher also turned up an unsettling detail involving yet more of the girl's clothing: Constance had apparently made the journey to Bristol with boy's clothing and her hair cut short in hopes of going to sea along with her brother as cabin boys, and on the day they left home she had concealed her dress and shorn locks in the outdoor privy, which was used for a much more sinister concealment a few years later.

Whicher's rounds also included interviews at Constance's school in Beckington. Emma Moody, one of Constance's friends, related that Constance had complained of feeling reduced to second class status in her own home after her father started his second family. Constance had been very candid about resenting the new baby, Saville, in particular. The Kents' doctor, meanwhile, was equally unambiguous in giving Whicher his own view of the case: Saville had been partly or completely suffocated, before his murderer proceeded to slash at the infant with a knife, and in Doctor Parsons's view that murderer was none other than Constance.

And then there was a further curious bit of gossip about the Kents that reached the detective's ears as he crisscrossed Somerset and Wiltshire. About a year earlier, so the story went, the Kents' nurse had risen one morning to find her infant charge lying exposed in his crib, stripped of all clothes and covers. This at time when "catching one's death of cold" was in vogue as a very serious terror. For Whicher, the eventual conclusion of his investigation looked increasingly inescapable: Saville Kent had been murdered by someone within the Kents' household, who had borne malicious feelings for the child for some time, and whose resentful attitude and actions on the night of the murder, both, matched very closely with the history of Constance Kent.

Whicher, at this point, must have felt fairly certain that he had solved the mystery of the Road Child Murder. The problem was that for all the affair's similarity to a mystery novel, it was still a real police investigation. Whicher had a compelling explanation for Saville's murder, but in the real-world legal system that wasn't the same thing as having a convincing case against his suspect. In fact, the case against Constance was, at this stage, largely circumstantial, and for all his patient scrutiny of various garments and other bits of material evidence, nothing Whicher had found amounted to incontrovertible proof that Constance had committed the crime. He had neither smoking gun nor bloodstained nightdress.

What he did have, unfortunately, was pressure to resolve the case that the press continued to proclaim as, "for mystery, complication of probabilities, and hideous wickedness... without parallel in our criminal records." And while the *Morning Post* and its ilk tended toward sensational views of most things, the legal justice system demonstrated scarcely more patience with its investigator. On July 20, only four days after he arrived in Road, the magistrates listened to Whicher report his progress and developing suspicions of Constance and then pressed for the inspector to make an arrest. Whicher, very sensibly, was reluctant to be party to such a hasty proceeding. Despite her scheme to run away and go to sea a few years before, Constance hardly seemed like a serious flight risk. If nothing else, Whicher preferred that someone else make the arrest if there had to be one now, particularly given that he was still an outside consultant on the local force's case.

The Victorians' criminal justice system apparently kept a remarkably brisk pace compared with today's, however. And if Whicher had any realistic alternative to complying with the magistrates' insistence on proceeding, he went along with their wish all the same. That afternoon, he arrested Constance Kent; he was granted all of seven more days to assemble his evidence and be ready for the trial.

Whicher had bluffed suspects before, with much less in his hand, and he may have hoped he could do the same again. The shock of arrest might well lead his suspect to break down and confess everything. She was, after all, a sixteen-year-old girl. As it turned out however, she was a decidedly formidable sixteen-year-old girl. She was definitely not an old lag, wanted for nothing worse than horse thieving and accustomed to "the way the game was played," who would demand only one last brandy for the road and then cooperate. What had worked with Tally-ho Thompson and others did not work with Constance Kent.

The young woman's consistent cool reserve, throughout the murder investigation and now arrest as well, convinced Whicher more than ever that here was someone capable of carrying out a brutal murder in her own home and then calmly returning to bed as though nothing had happened. This, though, would be no more help in winning a conviction than any of the other subjective observations of Constance made by Whicher and others. He needed more solid evidence, and if in an ideal world the evidence would have come first and the arrest after, the world he was working in had deemed it expedient to proceed the other way around.

Whicher had one week, and the record of his activities over those seven days suggests an increasingly desperate Scotland Yard inspector. He likely felt the pressure of time acutely, from the very outset. One of his first moves was to call for help: Sergeant Frederick Adolphus "Dolly" Williamson, regarded as something of an understudy to Whicher, rode out from London to assist his mentor, and they proceeded to search frantically for some further clue.

On July 21, another of Constance's friends spoke to the Inspector, but could add little significant information aside from Constance's iron determination and readiness to demonstrate it in fist fights. This might have been worth knowing before Whicher arrested Constance with some hope of frightening her into confessing, but was a day too late now.

On July 23, the saga of the missing nightdress continued as Whicher questioned the Kents' maid yet again about details of laundry loads from a month earlier. He also posted a reward of £5 for the elusive garment. On July 27, with his week nearly up and the magistrates interviewing Constance to confirm her fitness for trial, Whicher was ready to tear at the very scenery of the case. He hired men to dismantle the privy where Saville had been found: "Scour the cesspool and drain," they were ordered. The search revealed neither nightdress nor anything but the ordinary if unpleasant matter. Whicher had brought in reinforcements, had turned over every stone, and had effectively nothing whatsoever to show for a week of further effort.

As a result, he did not have a conviction either. The barrister defending Constance attacked the prosecution's case with ferocity and indignation, the public applauded, and the magistrates, with more restraint, had effectively the same reaction. Constance Kent was not actually acquitted but was released on the payment of a £200 surety by her father and, with that formality quickly concluded, returned home seemingly unruffled by the entire affair.

The fate of defeated Inspector Jonathan Whicher was far from being so mild. It's worth pausing to note that Whicher had not entirely *failed*, in a technical sense, given the outcome a non-acquittal dismissal for his suspect. And if he had been defeated, there were manifold reasons that were largely beyond his control. Whicher was brought into the case late, and specifically because of ineffective local police who had thoroughly trampled over the evidence and then been defensive and mostly unhelpful. Whicher was pressed into making an arrest after only days on the investigation, with a case he himself considered incomplete. And, perhaps the most important argument in Whicher's defense, he was given no real help whatsoever in court. Browne observes that Scotland Yard, at the time, "relied upon a legal adviser, who on this occasion seems to have done nothing, or not to have been called upon to advise." In other circumstances the family of the victim might have hired someone to prosecute the case, especially if that family had the means of the Kents, but in this case the victim's father was also the father of the accused. Whicher's own report prosaically records that "there was no professional man to conduct the case for the prosecution."

All of which, however, did little to soften the reactions at the time. Scotland Yard's best detective, who had seemingly enjoyed a charmed existence before the Road Murder case, was now denounced in the press and even Parliament. Meanwhile the investigation into Saville's murder dragged on: the Home Secretary appointed a solicitor to investigate the matter, who poked around for a while and had Elizabeth Gough arrested at one point, and Saville's body was even ordered exhumed. The further efforts did nothing to resolve the mystery. They did much to prolong the public's feelings of frustration, which it took out on the most convenient scapegoat, Whicher. Letters from armchair detectives expounding various crackpot theories and the writers' analysis of Whicher's errors did little to keep the detective's spirits up.

In fact, Whicher was badly broken up by the rejection of his case and subsequent public drubbing. He tried to carry on with work, and made an honest trial of the consoling belief that one defeat would not unmake an entire career. The following year, he enjoyed a taste of success again, capturing a clergyman who had forged his uncle's will to cheat the estate of £6,000. That summer, however, also saw Whicher on his first murder investigation since Road a year earlier, and the results must have been devastating. It was in outline a complete reenactment of the earlier disaster, with Whicher once again sure of his conclusions, but unable to convince a jury who sent another suspect home. The year after that, Whicher was sent to Warsaw with another officer to advise the ruling Russian government on a national police force, but it's hard to say whether this was a sign of enduring faith in its man by Scotland Yard or of a wish to send him away and forget about him.

Whicher, in any event, toughed it out for another year or so, then retired early, aged 49. Browne describes a general belief that Scotland Yard and particularly Commissioner Sir Richard Mayne very plainly wanted Whicher's departure. Faced with this, as well as the very real concern that he had "lost his touch," Whicher called it a career a bit shy of 25 years. His discharge papers cited his official reason for retirement as "congestion of the brain."

At this point the once celebrated detective seemed, in contrast to his only recently deceased forerunner Vidocq, as though he might simply fade away. Whicher's life for the next 12 months seems like it must have been remarkably quiet, even empty, after the decades of activity and renown. No more job, no more duels with villainy, no more write-ups by Dickens, just a defeated, unwanted man in an empty house.

And then the unlikeliest twist imaginable intervened to turn everything around with a suddenness that no fictional narrative would have dared. Almost five years to the day after Whicher staked his case and career on the hope of Constance Kent confessing to murder, she walked into the Bow Street magistrates' court and did exactly that. What sudden arrest did not achieve, something else had, whether the gnawing of a conscience, five years' further maturing, the influence of the clergyman she first told of her deed, or some other unguessable factor. Whatever its reason, the results were dramatic—the written confession that Constance pressed upon a reluctant chief magistrate may just as well have been a thunderbolt.

Strangely, of all those who had closely followed the case's tortuous opening acts (which must have included much of England), the one who seemed least affected by this revelatory announcement may have been Whicher himself. Apparently his reaction was simply numbness; he did not celebrate, or weep, or declaim at the unfairness. Yet, if Constance's confession seemed to elicit no significant reaction from Whicher, his life nonetheless transformed in its wake, as much as it had as a result of her silence years earlier. Even though she had confessed in writing to the murder of her stepbrother, and steadfastly stood by that confession, the never-actually-acquitted suspect was to undergo every step of the crown court process with no feature spared. Including the detective who had originally investigated the crime and named her as the guilty party. If Sir Richard Mayne had put pressure on Whicher to quit Scotland Yard's service, he apparently managed to master any awkwardness about asking Whicher's return to work, at least on a temporary basis. Once again, Whicher was in an odd circumstance, this time investigating a case after the suspect had surrendered and confessed, but at least it was a happier circumstance. So he emerged from the forgotten corner, bringing along his "relics" of the case, the original arrest warrant and some bits of evidence that apparently no one else had considered important to retain. He lent assistance to his former protégé "Dolly" Williamson, who had been assigned to assist Whicher the last go-around. He testified at the trial, likely much more comfortable in court in a supporting rather than leading role, and tracked down Saville's old nursemaid Elizabeth Gough to secure her testimony as well.

All of this proved little more than a formality, because Constance pleaded guilty in court. She was sentenced to death, but the public that had been scandalized by her accusal for the crime she now admitted apparently held no grudge, and rallied to her defense again. Queen Victoria commuted the sentence to life imprisonment. Constance Kent served 20 years of her sentence and ended her days in Australia in 1944, a survivor from a very distant place and era.

Back in Victorian London, another kind of survivor presented his contemporaries with something of a puzzle, i.e., what to think or do about retired Inspector Jonathan Whicher. Whicher had essentially been vindicated, although as is inevitable in any mystery studied so intensely there were doubters insisting that this or that point remained unanswered. Whicher's suspect had, nonetheless, confessed to the crime, and her guilt is more than credible, as Whicher had found all the way back in 1860. He hadn't won a conviction at the time, but that was not really his own failing, and now his suspect had been convicted after all. Some in the press did attempt to reverse the earlier judgment of Whicher, though on the whole there was little enthusiasm to refurbish his reputation; perhaps most people were, understandably, simply tired of the whole case and anything related to it and preferred just to move on in all ways.

Scotland Yard seems to have shared this preference and made no attempt to restore their estranged colleague to the fold permanently once his work on the trial was complete. And perhaps Whicher was entirely content with that, for having re-entered life after something of an absence, he seemed ready to make a new start as well. He found a congenial companion very near to home in the person of his landlady, Charlotte Piper, and on August 21, 1866, they were married. And early the following year, though the new household had a comfortable living from the pensions paid to both Mr. and Mrs. Whicher, Mr. Whicher decided to make his work as a consultant into a full-fledged second career and go into the private detective business.

As with his first career, Whicher was hardly selecting a profession enjoying high regard or status. If London had been won over by the metropolitan police force and then by its detective branch, at least as concepts, the very idea of the private detective was still viewed with suspicion. Dickens, who had been among the few to embrace the Scotland Yard detective branch from its first days, criticized their private sector counterparts in a rather acerbic, sour essay even though his friend Field was one of their number. And if Dickens was perhaps playing up his misgivings about private investigators for his audience, the PI is still fundamentally an imperfect fit as a popular hero, at least outside of fiction. Over the years a few real detectives have been celebrated as heroes, but it proved a rare and generally unstable balancing act. Not least because the private detective's employers often emphasize keeping his work *private*, and even the consummate showman Vidocq's famous cases are nearly all cases from before he entered private practice.

Jonathan Whicher was one of the first big exceptions to this rule, because the case that defined his career as a private detective was simply seized by the public and gripped tightly for more than seven years as an unabashed national obsession.

Of the Tichborne Claimant Case, contemporary observers were rather typical in the bombast and grandiosity of their assessments. *The Daily Telegraph* called it "the most daring and sustained imposture that ever afforded the measure of the possible wickedness of man," and *The Observer* declared that "For the greater part of the seven years since the Claimant appeared on English soil it may be said that no subject whatever occupied so large a space of the human mind." More recent observers have reviewed the whole affair and been scarcely less grand in their estimates of its scale. Douglas Woodruff, writing 90 years after the events in *The Tichborne Claimant: A Victorian Mystery*, said that "The public of Victorian England quickly became passionate partisans in a controversy which went on all over the country, and in and out of the Courts of Justice, through the longest civil action and the longest criminal trial on record, for the next ten years and beyond." Just within the past few years the latest chronicler of Whicher's famous cases, Kate Summerscale, wrote that "Over the next seven years the case claimed not only Whicher's unceasing attention but the attention of the whole country. It was a puzzle so confounding that it brought on a kind of national paralysis."

As with the Road Murder case, the detective once again found himself tasked with curing that paralysis and soothing an anxious nation with not only a solution, but a solution that would convince, even in court. Unlike that case, however, Whicher was not seeking an unknown person who had committed murder so much as seeking to resurrect a person, or at least an identity, whom a very conspicuously known person preferred to keep buried. The known person was Sir Roger Tichborne, or claimed to be, and the legitimacy of that claim was the focus of all the bewildered, fascinated attention.

This man, whom even recent histories refer to simply as "the Claimant," was at the heart of the whole Byzantine affair. Among the few points of agreement between rival sides in the case was that a real Sir Roger had existed at one point and was the heir to an immense fortune. And that he had been lost in a shipwreck, in 1854. Beyond that, fierce argument engulfed nearly every single point. The Claimant insisted that he was Sir Roger Tichborne, returned at last after years in Australia and South America in response to newspaper advertisements placed by Sir Roger's mother, Lady Tichborne. Various allies, including Lady Tichborne, were convinced of his assertion. Yet in addition to various much-contested inconsistencies, the Claimant's story was plainly incredible, just in general outline. Lady Tichborne was convinced, but other members of the family were just as convinced that she had been taken in by an imposter. As they believed that the real Roger Tichborne had died in 1854, however, the most effective way to prove whom the Claimant was not was to prove who he really was, instead.

Precisely why one of the doubters, family relation Lord Arundell of Wardour, hired Whicher for the case is an interesting question itself. It's possible that he had encountered Whicher somewhere, though perhaps a bit more likely that he received a referral from some friend who had. Whatever his reasoning for considering the detective, Wardour's actual reasoning for choosing him intrigues. Whicher's record at Scotland Yard constituted a strong résumé, of course, but his resignation and most of his last few years at the Yard had taken place under a cloud. Whatever Whicher may have achieved by that very early stage in his career as private detective had not included anything distinguishing. It is thus tempting to imagine that the only notable event in Whicher's recent history, the re-evaluation of his personally disastrous conclusion in the Road Murder case, actually helped lead directly to his great second chance by convincing Wardour that here was a man who saw what no one else had been able or willing to see.

The actual "why" of selecting Whicher to unmask the Tichborne Claimant must, ultimately, remain speculation. The wisdom of the selection is rather more easily judged. Assuming that the man professing to be Sir Roger was, in fact, some swindler who had vanished into a false identity, ex-Inspector Whicher was on very solid ground. Or was, at least, very sure-footed in finding a way through the shifting terrain of such phantoms. Summerscale is persuasive in describing Whicher's qualifications for the task:

> Through the 1840s and 1850s Whicher worked on sleights of hand and the mind. He dealt with criminals who slipped away into alternative identities, melted into the streets and alleys. He was set on the trail of men and women who counterfeited coin, signatures on cheques, money orders, who escaped from alias to alias, shuffling off names as snakes shuffle off skins.

Vidocq had pioneered this territory, as with so much else, employing his own considerable firsthand knowledge of such dissimulation; Whicher seems never to have adopted the earlier detective's enthusiasm for disguise, personally, but he knew his stuff. And he would need it against an opponent whose real identity had been left far back along a trail as devious as that of Tally-ho Thompson and scaled up across the whole world map. Unlike Vidocq's Paris, Whicher's London was a busy, port city capital of a maritime nation that surveyed an empire circling the inhabited world. In tracing the movements and identity of the Tichborne Claimant, the man who had begun his career patrolling the Holborn on foot was, 30 years on, directing a global enquiry like none in the history of detection to that point.

The essential break in the case was made by Whicher, in London, but resulted from his correspondence with a detective in Australia. Acting on this antipodean intelligence, Whicher began asking questions in the Thames-side neighborhood of Wapping. There he heard curious stories of how the alleged blue blood Sir Roger, upon his arrival in England, had paid a number of calls in the area to inquire after a working class family, the Ortons. The landlady at the Globe public house, a Mrs. Jackson, recalled for Whicher a "heavily built, muffled stranger" walking in from the cold the previous Christmas. He made various chit-chat, but kept bringing up more questions about the Ortons whose house had been a few doors away. He had stopped there already, in fact, but found no one home. Mrs. Jackson explained that the family had moved and provided an address for one of the grown children, Mary Ann. Mrs. Jackson told Whicher that, after talking of the family at further length, her mother noted their visitor's likeness to the late father, George Orton. At which the stranger said that he was "a friend" of the Ortons' missing son, only, and had come to help out the family as a favor to his friend.

That "friend" was Arthur Orton, who had been away from London for some years. Whicher began to investigate Arthur Orton's travels abroad, while continuing to pursue inquiries locally. He found the family members still in London and asked the surviving sisters if they knew a "Henry Orton;" they denied knowing any such person or recognizing a photo of the Claimant presented by Whicher as the man he sought, even when the detective suggested they might be in line for a large inheritance. Nonetheless Whicher continued to uncover more and more instances of the stranger from the Globe—whom he believed to be the Claimant—visiting people on the basis of acting for his friend Arthur Orton.

Whicher's instincts had suspected Constance Kent as soon as he began looking around, in the Road case, and it's almost certain that they quickly suspected that this "friend" of Arthur Orton was Orton himself. And that, if the information from Australia was reliable, Arthur Orton was the Tichborne Claimant. As the result in Road had painfully emphasized, however, deciding whodunit mattered much less than being able to prove whodunit. Fortunately, Whicher had time now and used it well. He turned his experience at tracing people to locating a variety of people who had known the man, Arthur Orton, whom this stranger had claimed to represent. And then arranged for as many of them as possible to get a quiet look at the Claimant in person. Orton's sisters, whom Whicher had shown a photo, denied that it was a face they recognized and they never wavered from that, but most of those Whicher showed the real article to had a different reaction. Including, significantly, Orton's abandoned teenage sweetheart; in his history of the case, Woodruff notes with much understatement that "It was not the least of Detective Whicher's Wapping successes when he found Mary Ann Loder, the girl whom Arthur Orton had been 'walking out' when she was no more than fifteen."

If this case allowed Whicher the time he had wanted in Road, it did not allow him any more freedom from public scrutiny or sharp criticism. As before, Whicher fixed upon a guilty party early on, and many skeptics, perhaps forgetting how his early instinct on that previous big case had eventually turned out, said that he was once again getting ahead of himself. Whicher patiently kept on building his case, and as he did so came in for outright vilification from the opposing camp, which, unable to dismiss his evidence, began to denounce it as a conspiracy. This outrage met with wider sympathy for a time when Lady Tichborne died and the nosey, prying detective seemed to contrast badly with the Claimant's display of mourning. That detective had apparently emerged from his earlier crisis a wiser and more self-assured man, however. He seemed to slough off the denunciations now and go right on with the job, confident that this time would turn out differently. In 1873, as the arguments' ferocity reached a climax, Whicher closed a letter to a friend with a brief remark on the critics:

> I daresay you hear me frequently abused in reference to the Tichborne case, but whether I shall live (as in the Road Murder case) to outlive the innuendoes and slanders [...] I know not, but that the Claimant is Arthur Orton is as certain as that I am —
>
> Your Old Friend, Jack Whicher

"Jack" did respond to some of those lined up against him, in due time, in a very novel and effective manner: by winning them over. In securing the defection of the Claimant's landlord, a Mr. Rous, Whicher's patience, confidence and skill were absolutely masterful. By late 1868, the members of one side of the very public battle were almost as well known to their opponents as to their allies, as were much of their activities. Whicher had observed disagreements between Rous, the Claimant, and an attorney, Holmes. When the arguments produced an overt breach, Whicher passed through the doors of Rous's inn, the Swan, and stepped right in.

The detective insouciantly ordered dinner and afterward strolled into the bar to light up a cigar and enjoy "a glass of grog." After a while he struck up a conversation with Mr. Rous and then took his time in broaching the Claimant's validity as Sir Roger Tichborne. Only then did Whicher begin his pitch with directness. "Mr. Rous, don't you believe anything of the kind," he warned. "You may depend on it, he is no such person. What I shall tell you will make you very uncomfortable." Whicher proceeded to deploy the arsenal he had stockpiled for more than a year by that point. He had the Claimant's activities in Wapping, and the testimony of witnesses identifying him as Orton, including Mary Ann Loder who had fainted into detective Whicher's arms after gasping that the Claimant was indeed "her Arthur." Whicher also had found one member of the Orton family who did not disclaim any familiarity with the Claimant; Charles Orton had, to the contrary, made a formal affidavit stating that he had been in the pay of the Claimant for months. (Though it was apparently a very poor return on the expenditure, for the Claimant.) The detective's correspondence with distant climes had borne fruit, as well. In addition to tying the Claimant more firmly to Arthur Orton's sojourn in Australia, Whicher had traced his man to Chile, where Orton had worked as a butcher for a time, and, per the Castro family, had served them for two years as a bullock driver.

And Whicher's Chilean investigations were not yet complete; he was in the process of finding witnesses who could appear before the Claimant in London and judge whether he was the man they had known in South America by another name. After laying things out before Mr. Rous at the Swan, Whicher prudently backed off and left his new acquaintance to consider what he had been told, in peace. He had sown seeds of doubt and could wait for them to sprout. They did just that after the Claimant, invited to meet some Chilean acquaintances of Arthur Orton, politely but firmly declined any meeting whatsoever. The Claimant lost an ally, and Whicher scored another point.

If the Road Murder case was a sprint, the Tichborne Claimant case was not so much a race of any kind as a parade. In more than one sense probably, but certainly in proceeding very slowly along a winding course, and in being difficult to assign one exact moment when it ended; a variety of answers are possible depending on the observer. For Whicher, his own years-long involvement with the case culminated between 1871 and 1872 with the Claimant's suit for Sir Roger Tichborne's inheritance. Both sides had been able to spend years preparing their evidence and arguments by then, but one seemed to have benefitted considerably more from the time. Whicher had an array of evidence, and was well practiced with it after persuading even highly skeptical audiences like Mr. Rous. In addition to the reports and testimonies he had assembled, Whicher confronted his opponents with one item of documentary evidence that the opposition found terribly awkward. The "Richardson letter" backed up the stories Whicher had gathered about the Claimant's odd interest in the Ortons, with a written inquiry about Arthur Orton, incontestably sent by the Claimant. The detective scored again, dramatically, when he asked "was there anything important you desired to communicate to Arthur Orton" and left the Claimant with a very awkward time explaining his refusal to answer. "It might have a tendency to criminate myself" was the embarrassing, if probably very honest, answer.

The testimony of one witness after another, that he or she recognized the Claimant as Orton, was Whicher's most important weapon. Despite her melodramatic fainting spell earlier, Mary Ann Loder proved an excellent star witness and unshakable even in the face of lengthy cross examination. Yet quantity may have counted for just as much as quality in the end. Woodruff presents a brief but effective summary of the entire trial's character when, commenting on the witnesses other than Loder, he writes "there were far too many and too much sameness in their testimonies to justify going through them all." This was a painfully obvious contrast to the Claimant's denials, evasions, and hesitation for fear of "a tendency to criminate myself."

As a result, this verdict probably came as little surprise for Jonathan Whicher, just as with the verdict in Road. But this time the verdict he suspected was the verdict he wanted and the verdict which the court agreed he had earned: the Tichborne Claimant's suit was defeated.

The loose ends from the Tichborne case strung out for a while longer. The Claimant, or as he may reasonably be called, Arthur Orton, was to face worse than being unmasked and denied his bid for Sir Roger's inheritance. After his long and costly court action the crown, understandably if not quite logical economically, brought him back to court and sued him for perjury. Orton lost this time, too, and his fears that he might "criminate" himself were entirely justified by a 14-year sentence to Millbank prison.

Whicher, by contrast, profited from his involvement in Orton's masquerade, though not really in the way that the former Claimant's partisans insisted. The diehards maintained that the courts had committed an injustice, either in collusion with or as a dupe of the anti-Claimant conspiracy. Whicher had somehow masterminded a plot involving, per Woodruff, "the bad faith of at least three or four men... the complicity of four women [and] the compliance, suggestibility, self-interest rather than any willful perjury of the others who testified that he was Orton." And in return for this service, the theorists persistently and very precisely charged, Whicher received £2,000; arguably a bargain in return for the manipulative wizardry the detective was alleged to have performed.

Lord Arundell probably did receive remarkable value from his choice of detective, whose honest work was purchased for no more than a fraction of the claimed £2,000. But Whicher could have counted himself well satisfied with the outcome, too. He hadn't gone back to work for want of money, anyway. And, if he had wanted to supplement his and Mrs. Whicher's pension income, he could have found easier work, even as a private detective, than a sprawling investigation that exposed him once more to intense scrutiny and criticism and consumed much of the prime of his life. But then, what price redemption? Whicher did not leave a diary, or lengthy interviews, or a memoir. It's nonetheless difficult to review the arc of his life without suspecting that the Tichborne Claimant case, and most of all the final result in court, were tremendously satisfying. The much-after-the-fact confession of Constance Kent had suggested that he had good instincts at least, but not necessarily the ability to handle a major case. By taking on a second such labyrinthine job, with more time but otherwise reliant entirely on his own resources even moreso than in Road, Whicher demonstrated ability that places him on par with the greats of his field. Never mind what compliments or rewards he was paid. Whicher had proved himself, to himself, and had learned that this mattered most in the end, regardless of the judgments of doubters or detractors who did not know him anyway.

The Whichers remained in London for several years after the Tichborne Claimant trial. Mr. Whicher probably continued working as a private detective, at least occasionally, throughout that time. His much publicized success must have drawn further clients seeking his aid, even in a city with at least one other celebrated sleuth in those years. He worked no more especially notable cases, at least in public records, and having achieved an important object with his victory over Orton, he may have settled gradually into semiretirement. He retired officially, again, around 1880, moving to suburban Battersea with

Mrs. Whicher. If this second retirement was happier than his first, it was unfortunately much the shorter of the two. Whicher suffered from stomach ulcers and gastritis and died June 29, 1881, of a perforated stomach. The *Police Gazette* noted the life of one of Scotland Yard's original eight detectives and "one of the most successful and most unlucky of detectives" with a three sentence obituary.

Detective-inspector Jonathan Whicher did not fade away entirely, all the same. He had the fortune of finding an early chronicler, in an author whose novels are now firmly shelved in the "classics" section, and as long as Dickens remains there, even his minor early writing will have readers. And Whicher had played central roles in not one but two enduring mysteries. Both the Road Murder and the Tichborne Claimant case remain popular largely *for* their mystery, though, just as Stonehenge or the death of Tutankhamen will probably always be approached as mysteries no matter how definitive archaeologists' solutions. Similarly, Whicher's own solutions as a detective tend to be underplayed, particularly as the Road Murder case has proven more popular than his later, more conclusive vindication. In addition to Summerscale's book, the Road Murder has been the subject of television documentaries as well as fictional works beginning with Wilkie Collins' *The Moonstone* in 1868 and continuing through the modern era.

All of which the detective himself likely would have found amusing, but of relatively little serious import. Whicher was, after all, ultimately a working class man of a talented but practical, down-to-earth mind. For all the importance they may have had for him, at the end of the day he had featured parts in two great cases simply because they were jobs that demanded someone step forward and try to prove equal to them. Solving mysteries was an interesting challenge Whicher enjoyed, along with praise if it was offered. But the real object was, all the same, to get a villain off the streets, not to get a detective into legend.

CHAPTER THREE
ALLAN PINKERTON

"We Never Sleep."

(Motto of Pinkerton's National Detective Agency)

THE UNDENIABLY, INDISPUTABLY GREAT pioneers of detection are few in number. One of this elect, who was eventually one of the most widely known and influential detectives in history, began life in acutely humble circumstances. He spent much of his early adulthood living an itinerant existence, at times to avoid authorities of the law, which he brazenly defied more than once during his lifetime. It was only by chance that he found himself chasing criminals on behalf of those authorities, instead, though once commenced on a career in detection he applied his singular energy and inventiveness wholeheartedly. Beginning as a kind of freelance agent for established police forces, he later joined their ranks on an official basis, then went on to create a groundbreaking private detective business. His agency soon enjoyed tremendous success serving the exploding market of private clients, though he continued to place his celebrated skills in the service of the day's governments as well, particularly when revolution threatened the stability of the nation itself. His work brought him in personal contact with many of his era's most notable figures, and he became a legend himself during his own lifetime, writing and inspiring popular detective stories both real and imagined.

"He" was none other than the Scottish-born American private eye, Allan Pinkerton. All of the preceding paragraph could be applied just as accurately to Eugène François Vidocq, however, the French detective who began the profession a generation before. Given the widespread fame Vidocq enjoyed from the 1830s onward, he was almost certainly known to Pinkerton, and an important inspiration when the Scot set out on his own unlikely odyssey as a detective a dozen years or so later, as well. But beyond the outline of their lives, Pinkerton was remarkably unlike Vidocq, as a detective and as a man. His personality was as ill suited to the Frenchman's drama and fast living as were his wire brush beard and thick Glasgow accent to Vidocq's play with disguise and false identities. Pinkerton married once, while young, and his wife and family's only rival for the breadwinner's attention was work, very nearly the far more intense man's only passion in life. Yet the arch law-and-order capitalist Pinkerton also was much more rebellious than the mostly apolitical Vidocq in ways that are still relatively little appreciated.

Though well documented by multiple biographers, the complete story of Allan Pinkerton remains almost obscure in comparison with the simplified but thriving *legend*. Of all those who have plied his trade, no other detective has exceeded Pinkerton's fame over the long term, outside the realms of fiction. For decades, "Pinkerton" was synonymous with the very word "detective," itself. The Pinkerton agency remains active, today, though detection accounts for no more than a fraction of its work. Meanwhile, even with a much lower profile in today's world, Pinkertons' historic fame and that of its founder during legendary parts of America's past keep the storied name in circulation. The Pinkertons were effectively the nation's law force during the Civil War and the Wild West era. Allan himself planned strategy with Abraham Lincoln, hunted fraud for the great railroad magnates, and waged war against the Renos and the James Gang. With such famous company, Pinkerton and his agency never vanish for very long before some new retelling or re-imagining, from a children's book, to a television documentary, to the fictionalized historic background of a Batman graphic novel. More than any of his successors or rivals, Allan Pinkerton still holds the office of America's great detective.

*

In early 19th century Glasgow, such a destiny must have seemed very remote. As must the prospects of becoming a great anything, particularly for a child born to poor parents and given little formal education beyond the age of 10. All the same, Pinkerton's rise from humble beginnings fit a kind of pattern. The entire Scottish nation has, like their fellow Gaels across the North Channel, somehow "punched above their weight" through more than 1,000 years of history, despite being small and relatively poor compared with their neighbor to the south. *The Wealth of Nations*, television, and the fictional detective whose fame eventually eclipsed all rivals real and imagined—all were the products of Scotsmen. It's fair to say that Allan Pinkerton, if less appreciated than Smith, Baird, and Doyle, still earned a place among the many sons of Scotland who had an influence stretching far beyond their rugged home.

It's also fair to say that whatever Pinkerton achieved was hardly a product of early advantages. The future detective was born July 21, 1819. Many sources give the date of August 25, but the more recent research of James Mackay, author of *Allan Pinkerton: The First Private Eye*, points to this as the infant's baptism date. Allan was also the second child of that name born to William and Isabella, after a previous boy had died in infancy, and, per Mackay "Myth, legend, distortion of the truth and controversy would surround this Allan all the days of his life." In his first years of life, a decidedly rough neighborhood surrounded Allan Pinkerton as well. He would know worse, eventually. All the same, it seems no one had anything particularly good to say about Glasgow's Gorbals neighborhood in the 1820s. It's unsurprising that young Allan left to seek his fortune by age 19. After his father died, while the boy was only 10, whatever resources the Pinkertons had were reduced further and Allan's formal schooling was "interrupted." Pinkerton picked up the trade of barrel making and, in 1838, set out on the tramp as an itinerant cooper. He had no particular destination, possibly. Just somewhere, anywhere, away from the cramped and impoverished world he had known his whole life.

For a young laborer with perhaps five years of formal schooling, however, Pinkerton's worldview and political ideas ranged well beyond parochial expectations. Nearly a decade before attempted revolutions throughout Europe, which brought France's great detective back into active service, working men like Pinkerton and other reformers challenged the established order in Britain with ambitious proposals published in a series of charters. Nearly all of their ideas are taken for granted in Britain and much of the world, today. But at the time the Chartists were truly a radical movement in a nation where the capital had only established a metropolitan police force in 1829. For more than two years, Pinkerton devoted much of his energy to this cause, even organizing the Northern Democratic Association. His dedication extended to more than words, too; he insisted on the validity of physical force in the pursuit of reform if necessary. This was a minority view among fellow Chartists, though hardly astonishing given both the limited voting franchise, which was one of their central complaints, and Pinkerton's later two-fisted approach to most opposition.

It was also enough to make Allan Pinkerton a wanted man, at least allegedly. In later life, Pinkerton recalled the circumstances of his emigration to America in dramatic fashion and how he fled old Scotland with "a price set on my head." Mackay, at least, suggests that these stories were either an exaggeration or the product of memories grown hazy with age, and that broader rebuffs to Chartism as a movement, the emigration of friends and relatives, or simple hope for greater opportunity and adventure were more significant in sending Pinkerton overseas. Whatever his reasons, Allan did not set off alone, having married Joan Carfrae shortly before embarking. For what it may be worth, the Pinkertons' marriage was arranged in something of a hurry, too, even if the threat of arrest as a radical agitator was not the reason for urgency. If Pinkerton did leave Scotland with some anxiety about the authorities, it's just possible that the explanation had less to do with Chartism and more to do with Joan's age; the new Mrs. Pinkerton was, apparently, three years short of her claimed 18 years.

Pinkerton and his very young bride's subsequent adventures reaching the New World seem even more outlandish on the surface, though they can be better substantiated by ship schedules and news reports. The first leg of their voyage to North America ended in sudden and dramatic fashion, when the *Kent* struck a rock. Allegedly this misfortune was then compounded by a band of

Indians camped on the otherwise isolated northern shore, who robbed them of what little they possessed. Even then, the Pinkertons were still relatively fortunate; another ship on which they later arranged to continue their journey, before changing plans, suffered a boiler explosion on the trip and was lost.

One way or another, Allan and Joan reached the United States, more or less in one piece, in the spring of 1842. The nation was in the midst of an eager, aggressive westward expansion. Within a generation, land grants and railroads would settle much of the present lower 48 states with European populations. At the Scottish newlyweds' arrival, much of the continent west of Pennsylvania was still in a very early stage of settlement, however. Throughout his life Pinkerton would refer to Chicago as part of "the West," and if that seems eccentric based on modern geography it did not at the time. Permanent settlement in the United States was still mostly confined to the east, and almost everything beyond was genuinely frontier territory and very reasonably seen as part of a great West.

That included Pinkerton's future world headquarters. Though European settlement had commenced more than 20 years earlier, Chicago remained little more than a swamp and a few rough shacks when the Pinkertons arrived to meet an old friend from Allan's Chartist days. Even the Gorbals would have seemed an orderly and sophisticated urban center in comparison. Chicago was, in fact, about to launch the first decade of breakneck growth that would make it first a boom town and eventually one of North America's leading cities. But on their first visit, the Pinkertons would have seen little to encourage a long stay. After briefly resuming cooperage work, probably to replenish the household funds, Allan and Joan continued northwest across the inland sea of waving prairie grasses.

For most of the next five years, the Pinkertons made a home in the village of Dundee. Today, East and West Dundee mark the far fringe of sprawling greater Chicago. But in the 1840s, it was a small, rural prairie community and probably an idyllic new home for two young refugees from the Old World's urban slums. Allan found an adequate market for barrels, and within a few years the young couple appeared to be settled in comfortably. In 1846, their first child was born. Yet that settled, quiet domesticity was to prove only a temporary pause. It seems as though some urging to greater things, for both father and tiny William as well, must have kept Allan watchful. Even Joan, though content with their simple existence, seemed aware of it; years later she recalled "They were bonnie days, but Allan was a restless one."

A restless nature may well have drawn Allan Pinkerton into his first effort at detection, as may curiosity, adventurousness or, just perhaps, a sense of destiny. On the other hand, it could be that none of these were as important as an archetypal Scottish thrift. Pinkerton, as a cooper, needed lumber to form into barrels. As a rural cooper living in a relative wilderness, however, he saw no need to pay for lumber when he could collect it himself for free. And it was just such a foraging expedition that led, ironically, to the beginning of the end for his barrel making career. The expedition's goal was a small island in the nearby Fox River. Pinkerton presumably found satisfactory raw material for wooden staves, while there. He also found the remains of a cooking fire and other signs of recent visitors, which made him suspicious. The modern idea of camping as recreation didn't really exist yet in 1847. A camp site on the small, secluded island still might have meant any number of things, but Pinkerton's instinct saw clear evidence that someone, in some way, was up to no good.

And here, at this point, some out-of-the-ordinary predilection for mystery and adventure can no longer be denied. Pinkerton's life until 1847 had been ordinary enough for its day, but his next action was probably not, even for a frontiersman. Pinkerton decided to stake out the island. For several days at least he made repeated visits to the site in hopes of discovering who had made a fire there, while taking care to keep his own presence unknown, in turn. When this produced no result, he began observing the island at night. One can only imagine what Joan must have thought of it all. But finally, her husband's determined curiosity met with result. One night he observed a group of men arrive on the island, by rowboat, then begin some sort of activity around a fire.

This was, at last, undeniably odd and at least suggestive of some clandestine purpose. When Pinkerton reported his discovery to the Kane County sheriff, as an ordinary person might have done in the first place assuming the camp site had seemed worth noticing at all, the sheriff did not simply dismiss the local cooper as a busybody. Instead, he briefly checked into what Pinkerton had reported and, after confirming it planned a raid on the site. Assembling a posse, Pinkerton among its membership, the lawman led them up the Fox River to the island base of a counterfeiting band and captured the surprised gang, along with their tools and a bag of entirely unauthorized U.S. dimes.

The very idea of counterfeit dimes must inevitably risk a chuckle or two from the modern reader, even with an understanding of 165 years' inflation. But counterfeiting of both paper notes and coinage was every bit as serious as it is today, and the 1840s Treasury had neither Secret Service nor holographic security foil to combat it. Frank Morn, in *The Eye that Never Sleeps*, suggests that even Pinkerton's personal intervention in the "Bogus Island" case and other counterfeiting operations was not so eccentric as it may seem:

> Counterfeit money did not directly affect Pinkerton's cooperage, but it harmed those upon whom he depended for business. He had a vested interest in the smooth working of the community, and it was no surprise when Pinkerton accidentally discovered a counterfeiter's camp in 1847 that he returned with the county sheriff to make an arrest.

The argument is interesting, though it seems to imply a demanding standard for truly surprising behavior. After his role in the island gang's arrest, however, word of Pinkerton's successful vigilance spread. It impressed enough people that he received encouragement to keep up an ongoing, if unofficial, watch for counterfeiters. Within a year, that unofficial, general watch became a semi-official, active effort against a specific target, when store owners approached the emerging local expert for help with another counterfeiting problem. The merchants explained that someone had been faking the private "scrip" issued by a local bank. They suspected a man named Crane was involved. But they lacked any kind of solid proof, so asked Pinkerton to see what he might learn.

In accepting this commission, Pinkerton took further important strides from village cooper to detective-entrepreneur. He was now intentionally investigating crime at a client's behest, essentially providing a private detective service, scarcely more than a dozen years after the Bureau de Renseignements had opened in Paris. And in pursuing the case he began to develop, in rudimentary fashion, the clandestine observation and infiltration methods that would continue to characterize his approach long afterward, even as head of an entire network of agents. Out of necessity he was feeling his way toward a system of detection, and a counterfeiting suspect, both.

Learning of a "well dressed stranger" who had recently arrived in the area seeking directions to the Crane home, Pinkerton soon found the man, John Craig, at a saddlery. There, Pinkerton managed to prompt Craig into repeating his inquiry about where to find Crane, information Pinkerton helpfully supplied along with a subtle but significant endorsement of the gentleman. This and further hinting eventually led to a rendezvous outside town. At the meeting, Pinkerton succeeded in negotiating the purchase of some counterfeit scrip from Craig. Some days later, having demonstrated himself an apparently trustworthy customer, Pinkerton arranged an even larger exchange to take place in Chicago. When Craig duly arrived with stacks of counterfeit notes, he discovered his woeful error in judgment as he found himself under arrest by the Cook County sheriff.

Pinkerton discovered an error of his own when he approached George Smith, whose bank's scrip Craig had reproduced, for compensation. Smith paid the freelance detective, but only after a stern lecturing on his audacity in taking such a job, without formal authorization, and then demanding a fee afterward. Pinkerton's progress as a businessman, too, thus took a step forward in the Craig case.

Like the majority of private detectives then and now, Pinkerton would nonetheless spend time learning his trade on the public payroll first. In Dundee, his rising reputation led to a job offer as Kane County deputy sheriff. He accepted, and, for the next year or two, life otherwise continued along familiar patterns for the growing Pinkerton family. Allan still made barrels in addition to his duties for the sheriff, and Joan gave birth to a second son, Robert, in late 1848. Around that same time, though, Allan resigned his job as deputy sheriff, then left it, coopering, and Dundee for good. Once more, he may have had various reasons. A disagreement with the local church congregation allegedly played a role, although for most of his life Pinkerton was an avowed atheist, and the ambitious "restless" character that Joan observed was probably a bigger factor. Why the Pinkertons packed up and left was in any event less important than where they went. After six years of (mostly) quiet, slow rural life, they set their faces once more toward Chicago.

Allan and Joan had briefly lived in Chicago already, but it was, for all practical purposes, an entirely different city in which they now made their home. The population had swelled to 14,000 by 1846, on its way to 75,000 by the mid-1850s. The writer William Cullen Bryant was just one of many who made visits to Chicago during this period and reported difficulty in recognizing a single thing after no more than a few years' absence—the only constant was probably an improvised, ramshackle appearance that persisted even as all the details changed.

Bryant's disorientation was less an issue for permanent residents, but the material problems of growth were greater. The community was making some efforts to tackle them. To help with the mounting garbage problem, for example, scavenging pigs were set loose in the streets. Local government's response to the crime that accompanied status as a fast-growing city, especially on the frontier, was by contrast somewhat more formal. It was probably also more helpful. The tough Scotsman who had made Kane County unpleasant for horse thieves and counterfeiters readily found an appointment as deputy sheriff for Cook County, where the job was no doubt a more reliably full-time occupation. As, no doubt, was being the city's first detective, a post Chicago's mayor created in 1849 while reorganizing the city police. As Chicago's one detective, Pinkerton, like most who held such early roles, was faced with a constantly growing and shifting criminal population. Many were tough men of the frontier, just like him; during his tenure as city detective Pinkerton was shot in the arm by one particularly determined bad man. As Mackay writes, "The responsibility for solving crime in a rumbustious city of thirty thousand... must have been a daunting prospect."

It became someone else's problem after less than a year because Detective Pinkerton resigned citing "political interference." And here, at least, is an entirely plausible explanation; given that he had been a self-employed trades- man most of his working life, and later on became an emphatically hands-on manager, Allan Pinkerton was almost certainly of that type who can never be satisfied working for another and simply has to be his own boss. He gave government employment one more go, as a Special United States Mail Agent, though he may even then have been setting up his ultimate posting as a pri- vate detective. But first he gave his profile one more boost with a very tidy little investigation into thefts from the Chicago post office, in the process demonstrating impressive skill for a minimally educated immigrant who had been making barrels in a country village only a few years earlier.

In seeking the thief, Pinkerton staged his first serious, extended under- cover operation. It was a small operation, admittedly; having no other agents to assign the job, he placed himself within Chicago's post office as a clerk and mail sorter for several weeks. Eventually, after what must have been a very tedious month or two for the ambitious detective, Pinkerton's investigations into his temporary colleagues revealed that one of the clerks had a brother once arrested for "pilfering mail." The long weeks of observation had begun to pay off, yet his next step was perhaps an even greater test. Pinkerton, in so much of his behavior and remarks, typically comes across as incredibly stern, gruff and impersonable; he may have been the most *serious* detective who ever lived. He could be very engaging when he chose, however, as shown by the many times he won people over in the pursuit of information. Now he applied whatever charm he possessed to befriending fellow clerk Theodore Dennison and was successful enough for his new friend to begin boasting, good naturedly, of his magician's dexterity in handling letters and packages. He even demonstrated these talents for Pinkerton, who watched the fleet fingered clerk show off with considerable interest.

In fact Pinkerton was curious enough to want another look, although he politely decided against bothering Dennison about it. Instead, he watched the other clerk go about his ordinary business, which proved to be somewhat out of the ordinary; watching "from behind a mound of packages" Pinkerton observed Dennison slip several envelopes out of the mail and into his own pocket. Having seen enough to consider the mystery solved, Pinkerton contacted the new deputy sheriff—presumably more for official authority than for physical back-up, as Mackay notes that during the subsequent arrest "the sorter tried to run away but was felled by a flying tackle from Pinkerton."

Dennison had one more challenge to offer. The money he had stolen during months of undetected thievery proved much more elusive than the thief himself. Pinkerton, probably in company with one or more police officers, spent hours searching Dennison's boarding house room until it seemed impossible that the modest accommodation could possibly be concealing anything. But Pinkerton, stubborn, determined and probably approaching a state of fury, refused to quit. Instead he began removing pictures from the walls. If he sought a hidden safe, there was none; undaunted, he proceeded to pull the framed artwork apart and, at last, tucked inside the backing panels he found what he was looking for. A total of $3,378 in bank bills. Flush with success, Pinkerton deferred any celebration, considering his accomplishments up to that point incomplete. For an encore, he proved his aptitude for still another aspect of police work and secured a written confession from Dennison.

The *Chicago Press* considered Pinkerton's efforts, after the mail theft case was all over, and proclaimed that "As a detective, Mr. Pinkerton has no superior and we doubt if he has any equal in this country." This sort of boosterism was in no way unusual in America's competitive young boom towns, where everything was always the biggest and best anyone had ever seen. For once, however, the *Press* may not have exaggerated much. At the very least, Pinkerton was advancing rapidly in a new field that seemed to present endless opportunities, as his own succession of jobs proved. What's more, he was more than shrewd enough to realize it and conclude that if he did have a lead on competitors, he ought to capitalize on it before anyone closed the gap.

Officially, he therefore founded Pinkerton's National Detective Agency in Chicago, in 1850. Yet even recent biographer Mackay, who rules on so many other points of contention with confident finality, acknowledges the beginnings of the Pinkerton agency are "shrouded in mystery and confusion." All of the varied and fragmentary origin stories are, at the same time, largely compatible. It's therefore at least possible that all are true. In which case the establishment of Allan Pinkerton's private detective agency may have gone something like the following:

The Pinkerton "Detective Dynasty" actually began with another Pinkerton entirely, years before Allan's first brush with counterfeiters. Robert Pinkerton, whose emigration may have helped encourage his brother Allan's in the first place, arrived in America and promptly went to work for the country's expanding network of railroads. As subsequent events would show, the railroad companies had need of detective services, and Robert's work as a contractor soon evolved in that direction. As early as 1843, he founded "Pinkerton & Co." to serve railroad clients; eventually the firm provided security for Wells Fargo's stage coach lines, and expanded to several full-time employees. By the late 1840s, inspired by both Vidocq and another model much closer to home, brother Allan could see great potential in the nascent private detective industry. Having already pursued the counterfeiter John Craig on an independent commission, Allan therefore continued to develop private detective clients as a freelancer. Almost certainly while working as a United States Mail Agent, and possibly even when employed by the Chicago police; it may even be that "moonlighting" brought his job as city detective to an end rather than "political interference." Either way, with a growing reputation and clientele, Allan eventually organized The North-Western Police Agency in early 1850, along with a business partner named Edward Rucker. Their partnership proved brief. Following Rucker's departure later that same year, Allan dissolved the North-Western Police Agency and merged its small resources and client base with brother Robert's business. And though the latter was older and more established, the tireless Allan soon took the leading role in the combined firm, operating under an ambitious new name, Pinkerton's National Detective Agency.

At least some of this certainly did happen. Beyond that, specifics are difficult to verify due to the intervening century-and-a-half, the loss of records to Chicago's great fire of 1871, and the impossibility of ever knowing the exact inspirations or motivations of another person. But however it got there, a Pinkerton's National Detective Agency was operating in Chicago by the early 1850s, and it was absolutely Allan Pinkerton's agency.

*

Robert Pinkerton, whatever his role in getting the agency up and running, faded from the picture quickly. Allan had energy, ideas, and experience as an organizer from his Chartist days, and his brother may have simply decided to stand back and let him run. Robert, nonetheless, deserves credit for an idea essential to Pinkerton's becoming a genuinely national detective force, because work for the railroads pointed the way to the company's first and most important big clients. The American railroad network, which by 1850 spanned much of the nation from the eastern seaboard through the Mississippi basin, exemplified most of the factors that were creating demand for private detectives as industrial society evolved. The railroad companies were large and complex organizations and constantly growing, breaking traditional notions about security based on personal familiarity and trust. A railroad's payroll might hide countless Dennisons, all of them with ready access to money and valuables traveling every which way, day and night. And they were only the quieter, inside threats; bandits might strike at any point on the railroads' long lines, which often ran through sparsely settled territory where local law enforcement was undermanned or absent entirely. Those forces that did exist were Balkanized and uncoordinated, while criminals could range freely over territory a thousand miles wide aided by the railroads' own service. Biographer James Horan, in *The Pinkertons: The Detective Dynasty that Made History*, notes pointedly that "Allan Pinkerton filled a very large gap. The wonder is that it took the Federal government so long to emulate him." Until the United States created more effective national law enforcement, those with wealth to protect turned to a National Detective Agency instead.

The agency took on clients besides railroads. In 1852 Pinkerton traced two kidnapped girls to Rockford, Illinois, where he recovered them from their captors (one of whom he shot in the process). Significantly, this job was commissioned by the Cook County sheriff; quite possibly none of Pinkerton's other achievements represents a greater advance over Vidocq than this, part of his broader success at positioning private detection as a complement to public police forces rather than as a competitor. As Pinkerton built up records on crimes and criminals, he made these freely available to police departments rather than requiring them to raid his office. He also funded his agency through per diem charges, eschewing any rewards that were valued greatly by oft under-paid police in those years. His demeanor may have helped, too, in an odd way: it may have been easier for police departments to watch Pinkerton succeed if, unlike Vidocq, he didn't seem to enjoy it nearly as much. Whatever the reason, Pinkerton's agency became a trusted ally to official law enforcement, helping both to avoid problems and to provide access to even more case work.

Nonetheless, the expansion of Pinkerton's from a small office in Chicago to an agency national in scale as well as name was overwhelmingly carried out for, and funded by, railroads. The Illinois Central; Michigan Central; Michigan Southern; North Indiana; Chicago & Galena Union; Chicago & Rock Island; Chicago, Burlington & Quincy—all signed contracts with Pinkerton's in its first few years, providing funds for evolution into a regional business with branches in Wisconsin, Michigan and Indiana. Regular work for the railroads came with important extra benefits too, beyond healthy fees. Pinkerton's contracts generally provided him and his agents with unlimited free travel, significantly. The railroads introduced him to contacts that would also prove valuable, even if not always right away, such as Illinois Central executive George McClellan, as well as a Springfield lawyer named Lincoln who drew up the contract between them.

With so many clients whose businesses were perpetually in motion, Pinkerton never stopped anywhere for long after his agency got off the ground. Even if he was in Chicago for a few days, his family might have had their best chance of seeing him at his office rather than at home. The National Detective Agency centered its expanding empire on Chicago, and a three story office building marked with the agency's iconic, slightly unnerving emblem: an unblinking eye above the motto "We Never Sleep." It was powerful branding for its time. The Pinkertons quickly became known as "the Eye" among those it was their business to watch. And their distinctive symbol undoubtedly popularized, even if it did not originate, the very term "private eye."

Pinkerton's initial staff consisted of five PIs, a secretary, and a few clerks, though those numbers expanded quickly. In his judgment of potential employees and his hiring practices Pinkerton was generally as successful as in most other things, even if he indulged one possible eccentricity. Pinkerton, and Vidocq before him, had both worked for the police before entering private practice, but neither was really a policeman at his core. Vidocq had entered the field of detection as a reformed outlaw, and insisted on the need to employ other ex-criminals against crime; Pinkerton, for his part, had come up from a skilled trade and mostly hired neither ex-cons nor policemen, but tradesmen like himself. He probably had some reasoning to explain this preference, but whether it was strategy or simply bias, it worked.

It needed to work, of course. Even a human dynamo like Allan Pinkerton could not provide or even entirely manage detective services on a national scale alone, though he tried hard. His early hires were key to pulling off the transition from freelancer to corporation, and, unlike other early private detective agencies, a good deal of information is readily available about staff besides the boss. Many of them were British immigrants like Pinkerton, including Pryce Lewis and Timothy Webster; Webster, a former NYPD officer, was also a rare exception with any law enforcement experience. The others were fast learners, however. Pinkerton's very first full-time employee, George Henry Bangs, was a "natural-born detective" according to Mackay, and became Pinkerton's indispensable right-hand man for the rest of his career.

Pinkerton's most remarkable hire was probably Kate Warne, very likely America's first woman detective. Warne boldly walked into Pinkerton headquarters one day in 1856 and explained to the formidable detective tycoon that he needed women investigators, who could learn things in places and ways that a man simply could not. Pinkerton may have actually smiled, for once, at this young lady telling him how to run a detective business, but less from amusement than from recognizing a good idea, as well as a smart and enterprising potential employee. He hired Ms. Warne, who quickly joined Bangs as one of his most trusted agents and, by 1860, managed a several-employee "Female Detective Bureau" within the larger firm. In accepting women for police work, Pinkerton was once again decades ahead of most official law enforcement, as well as his own agency where later directors would promptly reverse this policy.

Allan Pinkerton
Pinkerton's National Detective Agency Records,
Library of Congress, Washington, D.C.

But none of the agency's later directors, though they would include some remarkable detectives, were Allan Pinkerton. A laborer and progressive activist who became a wealthy businessman protecting the profits of ruthless railroad barons, Pinkerton was an odd character in his own era and remains just as difficult to categorize relative to modern American society. His very appearance suggested contradictions. He had a grizzled quality, even as a relatively young man, and like his very close contemporary, Ulysses Grant, he managed to look slightly rugged, even rough, no matter how well dressed. Pinkerton was a pragmatic, workaholic businessman—as well as an atheist who was outraged at reports of employees letting religious fervor into the workplace at a branch office in the 1870s—yet throughout his life and career runs a curious streak of revivalist idealism. He could look at 19th century American capitalism and see entirely adequate opportunity for all free men, but practiced and encouraged sympathy for the lawbreakers his agency existed to persecute. And the moment he began hiring employees, he drafted a moralizing statement of General Principles to ensure his own standard of ethical conduct prevailed. Some of these were just good business, in fairness. Eschewing rewards and bounties for an up-front per diem rate made hiring his agency more predictable and attractive for corporate clients. Divorce work was seen as tawdry, and he could afford high mindedness with so much business for the railroads.

On the other hand, those railroads extended throughout not only the northern states but the slaveholding South, where Pinkerton's fervent abolitionist views were hardly likely to promote trade. Even in the North, his active efforts in the antislavery cause were awfully bold for a respectable businessman. While in Dundee, the Pinkertons made their home available to escaped slaves, and Allan saw no reason to distance himself from the Underground Railroad after moving to Chicago. As both a government employee and private detective, Pinkerton flagrantly violated the Fugitive Slave Act throughout the 1850s. This was not unique, or nearly as drastic as the lengths to which others went for the same cause; abolition certainly had more fervent proponents, such as violent insurrectionist John Brown. He too, however, was a repeated guest at the Pinkerton home, and in 1859 Allan not only provided the wanted man with a hiding place, but raised funds for him from attendees at the Chicago

Judiciary Convention who were given a choice of contributing to Brown's escape or else having him join them at the convention, in a mood to raise Hell. When Brown was eventually captured, after the Harper's Ferry raid, Pinkerton used every connection he had in attempting to save his admired friend's life, though to no avail. That failure was possibly the most bitterly disappointing in his life—at least until another of his heroes was famously made a martyr to the antislavery cause as well, several years later.

If Allan Pinkerton's life was not entirely business, it was all the same very largely devoted to business, and that business had much less to do with the Underground Railroad than with the other kind. One of Pinkerton's cases from the late 1850s illustrates the kind of work that built up the agency; he recalled it years later in a book, *The Expressman and the Detective*. Pinkerton wrote or co-wrote a number of such accounts later in life, and in many, including this one, he certainly exaggerated or added various details for comic effect. (Even amid his overbooked schedule, Pinkerton apparently found occasional time to read for pleasure and specifically noted his appreciation for Charles Dickens's work.) Yet, setting aside some of the sillier diversions that pad out the plot, *The Expressman and the Detective* presents a real case and an informative look at Pinkerton's approach to an investigation.

Edward S. Sanford actually approached Pinkerton for help twice in what would become the *Expressman* case. Sanford was Vice President of the Adams Express Company, one of a number of firms that did not own railroads but employed them constantly in a kind of 19th century delivery and logistics service. Like the railroads, these companies would eventually become frequent customers of the National Detective Agency. Initially, however, Sanford may not have been entirely sure how a private detective even operated. He sent a letter describing the disappearance of $10,000 from a money pouch carried on one of their routes through Georgia, provided what details he knew and asked the detective to help. Pinkerton was tempted to ignore the oddly random epistle, but considered it over the weekend and wrote back suggesting that Adams's Montgomery office manager Nathan Maroney was the thief. He then heard nothing further, and forgot about the matter.

Pinkerton eventually heard from Sanford again, nearly a full year later. This time word arrived by telegram rather than by post, and the Adams VP was correspondingly much more anxious for a reply. After another robbery, he had charged Maroney and had the man arrested, but the move backfired disastrously. Friends rallied around the popular gentleman and raised the necessary bail money after it was reduced from $40,000 to $4,000 in light of Sanford's circumstantial and fairly weak evidence.

With a much clearer commission, his correspondent wasted no time in dispatching agents to the south and east. (Adams had originated in the North, but operated throughout the Southern states as well by this time; like Pinkerton, however, they could not keep their business interests entirely separate from the deepening conflict over slavery and split in two along with the nation a few years later.) Pinkerton, as a detective, was canny and effective, but his true genius was mostly administrative; his tactical approach to detection, by contrast, was generally as simple and direct as possible. Essentially, send in a man to watch and listen, and, if necessary, another man (or woman) and another, until eventually someone gave something away. He might elaborate or refine this in various ways and supplement it with other methods, but this was the core of Pinkerton's methodology throughout his tenure as chief. It was not entirely without some element of theory. Pinkerton believed that a crime never occurred without more than one person learning something of it and that criminals invariably had to confide in someone. As criminology theory, it was still primitive by modern standards, but as was usual with Pinkerton it worked fairly well, if only because the idea was implemented with his relentless determination and activity.

He now put these to work on the Adams thefts, placing agents around both Maroney and his wife. One trailed Mrs. Maroney through the South and observed her mailing a letter to Jenkintown, Pennsylvania; upon this report, Pinkerton promptly dispatched another agent to Jenkintown where he set up shop as a watch repairman and discovered various relatives of Mrs. Maroney living in the area. When Mrs. Maroney joined them, Pinkerton reinforced the watch repairman with Kate Warne, who arrived in town as "the wife of a wealthy forger" and found an understanding friend in the wife of the suspected thief, Maroney.

Kate Warne's friendship and sympathy may have been provided with extra appeal to Mrs. Maroney, meanwhile, as Pinkerton had directed Sanford in having Maroney re-arrested on charges of conspiracy. Upon which Maroney, too, found sympathetic new friends including a cell mate held on forgery charges (actually agent John White) and his attorney (actually George Bangs). Then for good measure, Pinkerton supplied Maroney with a new antagonist as well, sending him anonymous notes about his wife spending a great deal of time with a handsome stranger; another agent dispatched to Jenkintown lent substance to these rumors.

All of which, combined, ends up seeming like almost comic overkill, and even more so in *The Expressman and the Detective*. If Pinkerton exaggerated some things in its pages, he can hardly be accused of claiming omniscience as a detective, instead standing by in frustration as a small army of agents followed Mrs. Maroney's every move for weeks, without discovering a thing. For those used to dramatic feats of deduction or forensic analysis, Pinkerton's work seems laughably ham fisted. Yet in contrast with many who won fame as detectives, Pinkerton had no affinity for showmanship or dazzling flourishes. He promoted himself and his business through bottom line results, and if his methods were unimaginative, they won a strong record of both convictions and recovery of stolen property.

Eventually, he added the case against Nathan Maroney to that record, through patience plus a steady pressure to help things along. In combination with the anonymous notes, encouragement from White stoked Maroney's resentment, and receptiveness to the suggestion of simply buying his way out of jail. When Bangs arrived one day to announce that he had gotten his client, White, free of the charges, Maroney finally cracked and asked if Bangs could do the same for him. The pretend lawyer readily asserted that he could for the appropriate fee. So Maroney prevailed upon his newly free friend White to pay a visit to Jenkintown, as a favor, and secure the necessary funds from Mrs. Maroney.

When this stranger arrived, claiming to be an emissary of her husband, Mrs. Maroney had very reasonable suspicions. She sought advice from a friend, and hemmed in on nearly all sides by undercover detectives as she was, that friend was almost inevitably a Pinkerton agent. Just as inevitably, Kate Warne advised Mrs. Maroney to trust White with the money; appreciating her good friend's advice, she did just that. The stolen funds promptly made their way back to Sanford rather than their intended recipient, Maroney. He remained in jail awaiting the trial. When it arrived, Pinkerton secured not only a conviction but, at the end, even did so in a fairly dramatic fashion. When White entered the courtroom as a witness for the prosecution on the second day of the trial, an ashen faced Maroney surrendered and pleaded guilty.

Though achieved only after a grinding and expensive effort, the agency's success in the *Expressman* case impressed the business community. More and more work followed, both for Pinkerton's detectives and for the uniformed guard division introduced as a natural extension of their security work. By its tenth year in business, the National Detective Agency had ongoing contracts with Adams and its largest competitor, too many railroads to list, and Pinkerton's old employer the Postal Service as well. A great deal more government work was soon to follow, too, when Pinkerton nearly doubled his responsibilities upon the outbreak of the Civil War.

Officially, America's bloodiest conflict began on April 12, 1861. But, for many, the fighting at Fort Sumter marked nothing more than a new and more open phase in a struggle already under way for years. That must have been the perspective of Allan Pinkerton, who had kept his home open to fugitive slaves and seen his friend John Brown executed for violent action in that struggle well before northern and southern armies marched into the field. By the very beginning of 1861, moreover, Pinkerton was convinced that more men were plotting violent strikes of their own, though for an opposing agenda. The detective was not alone in his suspicions, as such views demanded little imagination in the divisive atmosphere following the 1860 election to the presidency of the Springfield, Illinois lawyer Pinkerton had met years before.

The months that followed saw various threads of Pinkerton's life—his connections in the railroad industry, his ties to Lincoln, his enthusiasm for the antislavery and Union causes as open rebellion loomed—all come together in the Baltimore Plot episode. A railroad client, the president of the Philadelphia, Wilmington and Baltimore, first approached Pinkerton about the possibility of some sort of danger in the large Maryland city in January. Samuel Felton reported that his company had received a variety of threats recently from Baltimore, which was considered rife with secessionist feeling. This was vague, but Pinkerton took it seriously enough to investigate personally, aided by several other agents. And, though perhaps the unlikeliest southern sympathizer ever, Pinkerton showed his peculiar charisma once again in befriending a secessionist who hinted at a dramatic plan to advance the cause: assassinating the president-elect.

Such talk can be cheap, and usually is. But by the next month, Pinkerton and Felton believed that their evidence was sufficient to take seriously and arranged to meet Lincoln himself. Unknown to the two men, Lincoln had already heard similar reports from other channels, and he found the additional warning from Pinkerton persuasive. The president-elect refused advice to leave Pennsylvania, where he still had public appearances scheduled, and immediately return to Washington. But with that exception, he agreed to place Pinkerton in charge of security details for the time being.

Whether a serious threat to Lincoln was present in early 1861 or not, this was certainly a good idea and another example of Pinkerton identifying needs for organized security and law enforcement decades before any official government agencies existed to address them. The Secret Service was not established for another five years, and then initially only to combat the counterfeiting problems Pinkerton had been battling since the 1840s; no permanent Secret Service protection of the president was authorized until 1902. When Abraham Lincoln finished his appearance in Harrisburg, Pennsylvania, on February 22, 1861, the responsibility for getting him safely back to Washington rested with the Pinkertons.

As history makes quite obvious, they succeeded. Allan Pinkerton and some of his chroniclers subsequently made much of cloak-and-dagger details: coded messages, a special train, cut telegraph wires, a personal escort for the president from Pinkerton himself, and numerous agents stationed along the route. Yet if the Pinkertons did thwart an assassination plot, they ultimately did so through deterring it rather than seizing an assassin in the act, gun in hand. Which, on the whole, is an entirely reasonable security policy. The Baltimore Plot's nature as a bomb that did not explode nonetheless led some critics to accuse Pinkerton of exaggerating or even making up the whole affair. And no one really had conclusive proof to offer otherwise.

Most of Pinkerton's biographers, including the often critical Horan, take the position that the threat to Lincoln was legitimate. Horan points to the angry crowd that mobbed Mrs. Lincoln's train car in Baltimore just two days afterward, as well as violent rioting in the city, in April, that fit with other information from the same sources that had tipped Pinkerton to a planned assassination. Ultimately, the best assessment of Pinkerton and the Baltimore Plot is probably that in urging Abraham Lincoln to arrange professional security against threats to his life, the detective proved, sadly, only too astute.

Pinkerton could not persuade Lincoln about the need for a permanent security detail, though, with results that remain well known 150 years later. But the Union government found plenty of other use for the National Detective Agency throughout the Civil War. Pinkerton even established a kind of secret service, though it was not for the president or the Treasury, but rather for yet another old contact from the agency's railroad work. Lincoln responded favorably when Pinkerton first offered his services for the larger war effort, but the press of events upon his taking office delayed any further discussion, and Pinkerton was left waiting around Washington; as he was never a man for sitting still even in peacetime, he was preparing to return to Chicago when he received word from George McClellan. The former Illinois Central executive was taking command of the new Department of the Ohio, and he, at least, was ready to put Pinkerton and his detectives to work promptly.

The result was an interesting partnership with results at least as controversial as the Baltimore Plot. Pinkerton served the Union government in a number of ways during the war, most of which added to his record of dependability and effectiveness. As a military intelligence officer, however, assessments of his service vary enormously. Pinkerton sent many of his best agents into the Confederate states and frequently joined them himself, traveling as "Major

E.J. Allen," in pursuit of information on the enemy. And the intelligence he brought back personally to McClellan was generally solid. But Pinkerton, who in many ways was always more of a spymaster than a detective, also needed to manage a large network of agents as complex as any he had attempted before, and in doing so he may have finally stretched himself too far. This is Horan's view in no uncertain terms: "Relying on what he saw or heard, Pinkerton was an excellent spy behind the lines, but as a front line analyzer of the reports of other agents, he would prove to be totally incompetent." As with most Civil War reputations, Pinkerton's remains the subject of ongoing battles. The more recent biographer Mackay argues that Pinkerton's wartime "secret service" work was brilliant, although Mackay finds few ways in which Pinkerton was other than brilliant.

Here, too, one may do best to look at the larger picture, in which Pinkerton did much good service for the Union cause, but was not able to do enough in his military intelligence role for General McClellan, whatever the actual quality of his work. By the middle of 1861, McClellan rose to General-in-Chief of all the Union armies, but that was the brief pinnacle of his success. Despite McClellan's relatively patrician background and his opposition to abolitionist ideas, Pinkerton liked and even idolized the general and was euphoric over his promotion to the top. He was thus dismayed, a year later, when McClellan was relieved of command as a result of both slow progress against the rebellion and growing unpopularity in Washington. The outcome must have been especially painful in light of the deep rift formed between McClellan and Lincoln, both of whom Pinkerton saw as heroes. Caught in the middle, Pinkerton resigned from the secret service he had established at McClellan's behest, but continued working for other government departments through the rest of the war.

There was still a great deal to do. If Pinkerton did fall short as a military intelligence analyst, he might at least be pardoned, given how much else he was trying to do at the same time. Among other things, even as he was trying to direct espionage against the Confederacy he was also working to prevent it from going the other way. His most challenging opponent in this game was running an entire network of spies and informants, including men in government, industry, and the military, and reaching from Washington, DC, to Texas. The contact for all of these agents was none other than a widowed southern belle in her late 40s named Rose Greenhow.

Pinkerton got his first clue to Greenhow's busy enterprise from a man he believed had been involved in the Baltimore Plot. Pinkerton kept him under regular surveillance, afterward, and this paid dividends in alerting the detective to Rose Greenhow's service to the Southern cause. Greenhow was openly sympathetic to the South—not uncommon in either Washington or the surrounding state of Maryland. But the scale of her support for the rebellion was something else entirely. Among the achievements that can be verified, Greenhow acquired the details of Union General McDowell's plans ahead of the battle of Bull Run and smuggled them to Confederate forces via courier, providing them a vital edge against the Yankees. Pinkerton determined to put a stop to this, yet he faced a formidable opponent. Greenhow's connections not only alerted her to Pinkerton's increasing surveillance, but allowed her to direct pressure back at him from members of the Union government he was trying to serve. The frustration was enough for Pinkerton himself to break into Greenhow's home illegally at one point, but for no result. Rose Greenhow seemed nearly untouchable. That sense of invincibility may have led to her finally making a fatal mistake that gave her adversary the break he needed. Pinkerton learned that a young captain, named Ellison, had been "borrowing" a number of confidential documents, and upon having the too careless mole followed, Pinkerton quickly had the long awaited connection between Rose Greenhow and specific, provable acts of espionage.

The saga of Rose Greenhow was far from finished, and would eventually offer up hardships of incarceration, scandal, sex, prison suicide and swallowed code messages. But while she remained a thorn in his side for some time, Pinkerton had effectively broken an important link in the Confederacy's intelligence service. Meanwhile, his attention remained divided between a number of full-time responsibilities. There was still a growing detective agency to run, which the boss remained determined to manage down to the last detail. There were investigations of corruption and fraud by war contractors, in which Pinkerton did signal service throughout the war. And, at least until

McClellan's fall, there were also personal spy missions into the Confederacy, as well as a certain amount of intrigue in Washington against the general's foes within the Union.

Though in the former, at least, Pinkerton had help not only from Kate Warne and other agents but also from the only employees he would ever trust more than Warne or even George Bangs: his two sons, William and Robert. In his later years, by which time Lincoln was a figure of another era, almost of myth, William recalled once meeting the president in the Oval Office, and Lincoln admonishing the elder Pinkerton in a friendly way about sending his sons into danger behind Confederate lines at such a young age. But for Pinkerton it was a mild moral compromise at most and an easy one given the alternatives. He believed too deeply in the Union cause to deny it his two strong, capable boys, yet like any parent he must have dreaded the idea of their charging into Confederate guns, even though many lads no older than William or Robert were doing just that. So instead, two more Pinkertons began learning the detective's craft from one of the best teachers, under some of the most unforgiving conditions. In the decades to come, both would put the experience to good use.

After the war, the restoration of nationwide commerce was good for the railroads. That was good for Pinkerton's National Detective Agency, which expanded its operations in Philadelphia and added a New York office. William and Robert, who had proven their abilities even against their father's high standards, were appointed co-managers, at least officially. Allan Pinkerton was still the one in charge, and had a lot of detecting left in him.

As wartime work for the federal government wound down, the agency's clientele resumed much of its antebellum form. The crimes they faced were another matter. In the 1850s, the Pinkertons had responded to evolving social and economic patterns with innovative systems and ideas. They were not the nation's first private detectives, but they quickly began operating at a scale unmatched by other law enforcers, public or private. They improved on Vidocq by adding photographs to their records as soon as it was practical, and if anyone has a compelling case for creating the first "rogues' gallery" it's probably Allan Pinkerton. They also combined this resource with another emerging technology, the telegraph network, to create a central clearinghouse for information between both their own branches and the nation's innumerable and scattered police departments. In Horan's phrase, "The Pinkertons appeared to be a crude but effective Victorian Age Interpol." But lawbreakers were responding with novel ideas of their own. In 1867, Pinkerton untangled a complex stock manipulation scheme that combined insider trading and tapping the telegraph network to plant false news stories. That same year he took his agency into an extended war with a gang that, in late 1866, had made history with the first major example of a staple of later Western legend: the train hold-up.

The thieves were certainly daring, if not foolhardy, as the $700,000 they stole was the responsibility of the Adams Express Company, which effectively guaranteed pursuit by the nation's leading detectives. The Pinkertons didn't have far to search, either. The gang had robbed the Express near Seymour; upon arriving in the southern Indiana town, Allan Pinkerton promptly found the Reno gang at large and well known.

As usual, Pinkerton assigned agents to the area for long-term surveillance. One of them, Dick Winscott, opened up a saloon and soon had members of the gang as regulars. He even persuaded John Reno and another gang member, Franklin Sparks, to pose for a photograph. Grinning for the camera while holding up mugs of beer, they helped themselves right into the Pinkerton rogues' gallery. Winscott also had little difficulty in confirming that the Renos were behind the train robbery. Yet making an arrest seemed a much more serious challenge. Winscott cautioned Pinkerton that trying to seize the men from Seymour was very likely to provoke a shootout, and danger to innocent lives would be unavoidable.

Pinkerton and his son William considered this, and they came up with a plan that later Western filmmakers might have admired. They obtained an arrest warrant and the cooperation of the Davies County sheriff, then used their status with the railroads to arrange a small favor. The Pinkertons arranged for a "special"—an unscheduled train—and spent the next two days in Cincinnati with steam built up and ready to make haste for Seymour at a moment's notice. Winscott, meanwhile, had worked to lure John Reno to the local train station on a pretext, and finally telegraphed that the bandit would be there waiting for a made-up friend to arrive on a regular express train. The Pinkerton special pulled into Seymour minutes ahead of the express, Allan and six of his detectives fanning out to surround Reno, then pouncing. Prisoner in hand, they quickly reboarded the train and pulled out of Seymour ahead of pursuit by Reno's gang, which had been alerted just barely too late.

A few months later, William led a raid in Iowa and captured other gang members who had gone into hiding. But arresting the Reno gang proved far more difficult than holding onto them, or keeping them alive. In later years, hold-up men like the Renos acquired considerable popularity as folk heroes, in the tradition of Robin Hood. In 1868, though, the Renos were far from well loved by a number of communities in which they had lived it up. Local resentment was so strong that as soon the Pinkertons' arrests fractured the gang's power, the detectives found themselves busier protecting the Renos from ordinary citizens than vice versa. Town jails proved no effective defense against vigilante groups, and Pinkerton needed quick work and large numbers, both, to keep gang members alive after arrest.

The Reno gang failed to appreciate the effort. Frank Reno and Albert Perkins managed to flee to Windsor, Ontario, where their eventual arrest started a drawn out, tortuous battle for extradition. And while in Windsor trying to move the process along, Pinkerton dodged not one but two attempts on his life by friends of the Renos. The still pugnacious detective not only survived these would-be assassins, but subdued and captured both men in almost contemptuous fashion. Hearing the sound of a revolver cocked behind him, Pinkerton spun around and jammed his finger through the trigger guard of Dick Barry's gun, then twisted the weapon away from him and delivered a good thrashing to the "noted cracksman" before marching him to the nearest police station at gunpoint. Two days later, a train robber named Johnson at least got off a shot, but missed and subsequently fared no better than Barry.

Ironically, after two assassins failed so completely, a careless boat pilot came much closer to ending the great detective's career. His business in Windsor finally completed, Pinkerton found passage back to the United States on a tugboat. (To the consternation of many of his railroad industry clients, no bridge existed at the time.) Unfortunately, Pinkerton's trip was interrupted when the tugboat collided roughly with a steamer. He was knocked over the side and immersed in the icy Detroit River before being pulled back out, no doubt chilled and infuriated at the same time. Having so recently demonstrated his vitality in dramatic fashion, Pinkerton's instinct was to shrug this off, to plow ahead with the million items awaiting on his agenda as usual. Yet even Allan Pinkerton had his limits. And in the year that followed, he was pushed up to and beyond them.

Outwardly, Pinkerton seemed hale as ever as he approached 50. But he had been driving himself relentlessly for more than two decades with overwork, incalculable stress, constant travel and minimal rest. The shock of his dunking in frigid water was followed by a prolonged cold as well as fevers and debilitating headaches. The beginnings of what proved a string of bad news did nothing to help matters. In 1868 he mourned the deaths of both his brother, Robert, and his invaluable lady detective, Kate Warne. Then, after years of acclaim for his successes, Pinkerton also met with some of the harshest criticism of his career during this period. A botched raid in pursuit of the Jameses, another outlaw gang, killed a young relative and injured other family members, generating a public opinion backlash. And skeptics of the Baltimore Plot received a boost when New York Police Chief John Kennedy loudly and publicly denounced it as a complete fabrication.

Conflict and loss were not new to Pinkerton, and he had always dealt with them by pushing harder. But now those around him found a man not only driven but increasingly angry and erratic, lashing out at anyone over the slightest offenses. Even his trusted and loyal ally, George Bangs, received a letter described as "astonishing" in its invective and bitterness. Pinkerton's determination to remain in control of everything, no matter what, had built up a pressure that no one could hold back forever.

In the summer of 1869, the dam finally burst. A massive stroke shattered the seemingly indestructible detective; in its wake, he was nearly paralyzed on his right side and could barely speak a word for more than a year. Physicians attending the broken man warned his family that Pinkerton would probably never walk again.

Their patient disagreed, however. The only thing Allan Pinkerton had no chance whatsoever of doing was quitting while he remained alive. That same stubbornness that had led him to overtax his body now allowed him to rehabilitate it beyond doctors' expectations. He needed such determination because it was a slow, frustrating process; he only regained basic use of his limbs after many months, and years passed before he could write so much as his own name. By autumn of 1871, however, he could get around well enough to return to work and did so whether anyone else thought he was ready or not. He must have recovered more resilience than friends or family suspected, for within a few weeks of his return he endured yet another major crisis.

Beginning October 8, the great Chicago fire raged for two entire days, devouring what had become the fourth largest city in the United States. Pinkerton's headquarters was destroyed, along with much of the agency's history. Early papers, the rogues' gallery, records from the Civil War—all were lost. Yet before the smoke had even cleared, Allan Pinkerton, who struggled to speak at all a year before, was voicing the same unshakable will to overcome that the whole city was about to demonstrate. "I will never be beaten, never," he swore. "Not all the fumes of Hell will stop me from rebuilding immediately." In the aftermath of the fire, his agency moved quickly to reassure a panicked city. Many other businesses had lost offices to the fire, of course, and amid fears of looting they worried for the contents of safes and vaults that had survived the inferno. The threat may in truth have been relatively minor, but Pinkerton vowed to extinguish it entirely, all but declaring martial law in his fury. "Death shall be [the] fate [of] any person stealing or seeking to steal any property in my charge."

Pinkerton's almost biblical series of trials would finally end, as they had begun, with an element of irony. Two years after he had dispatched armed men into the ash and smoke to protect the wealth of Chicago from burglars, both he and his clients suffered far greater financial losses from an entirely different quarter. The Panic of 1873 triggered an economic Depression in the United

States and Europe, lasting several years and doing the National Detective Agency considerably more harm than either fire or looters could have come close to. Business never dried up entirely for the Pinkertons, but the agency's upkeep had become considerable after 23 years of nearly uninterrupted growth, and cash flow problems therefore posed a very real threat. Its survival through these years owes much to hard decisions taken by its chief.

But Pinkerton's stewardship, for all of its impressive results over the years, was gradually coming to an end. It's difficult to say with certainty exactly how much Pinkerton ever recovered after the stroke that crippled him in 1869. He certainly returned to work in Chicago, and apparently resumed traveling to eastern branches in time, which suggests largely revived energy and mobility. In the immediate aftermath of the stroke, however, when Pinkerton lay paralyzed and helpless, his sons managed to maintain for some time that he had suffered no more than "a mild shock" and would be fine after a brief rest. So some consideration must be given to counter-propaganda in considering Pinkerton's subsequent health; a strong agency seemed unimaginable without a strong Allan Pinkerton, so long had he been the prime mover behind every decision and action.

Pinkerton himself had as much difficulty accepting this idea as anyone, as much *because* the obvious successors were his own children as in spite of that fact. His surprisingly progressive views on various issues of the day absolutely did not extend to patriarchal authority within the family. Inevitably, this created friction with three adult children longing to assert some independence. The Pinkertons' third child, daughter Joan, tried her father's patience by insisting on a social circle of her own choosing. Her brothers William and Robert, in turn, gave Allan fits with their notion of having some say in how the agency was run. As both men were now approaching their 30s, with more than a decade of experience, it seemed reasonable to them that they finally become "co-managers" in deed as well as in name. To their father, however, this was nothing short of high treason. Over the years, he reacted to such acts of "betrayal" with a combination of outraged bluster and melodramatic self-pity that must have sorely tested his sons' deep admiration.

In time, Pinkerton finally began to step back from the agency and, remarkably, even discover some of the broader life beyond. In middle age he took up yet another career as a writer, beginning *The Expressman and the Detective* and the other books in which he attempted to heal some of the bruises his legacy had taken in recent years. Meanwhile, his modest nod to the Great American Novel was complemented by a rather less modest venture at another enduring American notion, the dream house. While confined at home during his convalescence, he had begun contemplating a new, grander estate, somewhat more in keeping with the tycoon he had become. As soon as he was able, he began directing the construction of "The Larches," outside of Onarga, Illinois. Then an even bigger surprise followed: after getting settled on his splendid new estate, Allan Pinkerton felt the impulse to show it off, and actually began entertaining guests with some frequency.

But, then, The Larches' very location more than 80 miles from Chicago suggests a man at last coming around to the possibility of retirement as a real prospect. And so it proved; by 1877, William and Robert had effectively taken control of the National Detective Agency's operations, at least on a day-to-day basis. The fact that Pinkerton did not take to the field personally, even when his agency got involved in unraveling another conspiracy against Lincoln (this time an attempt to steal the late president's body), is telling. Pinkerton was not quite done; he organized and closely managed James McParland's 1876 infiltration of the Molly Maguires, a secret organization accused of terrorizing eastern Pennsylvania's coal mining communities. But that was the last major case in which Pinkerton played his accustomed role of directing every person and detail. (For his testimony, McParland himself was temporarily celebrated as "the great detective," though the case also stoked antipathy toward the agency among labor groups, who saw prosecution of the Mollies as union busting.)

If Pinkerton had to step away from the agency he had built from almost nothing, the late 1870s were about as good a time as any. Business had recovered from the crash, and the company was generally enjoying a high point in its history. Nearly every American railroad of consequence was a Pinkerton client. The agency was called in almost automatically after any major crime, by banks, insurers, and even many local and state governments. Pinkertons were operating more and more frequently in Europe, as well. William and Robert, after struggling for so long to get a real say in running things, were doing an impressive job and beginning to carve out reputations of their own as first class detectives.

In fact, by 1879, they apparently felt comfortable enough in their authority for Robert to admit struggling on one notable case and seek his father's advice. Another, better organized team of grave robbers had struck in Robert's territory of New York, making off with the body of merchant A.T. Stewart and demanding a large ransom. Allan agreed to review the case and sat down to conduct an investigation from his office using Robert's notes, just as he had with the letter from Edward Sanford about the Adams Express robbery more than 20 years before. His instincts proved still sharp. The body thieves claimed to have removed Stewart's remains to Canada, but Allan Pinkerton smelled a red herring. In rejecting an offer of $25,000 for the body's return, the thieves' letter protested that this was too low given all the difficulties they would face with customs. But they had never mentioned anything about entry *into* Canada proving in any way burdensome. Responding to his son, Allan advised that "I do not think this story of the body being taken to Canada hangs well together; I think the remains may be in New Jersey or at farthest in Pennsylvania..." When the body finally reappeared, it was no further from its original resting place than Westchester County, New York.

The last years were quiet ones for Pinkerton, probably more tranquil than any he had known in his first six decades. He had more books coming out, but did relatively little of the writing himself. Instead he spent time at home, enjoying his majestic estate. He went for walks, and probably even sat still and rested on occasion. It was on what should have been a pleasant stroll in June, 1884, that he took the unfortunate fall that eventually ended his remarkable story. He bit his tongue badly as he stumbled, and over the next three weeks endured gangrene, septicemia and incredible pain. His family realized before long that the old fighter would not pull through this time, though Pinkerton held out for days while those attending him were sure he was nearly gone. He was at last reduced to his final hours, on July 1, and with William and Joan at his side he expired at five minutes past three o'clock.

The New York Times led the many papers, throughout the United States and even overseas, that heralded America's famous detective. Their lengthy notice listed case after case that Pinkerton and his agents had solved, including a host of railroad and bank robberies, before declaring that "Very few crimes have occurred in this country in the last 20 years in the detection of which Pinkerton's agency has not had a hand." It was a legacy that endured long after Allan Pinkerton was laid to rest, in a great variety of ways. Of the many detectives who achieved a measure of fame, only Vidocq may surpass him for a literary legacy. Pinkerton wrote or authorized 18 books of his own, and was probably the inspiration for George Munro's Old Sleuth, the Detective. A decade after Allan's death, Frank A. Pinkerton (though no relation) began writing The Pinkerton Detective Series of mysteries, which enjoyed a long run; his use of the Pinkerton name to add a dash of real-life detective drama to his tales was the beginning of a tradition that continues to this day.

Pinkerton's legacy also manifested in other, more substantive ways. He had created a private detective and security service that, for good or bad, remained an indispensable component of American law enforcement for decades. His battles with counterfeiters and efforts to guard President Lincoln were a prototype for the Secret Service, which the federal government would eventually copy, long years afterward. And in his own summation of Pinkerton's life, James Horan considers a provocative suggestion that Allan Pinkerton effectively predicted the FBI as well:

> With some exaggeration, Murray Kempton believed that Allan Pinkerton had invented most of the devices used by [J. Edgar] Hoover. The director of the Federal Bureau of Investigation "found the tablets already engraved; no further exercise was demanded of him except some tracing at the edges." Hoover must be given more credit than that, but a comparison of the two detective administrators indicates that Hoover may well have been the twentieth century son of Pinkerton.

In considering Pinkerton's legacy to detection, it may however be best to close with his 19th century sons, William and Robert. They learned their trade at their father's side, led his agency to further heights, and carried on his methods and his literal DNA right up to the era of Hoover's FBI itself. If their names are less familiar today than their father's, they are hardly in unusual company even among the most distinguished of their field's history. A full account of the Pinkertons and of the great detectives must include their stories, too.

CHAPTER FOUR
'PADDINGTON' POLLAKY

"POLLAKY'S PRIVATE INQUIRY OFFICE.—
Mr. Pollaky has 27 years' experience in England
and with the Foreign Detective Police agents
abroad.—13, Paddington-green."

(Advertisement, The London *Times*, February 7, 1877)

T HE MURDER OF Francis Saville Kent in June 1860 was a tragedy for the infant boy's family. With time it also proved a disaster for one Scotland Yard detective, and a torment for a nation desperate for a resolution which could not be had. One small death caused so much suffering, and the anguish may have been even worse because of how pointless it seemed, a crime with no direct benefit to anyone, as in the end it proved. Yet not before one party was enriched, for a time, in an indirect sense. For in all honesty the affair was an absolute gift for the British press.

In the Road Murder, journalists had a mystery offering horror, intricacy, and longevity. Months after Inspector Whicher's prosecution of the slain infant's half sister, Constance, had collapsed, dispatches from the Temperance Hall at Road were still filling newspaper columns. Parliamentary outcry and investigations of investigations had kept the story alive through the summer. As autumn advanced, a Mr. T.B. Saunders took up the business, using his status as magistrate to conduct an otherwise unofficial, private inquiry. Meanwhile, throughout the multiple reinvestigations, the central mystery of *whodunit* pointed toward or intersected with a whole host of additional mysteries. *What became of the missing nightdress*, if there was one at all; *Did Mr.*

Kent have something to hide; and eventually, some years later, *Was Constance's confession the real truth of the case.* In November the papers made room amongst these to examine, briefly, another curious little mystery, of minor importance to the Road Murder but of considerable significance within the history of detection: *Who was Pollaky and what was he doing?*

The answer: Mr. Pollaky was a detective, and engaged upon some sort of clandestine business that prompted much speculation from the press and very little comment from Pollaky himself. Little more was known about his business in Road, in 1860; much the same could be said about his business in most things, ever. On the 13th of November, a London *Times* report on Saunders's inquest noted that "The mysterious Mr. Pollaky was there, and took notes of several parts of the proceedings." His "mysterious" presence was deemed worth noting in a number of dispatches from Road, in fact, and yet as one of them noted "the nature of his mission did not transpire."

This odd juxtaposition of notoriety and enigma characterizes much of the man's entire career. By the early 1860s, reporters and columnists regularly made reference to "Mr. Pollaky, the well known detective," and even began dropping his name in entirely unrelated contexts as a byword for sleuthing and furtive inquiry. For a time his surname even came into use by itself as an exclamation, "Pollaky!" It may indeed be that no other real-life detective has surpassed the currency that Pollaky's name achieved, in his day; others' reputations may have been bigger, or longer lasting, but "Pollaky" was for a time something very like a modern day pop culture phenomenon. His name appeared regularly in the news, his advertisements themselves developed a kind of cult following, and meanwhile the mysterious Mr. Pollaky's fame was attested by poetry, songs, novels, stage plays and even a Gilbert & Sullivan opera.

All of which begs the question of what all of the fuss was about. As the handful of reporters in Road asked 150 years ago: what was this man Pollaky really up to? Accounts of his doings appeared often in the subsequent two decades, but the picture they provide is often remarkably slight in detail compared with the seeming universality of his reputation within British society. A modern reader, especially, may legitimately wonder if the celebrity afforded

Pollaky wasn't simply some sort of extended, absurdist joke, indulged by a media-saturated culture with a capacity for self-aware humor rivaling that of today's online communities. One or two contemporary critics even crossed over from the tone of awe and mystery that otherwise prevailed in accounts of Pollaky, into overt sarcasm regarding his fame. Inevitable criticism of success? Or "giving the game away?" It seems difficult to believe that there was not some genuinely remarkable merit, somewhere, behind the widespread fame. Yet it is difficult to assess what precisely that may have been.

Pollaky seems to have tested the very limits of how private a private detective may be before vanishing into complete anonymity. He left no memoirs, and had no literary friend to fill out the spare accounts of newspapers with more-personal details; the closest anyone seems to have come to a real profile of Pollaky was a feature story published in an Australian newspaper, 16 years after the man's death. One cannot even be sure what he looked like. A caricature appeared in 1874 as part the *London Figaro*'s "London Sketch Book of Celebrities," depicting a strong, broad face adorned with bushy moustache and side whiskers. But the accuracy of this portrait can only be guessed at without photographs or detailed descriptions for comparison. Out of all the detectives who rose to celebrity status and who may have a claim to true greatness, "the well-known Pollaky of Paddington Green" was, more than any other, both professionally and personally a man of mystery.

For the early life of Ignatius Paul Pollaky, even the word "mystery" may be inadequate to describe the nearly complete absence of reliable information. Pollaky seems very nearly to have sprung into the world of London detectives, fully formed, in his early 20s. He arrived in London in 1850 as an immigrant, but even his nationality is open to question. News items variously refer to him as Austrian, Hungarian, or Polish. Pollaky was apparently born in Pressburg, Hungary, in 1828; at the time this was part of the multi-ethnic Austro-Hungarian Empire, and today the town (renamed Bratislava) is a part of Slovakia. Arguably, a young Pollaky would not have seen the issue of nationality the same as a 21st century citizen does, anyway. National identity remains a work in progress within Europe, but before the wars that welded together

Germany and Italy and broke up polyglot empires like Austria-Hungary it was arguably an entirely abstract concept. As a boy, Pollaky had one mother tongue, presumably, yet one would struggle to say what it was, as by early adulthood he spoke at least six. Victorian Britain might have simply classified him as a "Continental," which might be as appropriate as anything.

Pollaky himself seems to have felt little sentimental attachment to his original language and cultural background, whatever they were. In 1850 he left behind both to seek his fortune in London. Here, too, one can only speculate on the details. By the middle of the 19th century the once vigorous empire of the Habsburgs had arguably begun its long decline, at least relative to the rising Prussian state that would rout Austria in 1866. It was hardly the back of beyond, however, and most likely the twenty-something Ignatius Pollaky had other concerns in mind than the fates of civilizations. It may be that he imagined his fluency with several languages would be of greater value in Britain than continental Europe, where multilingualism was much more common. At the same time it may be that he simply yearned for adventure, or had some particular admiration for the English; an 1862 Naturalization application in Britain's National Archives could suggest both. Pollaky had apparently decided to adopt his new country wholeheartedly after a dozen years, or at least to attempt it. His application was, however, denied, with the amusing summary "Applicants of doubtful character: Ignatuis [*sic*] Pollaky, adventurer; certificate refused."

Regardless of his origins or his reasons for leaving them, no one seems to have held Pollaky's ethnic background against him. Early Victorian London was far from the diverse, cosmopolitan city that greets modern visitors, but it would prove fairly welcoming to the young man from Austria (or Hungary, or Slovakia). If Her Majesty's Secretary of State and others later regarded Mr. Pollaky with suspicion, it was because of the profession he had chosen rather than the origins he had left behind. Scotland Yard's official detective division was still only several years old when Pollaky first set foot in the teeming London streets, and private detectives were an even more recent innovation when he began attaching himself to that trade. Like the detective division before and the uniformed city force before that, yet another group of men nosing around would take getting used to. Under the circumstances, it was almost certainly Pollaky's means of earning a living, disdained as "adventurer," that resulted in his being censured as "of doubtful character" rather than any genuine instance of misconduct on his part.

Pollaky, like most who adventured in the detective business in its early years, probably had no intention of even doing so at first. His earliest appearances in the newspapers describe his role as that of an interpreter, usually in court. This, presumably, was a respectable enough career choice. It was probably his presence in court that ultimately led him astray into the world of private investigation, however, by bringing him into contact with Charles Field. One of the original detective-inspectors of Scotland Yard, Field proceeded to open one of Britain's first private detective agencies after his retirement from the force in 1852. He probably met Pollaky fairly soon after and quickly found work for the keen young immigrant, first as an interpreter and then in expanded roles as need and opportunity allowed. By 1860, Pollaky was "Superintendent of the foreign department of the private enquiry office, Devereaux-court, Temple" per *Lloyd's* newspaper.

His actual role was probably still fluid, in addition to being a bit less than the title "superintendent of the foreign department" would suggest. In March 1860, Pollaky accompanied city detectives on an arrest of four Prussians wanted in relation to the "Alleged Willful Sinking" of the ship *John Lugars*. Yet his contribution seems to have been simply identifying the men, for whom he had served as interpreter in an earlier court appearance. In all likelihood, the jobs of interpreter for police detectives and "superintendent of the foreign department" of a private detective agency blurred into that of an actual detective gradually, with Pollaky continuing to play other roles for some time afterward. The entire detective business was still new enough, after all, to make generous allowance for improvisation and flexibility.

If any particular date stands out in this gradual drift toward being a full-fledged detective, it is 1860. It was in that year that journalists referred to "Mr. Pollaky, the detective" in writing of his mysterious errands in the village of Road, although that mission may not have involved actually being a detective so much as posing as one. In *The Suspicions of Mr. Whicher*, Kate Summerscale suggests that Field dispatched Pollaky to Road mainly to intimidate Saunders, and perhaps thereby alleviate some of the pressure on Field's old colleague, Whicher, from endless second-guessing of his own work on the case. One of the reporters at the time had hinted as much, too, parting from uncertain colleagues and declaring that "Mr. Pollaky's business, it has transpired, has no connexion with the discovery of the murder, but is simply to watch Mr. Saunders in his extraordinary proceedings." That seems unconvincing as the entire reason for Pollaky's appearance, though, particularly as he reportedly "had been seen in Frome, Westbury, and Warminster, prosecuting certain inquiries" even after Saunders suspended his inquiry.

The genuine reason, or reasons, for Pollaky's assignment to Road will probably remain obscure. But that same autumn of 1860 did at last see a definitive if frustratingly abbreviated report of him not only represented as a detective, but acting as one, in the chase for Ernest Brewer. On September 20, Mr. Brewer failed to appear at the Throgmorton Street merchant house in London where he had worked for 20 years. The firm's owners, who may have been growing mildly suspicious even before Brewer's disappearance, promptly uncovered the reason for his hasty flight: it seemed that over two decades he had patiently and quietly embezzled the sum of £20,000. Believing "the Continent" Brewer's most likely destination, "the matter was placed in the hands of Mr. Pollaky," according to *The Morning Chronicle*.

The search for Ernest Brewer was probably the first of many such cases, which in time became a staple of Pollaky's detective career. His American contemporary, Pinkerton, directed much of his energy to thwarting counterfeiters and railroad bandits, while Scotland Yard's Whicher, working alongside Pollaky in London, was largely tasked with catching thieves and murderers. If Pollaky had a specialty of his own, it was what we would today call white-collar crime. It would prove a sizable market niche. Just as America's burgeoning railroad network met with growing pains as it expanded, so too did the riches of London-based financial empires make them the target of criminal entrepreneurs always busy with some new swindle or fraud. Significantly, many of these schemes at one point or another reached across to continental

Europe. For the English banking mogul whose fortune had been spirited away to those strange foreign lands across the Channel, a multilingual investigator familiar with Continental ways was an ideal agent to take up the trail.

In the case of Brewer, though, the trail to the Continent eventually proved to be a false one. Per the *Chronicle*, Pollaky "instituted the most vigilant enquiries, but for several weeks he was thrown completely off the scent" until he determined Brewer had gone to ground somewhere rather less distant or exotic and hidden no further away than Ireland. The *Chronicle* states that "the pursuit continued, but the culprit resorted to so many clever contrivances, that although he had one or two very narrow escapes, it was found impossible to capture him." It's no exaggeration to say that Brewer was resourceful, either. Pollaky had scarcely regained the fugitive's tracks and followed them to Ireland when he found that Brewer had crossed back to England, making for Liverpool. Following him there, Pollaky found clues pointing to a departure for New York aboard a just-departed Cunard steamer; in time, the lead was apparently corroborated by the Bank of England's receipt, via American banks, of some of the notes taken by Brewer.

Yet it was all a ruse. For all his facade of being an international criminal, Ernest Brewer seems to have been an oddly patriotic fugitive, never actually leaving British Empire territory. In 1860, this afforded him a much wider range of potential destinations than Liverpool or even Ireland, and by December he seems to have decided at last that the British Isles were too hot for him. He therefore booked passage for colonial South Africa, as usual taking pains to conceal himself from pursuit: despite his stolen fortune he traveled steerage, using a false identity as "a common labourer." But after keeping the chase alive for nearly three months, he finally moved just slightly too late, and too slowly. The *Lady of the Lake* departed a short time before Pollaky was able to confirm Brewer's assumed identity among the passengers, but in eschewing first class travel to disguise his movements Brewer had taken a berth on a sailing ship in an age of steam. Pollaky had time to procure an arrest warrant, and place it in the hands of a Scotland Yard detective who was able to overtake the *Lady of the Lake* in a steamer and finally bring an end to the long chase.

*

FIGARO'S
LONDON SKETCH BOOK
OF
CELEBRITIES.

POLLAKY.

A snapper-up of unconsidered trifles.
Winter's Tale, act 4, sc. 2.

Caricature of Ignatius Pollaky by Faustin Betbeder

From the *London Figaro*'s London Sketch Book of Celebrities, January 28, 1874.
The Ohio State University Billy Ireland Cartoon Library & Museum Collection.
Reproduced with permission.

If the Brewer case did represent a milestone in Pollaky's career, he was still finding his way the following year. In February 1861, he was credited with breaking up "one of the most notorious gangs of swindlers... in London," in the process recovering £10,000 belonging to one of their most recent dupes. But two months later, he behaved awkwardly in a court appearance against another professional rogue, one Edward Segers. Pollaky testified that he had observed Segers' alleged import business regularly for more than a year, and asserted that "I never saw any signs of business going on upon any of the occasions that I have been there." Yet his testimony became somewhat shaky on the matter of certain incriminating letters. First, Pollaky declared the handwriting to be that of Segers, presumably aiding the successful prosecution case. Yet at the sentencing hearing he attempted to hedge his earlier statement. This may have been no more than an honest man admitting second thoughts, but the sentencing judge was less than amused and delivered a sharp request that Mr. Pollaky either stand behind his earlier testimony or else firmly declare it to have been in error. Pushed off the fence, Pollaky affirmed his original conclusion, but this was all a bit short of the behavior of a polished professional. When, early the following year, *The Morning Chronicle* declared Pollaky "a gentleman of great experience and ability in these matters" it may have been welcome praise, but a bit premature.

If his reputation was leading his actual achievements, however, Pollaky was making a concerted effort to keep up. After a decade in London, the thirty-something immigrant seemed to have decided that if he still had things to learn, he was ready to move out of junior roles all the same and establish himself at last. The timing of his official exit from Field's service is typically uncertain, and may well have been a gradual process rather than a single event. He was taking on more independent responsibility by the beginning of the decade, conducting the pursuit of Ernest Brewer with apparently considerable latitude for initiative in 1860, and making an interesting appeal to the public during another investigation the following year. Though the ad requested any replies be directed to "C.F. Field, late Chief of the Detective Police of the Metropolis," it was typical of the intriguing, if enigmatic, missives that formed part of Pollaky's later legend. In this early example, seeking clues to a "mysterious murder, in Rhenish-Prussia, District of Coblenz, on the Rhine," Pollaky included a detailed description of the victim's clothing, followed by an interpretation of its likely significance. The observation that "The fine quality of the Materials and the elegant make of all these articles indicate that the victim belonged to a rich class" may not have been his own, or even an especially complicated, deduction, but Pollaky had learned from his years around the detective trade and become decidedly more than an interpreter.

Still, he remained adaptable, and even if he was determined to establish himself as a detective, it appears that he decided to have a go at being a spy, first. For many living at the time there seemed little difference, but Pollaky may have seen himself as more of a counterspy, in light of his assignment: keeping an eye on agents of the Confederate government. As another immigrant detective, Allan Pinkerton, was in the process of discovering, America's rebellious southern states managed large and far-reaching espionage activities in their war with the Union government. While Pinkerton applied himself to uprooting the Washington-based spy network of Rose Greenhow, other fronts of the intelligence war had their own heroes and villains.

One of these (which one depending on one's perception of the Civil War) was Henry Sanford. Officially Minister to Belgium, Sanford readily expanded the duties of his otherwise minor posting during the war. Hopes of support from Europe were key to the Confederacy's resisting the larger and more industrialized states of the North, and diplomats like Sanford busied themselves with thwarting those hopes at multiple levels. He lobbied overtly against Confederate overtures to the Belgian government for recognition as an independent country. He also worked behind the scenes to outmaneuver the Confederacy's own European agents.

Toward this end, Sanford hired various agents of his own. The rising young London detective Pollaky was one of them. The Sanford Historical Society, in the Florida town Sanford founded after the war, has preserved his papers from this time including dozens of messages from Pollaky, some of them in code. Those that relate specifics mostly involve Confederate attempts to obtain arms and ships; an account of August 1861 is representative of Pollaky's observations and their language:

[Regarding the *Thomas Watson*] I knew from her appearance that she could not have room for much more cargo than what she already had aboard which was said to be a cargo of salt — I ascertained today that she has not only salt but a quantity of firearms. She has also a long gun covered over in her poop cabin in readiness to be run out on the quarterdeck for use when required, and also another brass gun under hatchs. [*sic*] ... at high water this day she was towed out into the river quite unexpectedly ... she had scarce cleared the dock when she hoisted an immense Confederate flag and was towed up the river probably to display the flag to the Northerners. She then returned down the river and also I ascertained that a magazine boat was to meet her with a large quantity of powder...

One report stands out for urgency and content which is, if nothing else, intriguing:

Will you be good enough to let me know if, and at what time you expect to be in London, as I shall have shortly to leave England and as it would be highly necessary for my having a previous [*sic*] interview with you. Informations of the greatest moment have reached us concerning a wide spread conspiracy in the attack of New York.

Aside from a few acts of arson by Confederate sympathizers, New York never suffered attack as part of the Civil War, of course. Various transplanted Southerners well removed from the main fields of battle did attempt the occasional wildcat scheme, however, and Pollaky's information could have had some measure of substance. It's safe to assume that the bulk of his work for Sanford nonetheless involved keeping track of Confederate supply purchases rather than Confederate spy missions. But Pollaky's selection for the assignment reinforces the suggestion of early 1860s newspapers that he had built up a reputation of his own, and might very plausibly trade on it independent of Field's office.

At some point in 1862 he made official his intention of doing just that. Unfortunately there are few surviving details of precisely how or when he opened Pollaky's Private Inquiry Office, or for that matter where. An 1863 news item refers to "Mr. Pollaky, of George-street, Mansion-house," which may have been his home, office, or both; wherever he initially met clients, Pollaky did not take up the Paddington Green address that eventually provided his alliterative nickname until 1865. That same year, he also moved to a new home in Maida Hill West along with his second wife, and their domestic needs may provide one further clue to the why of his venture into independent practice. Pollaky married for (presumably) the first time in June 1856, to Julia Devonald. Sadly this early marriage had the same fate as that of Pollaky's fellow London detective, Whicher, and Julia died in 1859. Two years later, Pollaky wed Mary Ann Hughes, and their union would by contrast prove considerably more fruitful. Over the following dozen years at least four, and possibly several, young children joined the Pollaky household. Though the eldest, Pauline, was not born until 1863, it's quite possible that providing for a family was on Mr. Pollaky's mind when he decided to strike out and establish his own business.

The tireless assaults of swindlers, con artists and other frauds on London's riches created ample demand for Pollaky's business, and he was indeed on his way to being an "established" man by his mid-30s. He had a prosperous firm of his own, a respectable marriage to an English wife with the first of many children on the way, and he was by now routinely described in the press as "Pollaky, the well-known detective."

Not quite everyone was impressed, even then. The British government rejected his application for citizenship, as noted, and their official verdict of "doubtful character" was extended to the entire private detective profession in 1863 in *All the Year Round* by none other than the London detective's early booster, Charles Dickens. In the June issue of his periodical, Dickens published a jaundiced and very skeptical examination of the whole concept. Asking "what sort of inquiries are those in which the ex-detectives are ready to engage," and "What sort of people are those who apply to Messrs. Pollaky and Field for their secret services," the author proceeded to supply a variety of speculative, and very Dickensian, scenarios of middle-class neuroses that the professional snoop might indulge. Pollaky's name received frequent mention, but his former employer and Dickens's longtime friend Field was not overlooked. The great novelist may have changed his views on detectives or found the new private variety less to his liking than their public counterparts, or simply have sensed a general public skepticism, which might appreciate a bit of squinting in the private inquiry offices' direction. Whatever the reasons, his assessment of Pollaky's new trade was caustic: "Of one thing I am quite sure—there are more men to be seen standing about on the corners of streets than there used to be [...] that sinister office [...] There is something almost terrible about this licensed spy system."

On the other hand, Pollaky may have been less troubled by a rare if widely read critical voice than by the consequences of his own reputation becoming very well known and respected among the rest of society. Only a few years into his career as private detective, Pollaky found it necessary to appear in court to disavow and warn of "a foreigner" who had applied for money at various city firms, claiming to represent "the foreign detective establishment of Mr. Pollaky." "This proceeding," the genuine Pollaky testified, "was entirely unauthorized."

If the occasional con artist did seek to profit from Pollaky's reputation, he might almost have claimed it was no more than fair, as a good deal of that reputation rested on persecuting those who made a living by such dodges. In the late summer of 1863, Pollaky was recruited for another chase across the map of Europe, after "the now notorious Sigismund Ditrichstein." The Hungarian Ditrichstein had "absconded" from London with £8,000, upon which "Some of the most experienced detective officers in London at once interested themselves in his capture" per the *Liverpool Mercury*. Pollaky was among those "most actively engaged," along with a Detective Moss, of Scotland Yard.

One report describes Pollaky's role as interpreting for Moss, but by this point in his career it seems impossible that he would not have contributed considerably more to such an investigation. Particularly as the pursuit of his possible fellow countryman led to very familiar territory for Pollaky. Perhaps recalling the earlier chase for Brewer, the detectives began on the suspicion that their quarry would seek safety in familiar territory, which in this case backed up a theory of "fleeing to the Continent" rather than rebutting it. Ditrichstein and his wife had fled separately, possibly with the intent of making pursuit more difficult, though as a result they provided the detectives with the option of following whichever trail seemed more promising. Moss and Pollaky thus began by tracing Madame Ditrichstein, first to Ostend on the Belgian coast where they located her hotel, though she had already checked out after paying her bill with some of the stolen bank notes. The two detectives were close enough behind, nonetheless, to find Madame's trail still fresh. From Ostend they followed it first to Vienna, and then to a Hungarian city Pollaky had once known intimately: Pressburg.

The sparse newspaper accounts of Pollaky and his doings may never leave the interested reader more frustrated than at this moment. In addition to typically elliptical phrases, such as "They made all possible inquiries" and "A clue, after much difficulty, was again discovered," Pollaky's unplanned homecoming passes without any hint of what the prodigal thought or felt upon seeing his birthplace for the first time in more than a decade, under such odd circumstances. The unnamed correspondent of the *Mercury* may not even have known Pollaky's connection to Pressburg. It's certainly plausible that Pollaky did not see fit to mention it, either; for such a well-known figure he was, to all appearances, a remarkably private man.

It's also possible, if entirely speculative, that Pollaky had hoped never to see Pressburg again and had particular reason for making as little as possible of this otherwise interesting feature of the case. Whether joyous or miserable, his return was also undoubtedly brief. After finding witnesses who had seen Ditrichstein, as well as the mysterious "clue" of the *Mercury* article, Moss and Pollaky resumed the chase for Madame Ditrichstein to the Austrian border and then back across Hungary to the city of Pest. There, they had reason to believe, the two fugitives had arranged a rendezvous, and quick work along with the help of local police allowed them to catch up to and arrest their quarry at last. The eventual outcome of the long chase was nonetheless mixed, underscoring how the era's patchwork system of law enforcement made private detectives so useful while still limiting their effectiveness. Problems with extradition kept Ditrichstein in Austria-Hungary, at first, where authorities started a case against him and then abandoned it citing insufficient evidence; eventually he returned to Britain, where he was also taken into custody and then discharged. But Detective Moss's and Pollaky's efforts had recovered most of the stolen money, and they could return to London claiming a modest success for all of their time and miles.

"The well-known detective" wasn't—quite—always pursuing stolen Bank of England notes on improvised tours of Europe. He advertised a fairly broad range of services, including "election, divorce and libel cases" as well as the catch-all category of "discreet enquiries in England or abroad." He also applied his experience at finding people to cases where a missing person didn't necessarily want to hide, at least from the law. In 1864 he was commissioned to locate a French baron's young daughter who had run away across the Channel after "having formed an intimacy with a young Englishman," in the delicate wording of *Freeman's Journal and Daily Commercial Advertiser*. The following year, London's *Daily News* reported how "highly respectable" friends of another French youth, 16-year-old Edmund Renard, sought Pollaky's help in locating the boy after he, too, fled to London in company of a young Englishman. Pollaky found Renard and then, after further urging by his concerned friends, took him in at his own home in Maida Hill West before finding another billet for the young man with a Mr. Bucknell in Martin's Court. A few days later, Pollaky was summoned by Bucknell, who had returned from an errand to find Renard gone along with a silver watch and 10 silver spoons. Renard soon turned up, once more in the company of his older friend, and Pollaky had him taken before the police before he was fined, then released. At which point Pollaky may have entertained, with a sigh, the possibility that he was better off with reasonable people like Brewer and the Ditrichsteins.

Fortunately there were always more where they came from. Reading the frequent and rather casual accounts of Pollaky foiling yet another financial fraud, one is almost left with an impression that "swindler" was a mainstream career choice for men of the 1860s and '70s. In 1866 Pollaky accompanied an officer Webb of Scotland Yard to Europe, once more in pursuit of a con man, in this case insurance broker Lionel Holdsworth. As in the *John Lugars* case of several years earlier, a conspiracy to scuttle a ship and defraud the voyage's underwriters was the main crime, but otherwise Pollaky was closely re-enacting his more recent roles as manhunter. Webb and Pollaky pursued this latest fugitive's trail from Sweden to Denmark to Germany, finally getting a lead in Frankfurt that provided some hope of concluding a chase that had permitted little rest for the pursued and even less for the pursuers. After tracing Holdsworth to a hotel in Frankfurt, the detectives found that although he had already moved on, he had left a watch as security for his bill; unwisely, he subsequently sent money to the hotel management along with a request to forward his watch to a hotel in Basel, and the Frankfurt hotel thoughtfully got word of this valuable correspondence to Pollaky and Webb. They promptly relayed the information to police in Basel, who arrested Holdsworth when he appeared to collect his watch. The *Times* adds that "Thence the prisoner was conveyed to Frankfort [*sic*], where he was put in prison for 24 hours, to enable the officers, Webb and Pollaky, who in their search for him had not been in bed for seven consecutive nights, to have one day's rest."

The surviving accounts of Pollaky's cases present a credible argument for his being a detective of considerable talent. Among the details they generally omit, however, are specifics about the nature of that talent and how it was employed. As with other facets of the mysterious man, a few educated guesses about his methodology are possible, if not much more. Like any competent detective, he must have had good instincts for sizing up people and situations, and recognizing the out of place, however subtle. If he refined his approach to crime and its detection to form any detailed theories, he kept them secret. He performed his apprenticeship as a detective alongside serving and former Scotland Yard officers, so he may well have generally followed similar basic, no-nonsense procedures; his early employer, ex-Inspector Field, was rather atypically fond of disguises, but Pollaky seems to have dispensed with even that sort of trickery.

Eventually his Private Inquiry Office employed at least a small staff, but for the most part Pollaky remained a very hands-on, in-the-field detective. He was neither armchair sleuth nor string pulling mastermind. He made use of wider resources, but mostly in the form of a loose network of contacts. Like Vidocq, he seems to have built up a considerable knowledge of the criminal society opposing him, but Pollaky's network of contacts probably ran a bit less deep while being much broader, encompassing much of continental Europe as well as both sides of the law. The accounts of his partnership with Webb, in seeking Lionel Holdsworth, note more than once how Pollaky's "knowledge of continental languages and general experience rendered material assistance in detecting the fugitive." And by the late 1860s, authorities in Europe were referring plaintiffs to Pollaky in some cases, when his international experience might be more helpful than the local police. Though Pollaky never operated on anything like the same scale as the Pinkertons in other ways, the geographic range of his practice across Europe's own fragmented states may have made his agency, too, a modest start at "a Victorian Age Interpol."

No examination of the methods of "Paddington" Pollaky can even pretend to be complete, however, without remarking on his newspaper advertisements. His obituarist did so, more than 30 years after the last of them appeared in the "agony columns" (i.e. "the classifieds" per American usage), as did contemporaries. Before launching into his disapproval of private detectives generally, in *All the Year Round*, Dickens introduced the subject with what may have been the most familiar reminder of their activities, for literate Londoners:

> In the second column of the Times advertisement-sheet appeared, the other day, these mysterious words, "Audi, vidi, tace"—coupled with the announcement that a trustworthy personage was just about to start for the Continent with a view to certain "private inquiries." The advertisement was inserted by one Messrs. Pollaky and Co.

Pollaky's advertisements drew notice well beyond England, as well. The *Belfast News-Letter* suggested the pages of *The Times* as almost a second base of operations for the detective, in referring to "The mysterious and oracular Pollaky (of Paddington Green and the Times' second column)…" And when the *Brisbane Courier* published a feature examining the larger phenomenon of the *Times*' agony column and its following, their sampling of some ads of "the second class of the tragically mysterious nature" inevitably included an example from Pollaky. Apparently in rare form, the detective's notice read: "A whisper. Empty pocket. As quiet as a mouse. At Xmas. Pollaky, 13 Paddington-green." Most Pollaky ads were not quite this, probably literally, cryptic, though they often suggested mysterious affairs all the same. An early example, which established a pattern for many afterward:

If the Count de LUSI, Major, and formerly Aide-de-Camp to the Grand Duke of Weimar, will be good enough to CALL or SEND to Mr. Pollaky at 20, Devereaux-Court, Temple, he will HEAR of SOMETHING to his ADVANTAGE.

Other ads were nearly miniature case histories by themselves:

ESCAPED from a MAISON de SANTE, in Paris, a YOUNG GEN-TLEMAN, 20 years of age, 5 feet 8 inches in height, stoutly built, has a massive head, a peculiar drooping of the left upper eyelid [...] has soft winning manners, being most intellectually gifted, but in his paroxysms lies no moral perception whatsoever. His vanity then becomes excessive, and his irresponsible acts criminal. He assumes at times titled and high-sounding names, giving drafts on bankers and others where he has no effects. [...] Information to Mr. Pollaky, Private Inquiry Office, 13, Paddington-green.

Some were more amusing than anything else, if unintentionally:

Mysteriously left her friends, in Bayswater, a young Irish lady... finely cut features, but very irregular teeth... Information to be given to Mr. Pollaky, Private Inquiry Office, 13, Paddington Green

The ads were also a very engaging and, obviously, memorable form of marketing, even though the majority were seemingly meant as more specifically targeted messages. At least one observer questioned whether notices published to withdraw earlier requests, or express thanks upon the successful conclusion of a few cases of missing women, were not merely self-promotion cleverly disguised. Writing in the *Pall Mall Gazette* of September 5, 1866, the unnamed author argues, in surprisingly vulgar fashion, that:

> When a terrier bitch is lost, and a reward is offered for her restoration, the recovery of the erring dog and the payment of the reward generally close the transaction, and the fortunate owner does not usually advertise to thank the restorers and to withdraw the offered reward. But it would seem that in police circles the cases of strayed young ladies are dealt with more ceremoniously.

Had Pollaky seen this particular commentary, it's likely he would have been far from amused. He seemed to take particular interest in protecting young ladies from the various dangers that Victorian society feared might menace an unattended girl. Though any personal hobbies or interests remain largely unknown, Pollaky had a few professional sidelines complementing his main work as private inquiry agent. For much of his career, he was London correspondent for the *International Criminal Police Gazette*, and in 1867 the Metropolitan Police appointed him as a special constable for X Division, which encompassed his well-known Paddington Green address. And the following year, a *Daily News* account of a court case involving Pollaky included the information that "he is also a non-paid officer of the Society for the Prevention of Vice and for the Protection of Young Women."

Pollaky's association with the Society dated at least to 1866, when the *Times* noted their commissioning him to investigate certain rumors, to the effect that "at Hull a most nefarious traffic in abducted young girls from their homes and conveying them to Germany for immoral purposes was going on." This commission may have led to references, in later accounts, of Pollaky breaking up a gang of "white slavers" (per the era's euphemism for sex trafficking). The results of his investigation into six young women reported as missing, however, suggest that the rumors may have contained more scandal than substance. Pollaky located one girl with relatives, another with friends; two had already returned home on their own, and one turned up "at Grimsby, and her mother is going there in search of her." Per *The Times*, Pollaky discovered precisely one of the "missing" women among prostitutes—though not in Germany—and returned her to her family.

The reports of Pollaky's volunteer service to the Society for the Prevention of Vice generally suggest that it must have been performed out of genuine belief in the cause, for it seems otherwise to have profited neither the detective nor his reputation. A correspondent to *The Examiner*, in October 1872, expressed similar concern for the Society's mission but then charged that the Society's efforts in pursuing it were half-hearted at best, and perhaps even somewhat unsavory. The broadside's author firmly disapproved of the Society's association with Paddington Green's prominent detective as likely to do it more harm than good: "Mr. Pollaky, we are convinced, is open to a large contract to catch and convict dealers in obscene prints at so much per head."

No source accompanied that suspicion, but it was a nuisance Pollaky might easily have done without by that point in his career. Especially after his efforts at preventing vice and protecting young women had already led to considerably greater threat to his well-being four years earlier. That was the complaint he brought to court in 1868, at any rate, after one investigation for the Society met an even more hostile reception than that later published in *The Examiner*. Inquiring into a violent assault upon a girl at Margate, Pollaky found a woman to be responsible and subsequently saw her tried and convicted. Her husband or lover, one John Lomax, objected to this busybody interference. According to Pollaky he objected vociferously, abusing the detective verbally and then with threatening letters, one reported as declaring "Now, my cock, I have started and intend to go in against you and do not intend to leave you till all matters are finished." Pollaky, per the *Daily News*, "expressed his belief that his life was not safe while Lomax remained at large."

Mr. Lomax denied all of the charges and responded with a countercharge against Pollaky. A Judge Mansfield, tasked with sorting out these claims, understandably found his patience tried by what seemed a minor feud involving more noise than anything, and by a plaintiff who seemed awfully sensitive for a man who allegedly earned a living investigating serious crimes. Mansfield "said these ought not to have been brought into court. He believed there was no danger of a breach of the peace, and dismissed both summonses."

Pollaky survived whatever danger Mr. Lomax posed and continued his work, including that for the Society. Still, the episode may in one sense be somewhat less trivial than Judge Mansfield believed, if only to Pollaky personally. One account of Pollaky has suggested that while in most cases appearing a stalwart fighter against the criminal menace, he suffered increasing fear for his own safety through much of his career. This notion, though fascinating, was published years after Pollaky's death and apparently uncorroborated by other sources. Yet the Lomax incident suggests that at the very least, after several years on the job, Pollaky was already finding it a growing strain on his nerves.

At the same time, the affair carries an unavoidable element of the ridiculous, a problem shared by many of the cases from Pollaky's later career when they aren't scantly reported, too neat to be believed, or some combination of these. To most appearances, Pollaky's Private Inquiry Office continued to flourish through the 1870s. As of 1873, he employed "a large staff," he apparently collected decorations and honors from a number of foreign governments, and his name was seen and heard increasingly often in nearly every form of media. And yet... Even as "Alexander Ignatius Paul Pollaky Wolouski" strode the stage at the Prince of Wales Opera House in *Foul Play*, even as Gilbert and Sullivan's opera *Patience* paid tribute to "the keen penetration of Paddington Pollaky," the tireless manhunter of earlier years seems to disappear amid light diversions, and perhaps a few hints at greater affairs, but no more.

One cannot help asking, faced with Pollaky's fame as a great detective, where are the great cases? The contrast with his contemporary Whicher is significant, particularly as Whicher's several years' involvement in the Tichborne Claimant case demonstrates that there was at least one great case during this era and poses the further question: where was Pollaky? A decade earlier, while still establishing himself in the role of detective, Pollaky nonetheless managed a minor, walk-on role in Whicher's previous nation shaking investigation. Yet in the 1870s, as Britain's public and press were once more consumed by a sensational mystery, an internationally renowned detective was nowhere to be found. The job of unmasking "the most daring and sustained imposture that ever afforded the measure of the possible wickedness of man" went instead to a pensioned-off Scotland Yard officer, of whom little had been heard since his unhappy efforts in Road a decade before.

It's unreasonable to judge an entire career on one choice made by Lord Arundell of Wardour, for reasons that might have had nothing to do with Pollaky, of course. And to some extent the Tichborne Claimant case only became an extraordinary sensation after Whicher had been hired for the job. And yet, and yet, the available evidence of what Pollaky was occupying himself with, instead, still fails to assuage the doubts about how seriously he was really taken at the time, or should be taken now. It seems extraordinary that the many tributes paid him were all tongue in cheek, and yet there is reason to wonder. What else to make of the exaggerated response to John Lomax's bluster, or of a detective known for the classified advertisements as much as anything else. What, for that matter, to make of Pollaky's later cases?

Some of Pollaky's post-1865 news accounts were for commendable enough activities, but at the same time on the order of firemen rescuing a kitten from a tree. An issue of *Jackson's Oxford Journal* of December 1873 reports how not only Pollaky but also "a large staff under his own personal superintendence" set promptly to work when a Member of Parliament's daughter vanished, one morning, from her mother's carriage when briefly left alone. By 8 p.m. on the same day, detectives had traced the child, apparently through clothing already set out for sale at a local shop, to "a low part of Camden-town" where she had been abandoned "after her clothes had been taken from her, and others left in their stead."

The *Journal* commended Pollaky for his resolution of what, in fairness, must have seemed a dire situation for those directly involved. The following summer, however, a "London and Paris Gossip" columnist related another adventure of "Pollaky, the foreign detective" with undisguised cynicism. As originally reported in the pages of *Art Journal* by an S.C. Hall, a nobleman discovered a masterful though much worn painting in a West End pawn shop.

Purchasing the work, he diligently sought out its provenance, but could learn no information beyond the initials on the picture and a vague recollection among art dealers that the artist was still alive, though none could recall his name. The nobleman, having exhausted all other avenues, sought the aid of the Private Inquiry Office; Pollaky "knew nothing about art or artist, but he undertook to find the man." And, "after some trouble," he succeeded, finding the artist living in a corner of Soho, unnoticed and destitute. But in a happy ending that does, indeed, test the cynic's reflexes, the artist's discovery by Pollaky led to commissions from his nobleman admirer, better fortunes, and exhibition in the National Academy. In gratitude for the detective's role in his good fortune, the artist thanked Pollaky "with a fine picture which he is only too proud to exhibit to his friends." Concluding the story, the gossip columnist judged that

> It is a pretty bit of romance, and if Pollaky did not present Mr. S.C. Hall... with a handsome cheque for publishing that puff—and does not send me one for passing it on—I do not think Mr. Pollaky knows how to pay for his advertisements in a Royal style, still—it may be true.

Other cases from these years are less incredible but, instead, simply bizarre. The *Liverpool Mercury* of July 10, 1869, describes a Vienna gentleman swindled out of expensive jewelry in exchange for a bad check, while in London, and referred by consular authorities to Pollaky. The con artist "had made no false representations except by inference [and] according to English law the police could not interfere," but the consul advised that Mr. Pollaky was very familiar with these dodges and would certainly recover the lost property, at least. Pollaky did find this latest swindler, after following a well-marked trail of bad debts. But the search had an unexpected surprise at the end. The wanted man, it seemed, was in fact "a complete lunatic" and recently committed to an asylum when Pollaky at last tracked him down. The detective did succeed, fortunately, in learning the fate of his client's jewelry, and the *Mercury* speculated that while a costly intervention by lawyers would prove necessary, the Viennese gentleman would recover them.

Jewels were at issue in another case that Pollaky resolved handily, which combined a little of both the strange and the fantastic. His client was a wealthy woman who had also been deprived of expensive jewelry, though in her case it was only in an attempt at deception that deception was discovered. Apparently the woman needed money to cover racing losses, but wanted to keep the entire business secret from her husband (possibly as much for the scandal of her participation in an "unladylike" pastime as for the scandal of her financial predicament). So she conceived the idea of substituting a paste imitation for her own tiara, permitting a covert sale of the real item. Upon presenting the tiara for a jeweler to copy, however, she received a shock: the diamonds were already paste. Finding herself confronting a different sort of scandal, she enlisted the detectives of Scotland Yard, but they ultimately came up empty handed. The tiara had certainly been genuine originally, and subsequently never left madame's sight except when secured in a home safe or at the bank. The Yard's detectives suspected some sort of inside job but could take the case no further. Enter "Paddington" Pollaky, whose investigation confirmed that the thief had been a member of the household. Pollaky found that the inspiration of selling the tiara, after substituting an imitation so that the better half would not suspect one's debt difficulties, had not been an original idea within this couple: the husband had enacted the scheme before his wife ever conceived of doing the same.

As Vaughan Drydon noted in his telling of it, the whole affair "might furnish the material for a short story." The plot is certainly neat enough, and in truth almost too neat, in addition to being related only in second- or third-hand fashion with neither names nor details. Possibly very desirable for a private detective, especially under the circumstances. Yet that doesn't answer to the suspicious tidiness of the tale, or that of the struggling artist in which, one might suppose, names could have been included more freely.

To be fair to Pollaky, it may be that both stories seem too pat and easy because Pollaky could make things look easy. As with the reaction to Pinkerton and the Baltimore Plot, great efficiency may in fact make claims of brilliance less credible, not more. Yet they may be valid claims nonetheless. If contemporaries ascribed remarkable abilities to Pollaky, the simple and logical explanation might not be universal exaggeration but, instead, that his abilities genuinely were remarkable.

One final case note, from November 1868, does at least suggest a man with an extraordinary capacity to foil crime in a manner that seemed nonetheless offhand and ordinary. Photography, after a few decades of progress, was by this time practical enough to have been readily adopted on both sides of the Atlantic for police work. When yet another Austrian gentleman was cheated of some thousands of pounds, therefore, this latest dupe was able to provide authorities with a little help in the form of a photo of the alleged Englishman, "Grey," who had duped him. The local police distributed copies, along with information about the case, to other forces. They also naturally enough shared the photograph with the London private detective Pollaky, who had demonstrated a facility for these cases in both his adopted nation and on the Continent. Pollaky was already in Europe, moreover, possibly for a case although it was apparently not one of his breathless chases after a light-footed fugitive. The Glasgow *Herald* story on these events includes a rare glimpse into the detective's off-duty life, describing how he attended a play at the Stadt Theatre while passing through Hamburg.

Even off-duty, however, it seems that Pollaky still possessed a mind very "keen," per another theatrical production which later became part of his lore, in approaching the business of a detective. The seemingly idle gentleman "during the [intermission] passed his time in inspecting professionally the audience." Upon spotting another attendee resembling the photo of "Grey," Pollaky no doubt calmly slipped away to the local police. Then, with his familiar reputation and fluency in German, easily convinced them to take this tip seriously and make haste to the theatre. Afterward, this product of sharp-eyed people watching proved an especially fortunate discovery: "Grey" had already paid his hotel bill and made ready to leave the city the next morning, and moreover was not Grey or even an Englishman, but rather "a Frenchman, and the head of a band which has operated for years at Odessa, St. Petersburg, Munich, and other places." Pollaky's observation and quick action had secured £5,000 in ill-gotten gains, and the arrest of another internationally wanted criminal.

*

And yet, the affair looks awfully much like a lark all the same. Which just may suggest a broader reason why the accomplishments of "Paddington" Pollaky seem faintly unsatisfying in comparison with other celebrated detectives: something is missing. There are plentiful hors d'ouevres that succeed admirably in stimulating the appetite, there are delightful confections for dessert, there is even the scent of a great hearty feast, but nothing more than that; the main course is not to be found. Just what a reader makes of this situation might, in the end, have to rest on faith. One might believe the many rave reviews and trust that the "chef" was indeed brilliant; alternately, one might conclude him a fraud, and the "junk food" in evidence the entirety of his range.

On balance, the evidence for Pollaky as one of the great detectives seems deserving of some trust. It's possible, of course, that he was at most a competent PI with a gift for PR. It's possible that he simply tagged along with genuine detectives as an interpreter, and it's possible that by exploiting his knowledge of languages that they did not speak he was able to fool European police forces into believing his the real skill. It's possible that his cryptic advertisements alluding to cases in progress were nothing more than marketing ploys, and it's possible that they nonetheless proved such a novel entertainment that this can explain tributes in song and on stage. It's possible that his reported decorations from foreign governments were nothing but tin toys, or that they never existed at all; it's possible that one clever immigrant either fooled or co-opted journalists throughout the British Empire for decades through nothing more than a combination of luck, rumor, and smoke.

All of these things are possible. But the combination of all of them, which is necessary to dismiss Pollaky as a sham is, nonetheless, overwhelmingly improbable. Too many somewhat unlikely scenarios must be stacked upon one another and the whole simply cannot support its own weight. The alternative, that Pollaky really was a great detective, might seem less credible when compared with some or even all, individually, but compared with them as a group it proves the simpler, sturdier conclusion. Which still leaves the lingering question of why his record does not contain more persuasive accomplishments, but in this regard Pollaky was perhaps not very different from any famous detective. The private detective business is, after all, often a private one. And unlike Vidocq, Whicher or Pinkerton, Pollaky conducted nearly all of his cases as a private detective for private clients; police forces and governments often had reason to appreciate his efforts, but they were not his employer.

In the long run, moreover, exactly what constitutes a persuasive case for fame is relative. The fame commanded by all of the great detectives is largely forgotten and might seem just as incredible as Pollaky's to a modern man or woman in the street. If the arguments for Pollaky's own renown still seem a bit more vague, even on closer inspection, that arguably owes more to his chroniclers' nature than to his own. William Hoerr, writing in a journal devoted to another renowned London sleuth, observed that "Because [Pollaky] was very close-mouthed and lacked a literary friend, we shall probably never know just what his exploits were, but quite possibly he too had his Gorgianos, his Milvertons, and his McFarlanes."

For his own part, Pollaky seems to have had little use for fame anyway, despite the theories that his agony column ads were primarily a promotional gimmick. Journalists, playwrights and novelists wrote of him, but he did not court their attentions or seek to join in their efforts by publishing any stories himself. To the contrary, it seems that as the years went by Pollaky grew somewhat uncomfortable with society's widespread familiarity with his name and reputation, at least among that element of society of which his work inevitably made him an enemy. As far back as 1868 his appeal to the courts for protection, following the threats of John Lomax, suggested a man ill at ease with knowledge of people eager to do him harm. The balance of evidence suggests that this disquiet grew larger with time, not smaller.

With a family to feed Pollaky nonetheless bore up under this strain, to whatever extent it affected him, for many years. In 1876 he rebutted accusations relating to the "Turf Fraud" scandal while engaged in another enigmatic commission in Europe, at one point signing a letter to *The Times* "from Falkenstein-in-the-Taunus, Germany." (The conspiracies alleged by officer William Reimers turned increasingly ludicrous, eventually including not only Pollaky and multiple authorities at Scotland Yard but the Bonaparte family; the larger scandal eventually resulted in a reorganization of the detective branch, but the matter never involved Pollaky in any significant role.) Into the 1880s, Pollaky's advertisements continued to appear in the newspapers, though by 1880 he seems to have found that he could often omit details and rely on his reputation to supply the rest. In the May 26 *Times* of that year he published the positively spartan notice "POLLAKY'S PRIVATE INQUIRY OFFICE, No. 13 Paddington Green. W."

Significantly, that ad appears directly above a longer promotion for a rival firm. The private detective agency, once remarked on as a new and "sinister" phenomenon by Charles Dickens, had become almost an established industry. Pollaky's early employer and mentor Inspector Field had opened his office nearly 30 years before; the British expatriate Pinkerton had extended his American operation back across the Atlantic; Whicher had come and gone from private practice, retiring in 1880. Two years later, Pollaky finally had enough of matching wits and nerve with the criminal trade and, though younger than Whicher by nearly a decade and a half, decided to join him.

It's a singular example of synchronicity that just a few years after one celebrated consulting detective departed from London, another one arrived almost as though drawn by a vacuum in the absence of Pollaky. And it may be worth a brief digression, at least, to consider how the man whom *The Argus* described as "A Sherlock Holmes in Real Life" corresponds to his more famous successor in imagined life. Pollaky was a mildly eccentric and mysterious private detective practicing in Victorian London. For much of his career, his address at 13 Paddington Green was as central an element in his legend as 221B Baker Street is in that of its fictional occupant. Unlike Scotland Yard's men, Pollaky was primarily a kind of gentleman detective, untangling devious swindles, searching for wayward scions of the nobility and engaging in thrilling chases after white-collar villains. All of which would fit comfortably into the pages of "The Red-Headed League" or "The Three Garridebs."

The parallels extend only so far; there is no evidence that Pollaky played violin, used cocaine, or even smoked a pipe. As Hoerr noted, Pollaky had no loyal partner to chronicle his adventures for posterity, either, a difference more significant than any in the two famous detectives' very different places in subsequent history. Yet given the extent of Pollaky's celebrity in his day, in the 1870s and early '80s, it's very unlikely that he would have been unfamiliar to an educated young British doctor with an interest in criminology. Arthur Conan Doyle had a variety of inspirations for his most famous creation, including Vidocq, Dr. Joseph Bell, and even himself. Yet if the character originally named "Sherrinford Holmes" did not also take cues from the real detective "Paddington" Pollaky, the similarities between the two are a most remarkable coincidence. All the same, it is possible that some or even most of them are coincidence, particularly that which might be the most curious among them: in 1882, Ignatius Pollaky closed down his practice while in the prime of his life and enjoying tremendous fame and renown, and retired to the seaside where he lived quietly, well beyond the turn of the century, to great old age. Twenty-one years later, for reasons probably quite unrelated to any modeling on the earlier sleuth, Conan Doyle's enduring detective hero did exactly the same.

In Pollaky's case, retirement meant the southeast English city of Brighton, just across the Channel from the European chessboard where many of his cases were played out and yet a world away from the hectic London streets that had frayed his nerves. Life as a leisured gentleman was apparently much more to Pollaky's liking. To all evidence he was untroubled by the temptation of one last great encore, which over the years many of his colleagues found irresistible, at times to their misfortune. "Pollaky of Paddington Green" was by contrast quite satisfied to spend his days quietly, far from that famous address, either at home on Stanford Avenue or at the Brighton Pavilion, where he often enjoyed less hazardous chess matches in the sunlit Public Room.

The longtime fixture of *The Times'* agony column did not disappear from public life entirely. Indeed, in retirement, one of the most purse-lipped detectives ever seemed to grow more comfortable with expressing himself. Pollaky had written *The Times* before, taking part in a debate on credentialing servants in 1879 for example. But his correspondence from Brighton seems to display a bit more freedom, as well as a bit more flourish. When Parliament considered a new Aliens Bill in 1911, Pollaky "wrote instructively" on the matter in the later judgment of *The Times*, opposing unrestricted immigration. In 1914, he delivered his thoughts on "Touring Criminals." The ex-detective signed these missives, moreover, as "Ritter Von Pollaky, Criminal-Rath," apparently award-ing himself some small honors in Continental style, in recognition of what was after all a distinguished career.

Distinguished, though not exactly long; Pollaky's retirement ultimately lasted longer than his entire career as a London private eye. Which just might, in itself, constitute one final piece of evidence that he was no mere hack, famous simply for being famous. The Pollakys lived in comfort for more than 35 years after the breadwinner closed up shop, in an era well before any public pension or social security system. The fact that a single enterprising immigrant was able to achieve this, after a career that was relatively brief even by the standards of modern first world economies, certainly speaks well of the promise that the field of detection offered new entrants, and of the opportunities afforded by Victorian British society. It also speaks highly of Pollaky's individual skill and efficiency as a detective. If being in the right time and place helped, it would not entirely explain what must have been a small fortune in savings. If financial success is any guide, however approximate, to professional ability, "Paddington" Pollaky's suggests that he must have been a very good detective indeed.

He simply felt little need to prove it to anyone, it seems. Letters to *The Times* aside, Pollaky remained a quiet, private man. He wrote no memoirs and, far from pursuing hopes of a dynasty by bringing his children into the business, seemed content to leave detection behind entirely. The result must have been satisfying, at any rate for the most part. In June 1911, the Pollakys celebrated their golden wedding anniversary. And in 1914, Ignatius Paul Pol-laky finally became a naturalized British citizen, more than a half century after his first attempt was rejected for "doubtful character." For all that this was probably a happy moment, however, its timing in June of that year portended darker days. It would be quite a stretch to imagine that Pollaky, even in his prime, could have had advance notice that an assassin would shoot the heir to Austria-Hungary's dual monarchy, and thereby plunge Pollaky's former and adopted homes into war along with much of the world. But at the same time it hardly required "keen penetration" to recognize the risk of war, or that the pattern of European alliances would place resident alien Pollaky on the side opposing his home of more than 60 years.

Fortunately for the by-then-elderly retiree, his petition for citizenship was approved before the hostilities began, though the first world war must have been a difficult closing to what had been a comfortable and pleasant idyll for so long. It's open to question just how aware Pollaky was of it all, though. More than one source indicates that in his last years Pollaky's sharp intellect was eroded by some form of dementia, and that the ex-detective suffered from failing memory and even paranoid delusions of plots against his life, to the point of answering visitors to his home with a revolver in hand. Precisely when this decline set in is less certain; the name of "Ritter von Pollaky, Esq." appears in *The Times*' pages twice in 1915, expressing support for his adopted country and joining a list of contributions to the paper's Fund for the Sick and Wounded. Yet it's possible that Pollaky's wits had already begun to fail him and that these gestures were the product of lucid intervals, or even made in his name by his wife Mary Ann, poignantly tending the reputation of her ailing longtime partner.

Ignatius Paul "Paddington" Pollaky died February 25, 1918. His obituary does not state a cause of death, though either advancing dementia or simply "old age" are plausible; at 90 years old his death hardly required a great detective's skills to explain it, any more than did those of the much younger men named on the same page of *The Times* under the heading "Killed in Action." In other ways Pollaky remained an odd figure, even in death. His obituary describes him as "at one time well known in London as a private inquiry agent," yet devotes nine lines to the brief reference to him in the opera *Patience*, in addition to making "A Detective Mentioned in Sullivan Opera" the headline. Several more lines are devoted to Pollaky's agony column advertisements, as well as to his correspondence on the 1911 Aliens Bill. Not one specific case is mentioned.

Sixteen years later, Vaughan Drydon's profile of Pollaky in *The Argus* provided an account somewhat more commensurate with a figure once so prominent in his field. Even Drydon was ultimately somewhat vague in describing the details of Pollaky's career, though, as well as his origins, which for some reason Drydon concluded were Polish. And that was largely the last significant notice taken of a once famous detective, aside from the amateur scholar Derek Ross who has gathered many of the remaining loose threads from Pollaky's history in recent years. Otherwise his name is forgotten; *Foul Play* has long since gone out of fashion, and while *Patience* is still staged, five words hardly constitute the preservation of a legend, even in a Gilbert & Sullivan opera.

Such is the nature of fame, however, even for those who cherished it; having for his own part been a consistently secretive person, even in his own era, "Paddington" Pollaky would hardly be saddened at vanishing from public memory. It could well be that in this, London's "Sherlock Holmes in Real Life" would have as company the creator of his fictional successor, whom the public steadfastly refused to forget even when that creator might have preferred otherwise. Arthur Conan Doyle did not necessarily ever wish for obscurity, per se. But his attitude toward his own great detective was certainly complicated, as evidenced by three attempts at ending the character's career, none of which truly succeeded. Thus it's reasonable to imagine, at least, that if Doyle ever gave thought to the contrasting disappearance of a possible model for his hero, he would have concluded that it was no tragedy at all for a detective to enjoy success and acclaim, and then exit the stage without once looking back.

CHAPTER FIVE
ISAIAH LEES

"I noticed these facts and was impressed with them.
It simply happened that other people
overlooked them."

I T'S NOT UNUSUAL for vitriol to splash around when arguments become heated. In modern usage, the word refers almost invariably to caustic language, rather than any physical substance; one person will attack another with vitriol, but the "attack" consists of nothing more than words. Though intended to suggest ferocity, the vitriol of contemporary assaults is essentially harmless, in a tangible sense. But it was not always thus. Twenty-first century pundits' description of one of their number attacking another with vitriol is the legacy of a bygone era and some of its less genteel persons, among whom a caustic assault was no mere figure of speech.

When Captain of Detectives Isaiah Lees arrived at the cottage of Maria LaFourge late one night in 1856 to investigate a reported assault, the vitriol involved was only too real. Lees found the French prostitute mutilated by a literally corrosive blast, her face a ruin and her mind so gripped by pain that Lees could get nothing coherent from her. The population of San Francisco had grown enormously in the past several years, however (even if it was still a predominantly male population and thus rich territory for LaFourge and her colleagues), and even near midnight Lees had little difficulty finding other witnesses in busy Washington Place. They readily provided the beginning, at least, of an explanation for what the officer himself had just seen. From their own observations and what the woman had managed to relate in the immediate aftermath of the incident, witnesses gave Lees this picture of events: Earlier in the evening, LaFourge had stepped outdoors for a moment, drawn by "suspicious" sounds of some sort. Finding nothing, she was about to return to her home, when an assailant threw a vial of acid in her face. No one volunteered to name this attacker, but at least one witness acknowledged that LaFourge had run, screaming, to a nearby saloon and loudly blamed her estranged lover Thomas Chieto for the crime before agony overcame her.

Though a policeman for barely five years and, as was frequently the case before the 20th century, lacking any training beyond experience, Captain Lees had a sharp and confident eye for detection which was to take him far over the course of a long career. The vitriol attack on LaFourge, though a ghastly crime, was by no means the last such he would investigate. As always, Lees tackled the situation resolutely and methodically. After questioning witnesses, he examined the crime scene further. He noted small burns on a curtain and chair outside the cottage, which supported the reports of acid thrown at LaFourge, as did a small bottle wrapped in a man's handkerchief, which Lees picked up.

At this point, despite Lees's best efforts the investigation became somewhat disordered. Lees arrested Chieto—only to find him released on bail a short time later, and gone, along with evidence Lees had collected on his first visit to the saloon. Fortunately, the suspect immediately returned to the same spot Lees had found him in before, though as a result Lees ended up conducting two searches of the saloon. Working for a police force and indeed a city still finding their way, Lees was probably used to such crossed wires. While capable of anger, he could be endlessly patient in pursuing a case. Chieto stonewalled the officer and attempted to conceal evidence—even if he neglected to conceal himself—but Lees was a determined searcher.

In the end, he assembled a battery of evidence typical of his thorough style. In Chieto's rooms above the saloon, Lees found a trunk of clothes; some of these bore a laundry mark matching that of the handkerchief found earlier. Lees also took note of marks on the clothes Chieto was wearing, as his trousers bore small burns resembling those on LaFourge's curtains. After his release, Chieto attempted to hide that pair of pants, but his efforts at eluding the detective backfired disastrously. Lees found the pants rolled up beneath the bar, and damp, as though someone had made a hasty attempt to clean them. In the process, Lees also discovered new evidence he had missed on his first search. Sifting through "a pile of rubbish in a dark corner," Lees found a container of vitriol, while beneath the bar along with the rolled up pants he found a cork, which for some reason made him suspicious. Lees went through the entire bar seeking a bottle that this cork might fit, without success, before confirming what he likely expected all along. It matched the vial from LaFourge's cottage exactly.

When Chieto's trial date arrived in October, Lees presented all of this evidence against his suspect. He also provided the prosecution with a number of witnesses, including a druggist who had sold the larger container of vitriol, and Madame LaFourge herself, her face badly scarred and one eye lost entirely to the caustic fluid. With the persuasive evidence and witness testimony, Thomas Chieto was convicted and sentenced to 10 years. Captain Lees, in turn, was lauded for the case; the *Marin County Journal*'s comparison with Vidocq still lay decades ahead, but Lees's efficient work on this minor sensation launched his eventual legend, effectively. And appropriately, featuring as it did both patient detective work and success in the court room, as well as a disquieting element of horror.

Lees would chase down his share of frauds and forgers too, yet there is all the same a dark, gothic quality to many of his cases. In the rough boomtown environment of early San Francisco, Isaiah Lees pitted himself against crimes of desperation and even abject evil. He struggled against murderers and at times against some who seemed even worse, such as Chieto, perhaps, or Rose Church, who kept a missing man captive in a tiny room and so paralyzed by drugs that Lees could barely hear him croak "Thank god, I am saved" upon finding him. Lees himself acknowledged this distinct element to his career, compared with other celebrated detectives, and considered it nothing to be envied. "I try to forget that phase of my life when I go home," he once said, suggesting that it was never an entirely successful effort.

Lees was not really a brooding antihero, however, any more than he was an unerring, square-jawed western lawman. He had his faults and his failures, although these latter were vastly outnumbered by successes in a career of nearly 50 years. The sheer number of great cases closed by Lees and well documented by San Francisco's eager and competitive press makes it difficult to decide what to leave out. Unlike Whicher, Lees was in the spotlight many times, and unlike Pollaky he spoke readily of both his professional and personal life. Of these, his professional life usually took precedence. But plentiful records also describe Lees's family life; his finances; his friendships and quarrels; and his origins, which for variety and adventure might almost provide Lees "rank with Vidocq" as well.

Isaiah Lees joined the police force while still in his early 20s. Yet by that point in his life he had already been a cotton mill worker, a mechanic, a fireman, a gold prospector, a partner in a successful tugboat company, and a real estate speculator. He was also well traveled, to an extent Vidocq never approached, from his earliest years. Lees was born on Christmas Day 1830, in Liverpool, England, and was only an infant when his parents John and Elisabeth emigrated to the United States. Thus, unlike another British expatriate who found fame in the new world as a detective around the same time as Lees, young Isaiah effectively grew up as an American. Aside from growing up in Paterson, New Jersey, in somewhat more salubrious conditions than those of the Gorbals, however, Lees's youth was much like Pinkerton's in broad outlines. Isaiah's father died when he was only eight, after which the boy had to leave formal schooling and go to work. Lees nonetheless managed to learn a skilled trade, that of a mechanic like his father. He then went out "on the tramp" as well, traveling widely through New England and even visiting Cuba at one point. And Isaiah Lees's life also changed, forever, in the 1840s when he took a long voyage thousands of miles west of his home.

As Lees had already crossed the Atlantic Ocean, in his case this meant going further west, to California along with the rest of the Gold Rush. There is a modest irony, here: the moralizing one-time Chartist Pinkerton made his legend as a detective in private practice, yet Lees was arguably much more of a profit-driven entrepreneur at heart, even though his own detective career was forged as a poorly paid public employee. Aged just barely 18, Lees set out on his great journey west for no reason other than riches, and perhaps adventure. Like many other young men, the discovery of gold at Sutter's Mill lured him to San Francisco to try his luck.

Lees had little luck as a prospector, however. After one unsuccessful season in the gold fields he returned to San Francisco. He found it already much changed from the town in which he had embarked less than a year before, if still barely more than a sprawling temporary camp. (Here too, once and future Chicagoan Pinkerton would no doubt have related.) Looking for some other way to sustain himself, Lees found opportunities, if all too familiar in shape. An acquaintance from Paterson had established an iron works, which was prospering in an expanding community in need of not only mining tools but nearly everything else, too. Lees soon resumed his trade as a mechanic, along with another activity from Paterson; having served as a fireman in New Jersey for a time, Lees became a founding member of California Engine Company No. 4 and took pride in that elect position for many years after.

And yet, he had traveled a very long distance just to resume the same patterns of life in a rougher and more lawless setting. For a time, Lees seemed to go back and forth between life in San Francisco and life back east. Literally, in fact; in late 1850 he arranged working passage on a ship back to the East Coast, and a few months later married his sweetheart Jane Fisher. After a modest honeymoon, Lees left behind a pregnant Jane to return to San Francisco. He intended to get his life in California a bit more established first, then send for his new bride, and for the most part the plan worked out well. In October of 1852, Isaiah welcomed Jane and their first child Mary Jane to San Francisco. They soon settled into the relatively family-friendly new "Happy Valley" neighborhood, and Isaiah began settling in to his new venture running a tugboat in the increasingly busy Bay. A month before his family joined him, however, Isaiah Lees played a brief role in certain curious events, which eventually led him far astray from his prudent new career plans.

Like Allan Pinkerton's "Bogus Island" stakeout five years earlier, Lees's investigation of a brutal murder in September 1852 seems difficult to fully account for. Still just 21, Lees had already led a varied life and was obviously not shy about trying his hand at something new. It's also possible that as a volunteer fireman he felt just a bit more natural in stepping in to solve a problem, even when it did not concern him personally, than the average man. His readiness to intervene might be further explained by a frontier setting in which ordinary citizens had to do more for themselves, with formal authorities so few and far between—particularly detectives, which as an institution were still just a decade old, even in cities like Boston and London. Nonetheless, when Lees learned of a mysterious fatal stabbing, his decision to investigate personally still seems the stuff of novels, to say nothing of how effective he then proved as amateur detective. A believer in reincarnation might almost suspect that Lees had investigated crimes in a past life and was merely picking up where he left off.

The situation, upon Lees's arrival on the scene, certainly called for an experienced sleuth. A small crowd of witnesses had been drawn by the sound of screams to a bloody crime scene; there, they found a Spanish immigrant named Jose Forni stabbing another man. Forni immediately attempted to flee before someone blocked his escape. Dragged back to the scene, he then claimed to have acted in self-defense, after taking a knife from the other man who had used it to stab Forni's leg while attempting to rob him of $300. The other man had died within minutes of the stabbing, however, and while his 11 wounds made Forni's story highly suspect, no one could immediately disprove it or even identify the deceased, whom Forni claimed was a stranger to him.

Forni himself was a poorly dressed man of around 30 and professed to be a native of Valencia, Spain. The stabbed man was well dressed, but apparently lacking any documents or other clues to his name or origins. Two days after the stabbing, the small San Francisco police force had provisionally identified him as Jose Rodriguez, but otherwise the case seemed to be at a dead end. Upon appointing himself to investigate the case, however, Lees had a look at the body, and though he could not confirm or deny the man's identity he noticed something that might offer a clue after all. The victim's fingernails were outlined in a black material. Which, perhaps because of his own hands-on experience with steam age industry, suggested to Lees that the man may have worked in a coal yard. Lees recruited a few of his coworkers to ask around San Francisco's collier community. Eventually, at the yard of a Don Ventura Miro, Lees made a break in the case that had stumped local police.

Jose Rodriguez had worked for Miro, though no one had seen him since the last payday. Lees could turn to his own knowledge of San Francisco for where to look next. In a city overrun by gold prospectors, failed or successful, gambling was one of the best established local industries. As Doris Muscatine notes in *Old San Francisco: The Biography of a City From Early Days to the Earthquake*, "The gambling houses were among the most sizable structures in the community" and had taken in many a man's salary on the same day it was paid out. So, fanning out from Rodriguez's workplace, Lees began checking saloons and gambling halls and shortly found a dealer who recalled the slain man. Rodriguez, he told Lees, had enjoyed great luck at the tables at his last appearance. He continually tucked his winnings into a sash, then finally left—followed by Jose Forni.

Forni had claimed that the sash full of money was his own. But, in addition to the dealer's testimony, Lees spoke to a number of both Spaniards and Mexicans in the course of his inquiries, who left Lees convinced that a native Spaniard (as Forni claimed to be) would be very unlikely to wear "a cheap, Mexican sash" of that type. Lees reported this, along with his other findings, to the officer Hampton North who was officially assigned to the case. Within a month, Forni was tried, found guilty, and hanged. Reflecting years afterward, Lees recalled the incident with characteristic modesty, stating simply that "some of the boys at the Union Iron Works and myself dug up most of the evidence that convicted him."

For just over one year, his successful outing with "the boys" remained the beginning and end of Lees's detective career. A young family and a young business kept him well occupied, and in his spare time he began investing profits from the latter in property around San Francisco. Yet for all that this seemed as safe and reliable a lifestyle as a 19th century frontier city offered, Jane Lees was uneasy. She feared for her husband's safety, plying the waters of San Francisco Bay. She worried about a boiler explosion, telling Isaiah she had a terrible premonition and would not know peace of mind so long as he continued to risk such a fate. For Isaiah, whose analytical mind was probably bored of the long days of toil, acceding to his wife's pleas was an easy choice and small enough concession to a faithful partner. Particularly as his choice of replacement career, which would ironically pose considerably more danger by most standards, would also mean even longer hours away from home and would leave Jane to raise their family largely by herself.

But if Mrs. Lees had misgivings about Isaiah joining the police, she kept them to herself, satisfied that at least the evil vision of her husband being blown up by an overheated boiler had been thwarted. In the short term, it was nearly the only positive to come from Lees's new line of work. On October 28, 1853, Isaiah Lees was sworn in along with other raw recruits and joined a police force that was poorly equipped, outnumbered, and underpaid. In general this was merely par for the course in mid-19th century policing, admittedly. The situation in San Francisco was not especially different from any American city, at most a bit worse. The equipment may not have been much worse, though it still wasn't very good; many officers carried a knife for back-up when their pistols misfired. The teeming population was more transient and unruly. The low wages were certainly lower, especially after adjusting the city scrip's official face value for its invariably lower, real-world, value. Lees at least had the proceeds from selling his share in the tugboat firm, and rental income from property in which he was investing them. Most officers were not so fortunate, which explains much of the culture of eagerly chasing rewards and other opportunities to leverage the job for extra money that prevailed at the time.

Altogether, the San Francisco Police Department that Lees joined in 1853 was a rough-edged crew of just more than 100 men, tasked with upholding law and order in a city already exceeding 50,000 people. Like others before and after him found, such circumstances offered possibilities along with problems. An able man might find opportunity to learn quickly. In *Dark and Tangled Threads of Crime*, his biography of Lees, William B. Secrest writes that "This was the greatest training ground for fledgling lawmen in the world. There were confidence men, horse thieves, burglars, political thugs, and ex-convicts from all over the world." So it readily proved. Lees began his police career as an ordinary patrolman, but the city that had offered him a murder investigation while still a private citizen did not demand he wait for promotion before offering up further knotty mysteries.

Lees found the missing piece to one puzzle, first encountered while patrolling Kearny Street, late at night in a dark storeroom behind the kitchen of the El Dorado casino. Claims of a stolen diamond pin and a vanished thief had drawn Lees to join two other officers at the city's most lavish gaming house. But while examining the storeroom, empty but for a heap of rice bags of which the kitchen steward seemed suspiciously protective, Lees made one small discovery that led to a much larger one: the bags were filled with soil. Suddenly Lees called over his colleagues. "By Jove, Mac, we've got the biggest thing out. I see through the whole thing."

For nearly a week, Lees had heard what sounded very much like miners' picks at work beneath his feet as he walked his beat in the hours before dawn. The connection to these earth-filled rice bags was unmistakable, in his mind, although the rest of those present were still astonished when Lees began heaving aside the sacks to reveal a narrow tunnel. Lees had no doubts that it led toward the nearby Palmer, Cook and Company bank, but he suspected it might lead to something, or someone, else as well. Taking up a lantern, Lees crawled into the tunnel and disappeared from view. Minutes later the other officers heard a loud bang from some way inside the tunnel, then after a couple of more moments, Lees reappeared. Crawling out backward and sporting an ugly bruise from a crowbar, Lees emerged from the tunnel and then dragged out a wounded thief and the stolen pin. These he entrusted to the other men to take care of while he remained behind. Lees was invariably thorough, as well as observant. Even though he had solved one theft and preempted another, something else which he had *not* seen nagged at him just as had the nearly empty storeroom. Continuing to search the casino after everyone else had gone, Lees finally found the tools that he knew must have been hidden somewhere, and with them a selection of the more specialized implements of burglars and counterfeiters.

*

The combination of acumen, dogged effort, and results that Lees demonstrated at the El Dorado won notice from the brass. Barely a year and one month after being sworn in as a rookie, Lees was promoted to assistant captain of police. By the middle of 1856, still just 25 years old, he was captain of detectives. The young Captain Lees, who successfully investigated the vitriol attack on Marie LaFourge soon after his promotion, was well suited to the role.

In addition to the qualities of intellect and character that helped him piece together solid evidence, time after time, he looked the part. Allowing for differences of fashion, Isaiah Lees may have looked more "like a detective" than any of the field's other luminaries, most of whom were squat, stocky fellows. Lees was a taller, leaner figure. A photograph taken in his forties shows a man with relatively angular features, though becoming somewhat fleshy with age; dark bushy hair, probably combed as neatly as it would allow; and a long goatee. The general effect gives Lees a vague resemblance to Charles Dickens. But the eyes bring the portrait and its sitter to life. Shown in three-quarter profile, Lees's narrow eyes peer to the side, directly at the viewer. The face gives an immediate impression of a watchful observer.

All that Lees seems to lack is a pipe trailing smoke to complete the image, though his own tastes ran to a fine cigar. Outside of solving mysteries and occasionally, even long after retiring as a prospector, angling for treasure, Lees was a man of generally simple interests: a good cigar, spending time at home when he could get it, or visiting with some of his friends. His only notable hobby was book collecting, though he apparently pursued that with nearly as much diligence as he pursued San Francisco's criminals. Possibly even more, per *The San Francisco Examiner*, which suggested in July 1889 that

If Captain Lees tomorrow were to collar the Whitechapel fiend, and be able to establish his identity by the clearest of proofs, he would make no mention of the circumstance in the upper office, and treat it as an everyday occurrence. When he runs down and scoops in a rare specimen of criminal literature the case is different. He glories in his success, brags of his achievement and will spend hours telling his friends how he was enabled to make the capture.

Through the years Lees amassed a large library, and savored the occasional evenings at home when he could sit down with a book and a cigar and read quietly. As well he might, given their rarity. Lees had left behind a venture that was predictable, profitable and, Jane's fears aside, relatively safe; his career as a policeman by contrast involved turbulence of one sort or another from nearly the first day to the last.

If Isaiah Lees's path to rank was short, it was neither smooth nor direct. Multiple times, in the 12 months before his promotion to captain, it had looked more like he would be pushed out than raised up. In August 1855, a proposed reorganization of the department would have made American citizenry a requirement, disqualifying Lees who had lived in the United States nearly all his life but, perhaps for that reason, never gotten around to applying for citizenship. The plan was tabled, but more difficulties lay in store with the SFPD and, particularly, its marshal.

Just how Hampton North had felt about Lees coming in off the street to close a murder case North was assigned to is impossible to know. No accounts suggest that he bore Lees any grudge. On the other hand, nothing else in particular seems to account for Lees's suspension, in early 1856, along with three other officers. All charges against Lees were eventually dismissed. When reassigned, however, he found himself on a particularly notorious beat even by the standards of early San Francisco, and under personal surveillance by Marshal North. North kept the observation a secret from Lees—until one evening he found something else, in the Presidio neighborhood, which concerned him rather more. Observing from some distance behind as a large group of brawling soldiers began spilling into the street from a saloon, North caught up to Lees but was at a loss for what action to take or order to give. Lees was not. While he could be a cool, analytical reasoner when a case demanded it, Lees never hesitated to leap into action when a situation grew hot. In this instance he swiftly tore two pickets off of a fence, handed one to North, and charged into the saloon bellowing. His initial sally knocked down several of the brawlers, and most of the others fled. After the fight, North shook Lees's hand and declared that he would never mistrust him again.

North seemed to have great difficulty getting along with his men, and in spite of the marshal's pledge, that continued to include Lees. Several weeks later the two were at odds once more and arguing with such force that they nearly came to blows. Afterward, Lees spent the night in a cell. He was neither the first nor the last detective of note to do so, but Lees was left deeply pessimistic about his career; he still rented his family's own home, and he paid up the rest of the year's rent so that whatever else happened, they would at least be assured of a place to stay. As it turned out, he and Marshal North were indeed soon to part ways, but not as Lees expected. At a hearing, a parade of officers testified to Lees's good qualities, and even North himself joined them. Lees was suspended again, briefly, but his career would survive. North's would not. A few months after his fight with Lees, the quarrelsome North resigned, possibly in response to pressure from his officers, or dissatisfied citizens, or even one of the vigilante groups that intruded intermittently into the early days of San Francisco law enforcement.

His colleagues rallying to defend him and North's subsequent departure should have made a neat ending to Captain Lees's struggles with his employer. They might have, too, but for the police commissioners targeting San Francisco's force with yet another "reorganization" plan. This one passed, and brought about Lees's outright dismissal from the police at last, along with several other officers. After the year Lees had been through by the end of 1856, this last absurd twist seemed to suggest that the whims of fate were unguessable and worries over his career mere vanity. And Lees may well have smiled ruefully at the humor. But he also wanted to keep his job, as did his colleagues, and saw no good reason for what looked like entirely arbitrary meddling by the commissioners. A number of San Francisco lawyers agreed and offered to prosecute a case against the city, free of charge. The commissioners may simply have hoped, in the style of the day, to create some opportunities for political patronage, but they had miscalculated in trying to open up new postings in a hard working and respected police force. They quickly reinstated all of the dismissed officers, though to save face they spitefully brought the men, Lees included, back as patrolmen.

The ex-officers accepted this settlement, perhaps suspecting that their reduction in rank would be brief once the affair blew over. They were right. Lees regained his rank as captain of detectives, and had good reason to feel satisfied with his job, in spite of everything. His first years as a police officer were as far from a dull routine as he could have possibly hoped. He solved violent crimes and exposed devious plots; charged into riots; survived assaults by fists, crowbars and bullets; made headlines for remarkable adventures; and found himself suspended, locked up and dismissed from the force, only to return determined on making up for lost time.

During the first half of Isaiah Lees's long and eventful police career, San Francisco was home to another enterprising British expatriate who earned a measure of celebrity for himself. Significantly, a century and a half later, Norton I, Emperor of the United States, is much the better remembered of the two. That a failed businessman turned grandiose professional eccentric not only shared the acclaim of 19th century San Francisco with more serious public figures, but has in most cases surpassed it since, says something about the character of the city. In policing its population Lees confronted humanity's worst aspects time and again, and, per his own words, could only "try to forget" at day's end. Yet the same scrambling, tumultuous city of chancers which had such capacity for crime also had a flair for the absurd that set it apart, even from other of the era's rough boom towns such as Pinkerton's more business-like Chicago. This side of San Francisco was reflected in Lees's work as well.

The late 1850s, when Emperor Norton first proclaimed his reign, appropriately saw some of the first notable interludes from more serious police work in Lees's career. The affair of Archy Lee was serious enough to those most closely involved, particularly the contested slave himself; given the war that was eventually fought over the issues at stake, it was arguably of great seriousness for the entire nation. Yet Captain Lees's part in Archy's trials had an undeniably boisterous, swashbuckling quality.

On March 6, 1858, Lees and other officers joined a sizable crowd gathered at the wharf, straining to catch sight of Charles Stovall and his disputed property, Archy. Stovall had fought at length through California's courts to reassert his ownership of Archy, but per rumors had lost patience and decided to forcibly convey Archy back to Mississippi where the matter might be more readily settled in Stovall's favor. Police were ready to intervene and charge Stovall with kidnapping if they could intercept him. They had information that Stovall and his party would attempt to board the *Orizaba*, after it left shore, from a small boat. Shortly before the *Orizaba* cast off, Lees and two other officers quietly stepped aboard the craft, in plain clothes and largely unnoticed in the general excitement.

Among the three officers, Captain Lees would stand out once again through a mix of sharp observation with swift, decisive action. On the alert for any kind of signals, Lees noted a fellow passenger waving a handkerchief; then, casting his sight in the direction of the gesture, he saw a small craft and someone aboard waving back. The boat drew near, and those on the *Orizaba* could see that it was carrying Stovall and three accomplices, with Archy pressed down low and nearly concealed from view. Someone recognized one of the policemen and shouted a warning to Stovall, but he had no time to react. As the *Alta California* reported, "Lees sprang down into the boat, at the risk of jumping through her, and seized Archy by the collar." Chaos followed, with shouting aboard the *Orizaba*, and Stovall and his crew threatening Lees with every violence imaginable. But by this point in his career Lees was already inured to such abuse. He calmly hefted the astonished Archy out of the boat to the other officers up on the *Orizaba*, then arrested Stovall for kidnapping, loud cheers drowning out the voices of protest.

The following year, Captain Lees was involved in a different sort of maritime adventure, somewhat less heroic but equally daring. That February, crew of the recently sunken brig *Cornelia* arrived in San Francisco and told police how their ship's fate had been no accident. The Cornelia's captain and mate, per the crew's story, had sent them below decks while off Cape San Lucas and proceeded to move a fortune in Mexican silver ashore before ordering the ship abandoned and then scuttled. Lees's contemporary, "Paddington" Pollaky, earned favorable press more than once in his own early career for investigations related to this sort of scam. But in this case the local U.S. attorney decided that he had no jurisdiction in the matter, and with the field otherwise seemingly uncontested, Lees decided to launch a salvage expedition.

Hand-retouched portrait of Isaiah Lees
Courtesy of The Bancroft Library,
University of California, Berkeley, California.
Reproduced with permission.
[Lees, Isaiah--POR 1]

Organizing a few partners, the former gold-seeker and tugboat pilot captained a new mission in search of silver. With the reluctant help of the *Cornelia*'s captain, whom the police had taken prisoner, Lees and his own crew found the treasure cached at the southern tip of Baja California. They hauled it aboard, though the completion of what was already a highly novel mission was slightly delayed by two outright comic interruptions. First, the local village *alcalde* arrived to protest, before Lees distracted him from his intentions with a bottle of brandy. Then, before the crew could depart at last, they had to search for a missing crew member to whom locals had applied the same tactic.

Captain Lees's mission eventually made it back to San Francisco, entirely successful, although its claim to the silver was hotly contested. The coins' original purchaser, Thomas Bell, had declined an invitation to back Lees's expedition but considered that this in no way prejudiced his legitimate claim to ownership, and months of argument followed. It should be noted that, while the entire episode seems not only novel but highly inappropriate for a police officer by modern standards, the salvage partnership not only received much of the claimed treasure after eventual arbitration, but included San Francisco's police chief among its members. Though Chief Curtis even went to jail at one point during the legal battle, most of the community (which of course included many who had arrived just like Lees with dreams of finding a fortune in precious metal) applauded the episode.

The "salvage" of the *Cornelia* was by no means the only time that Lees sought to profit from cases in which funds were plausibly up for grabs, either, although it was by far the most successful. To a great extent, this sort of behavior was an accepted custom of policing and in no way unique to San Francisco. Both formal rewards and informal opportunities for enrichment predated professional policing and continued to exist long afterward. As a result, governments saw little need to provide decent wages to early forces; if expecting police to scavenge for themselves was somewhat unseemly as well as a distraction from their core mission, putting up with it was still easier than raising taxes. So America's police forces were low-paid, particularly in the rapidly growing cities. Police department budgets were likewise meager, and policemen often had to purchase even the basic tools of their job, let alone more advanced equipment. Lees and fellow officers paid for cuffs, pistols, and notebooks out of their own pocket. When photography became practical for police work, San Francisco was one of the first departments to adopt it; for many years most of the cost, not inconsiderable in those days, was however paid by none other than Captain Lees and Chief Curtis.

If the rules were somewhat different in Lees's time than in our own, there were still rules. And if overall standards were also poorer there were still honest, hardworking cops. Lees was one of them. Per the prevailing customs, he took part in schemes that would earn censure today, as for that matter might some of his two-fisted actions in the line of duty. But Captain Lees would probably have little difficulty with modern policing, all the same, at least with its overall approach. Though ready and entirely able to intervene in matters physically, Lees was a cerebral detective. Observation, careful assembly of evidence and patient handling of suspects marked his work. In a century when "third degree" interrogation was scarcely even controversial, Lees treated prisoners with respect and tried to advise them of their rights more than 100 years before *Miranda v. Arizona*. Admirable as such tactics may have been, getting results was still what counted, of course. Lees got results. As Jonathan Whicher was painfully reminded, back in the England of Lees's birth, a detective's success rests on not only solving a case but convincing a court of the solution. Lees had a natural ability for both and—along with adequate time to use it in most cases—was at least as effective in the work that followed an arrest as in the work leading up to it.

Not long after his return from salvaging the treasure of the *Cornelia*, Lees cracked a mysterious theft from a Freeman and Company express wagon, which arrived in San Francisco with leather bags containing paper-wrapped iron bolts rather than money. The detective traced the origins of the bolts, the paper, and the twine that sealed it, as well as the leather bags which he correctly suspected were replicas, until he had witnesses able to describe nearly every move of his suspect leading up to the crime.

Likewise, early the following year Lees carefully picked apart the complicated alibi of Edward Bonney, whose business partner Auguste Hirsch had been discovered dead by a roadside in East Oakland, his head nearly severed from his body. Bonney was ready, even eager, to account for himself, if not necessarily to do so truthfully. Lees managed to escort him back through his movements leading up to and after the time of the murder, and probe subtle flaws in the story without putting Bonney on his guard. Afterward, Lees retraced the route again, seeking witnesses and collecting evidence including two neckties, a support strut from a buggy seat and the distinctively flawed hoof print of a rented horse. Though mainly circumstantial, the *Alta's* correspondent noted that Lees's evidence was central to the court case that eventually convicted Bonney:

> Captain I. W. Lees, of San Francisco, the detective who principally 'worked up' the case, and who finally took Bonney into custody, was on the stand the whole of yesterday and nearly all of this forenoon... The importance

of his evidence was so obvious that the defense counsel resorted to every method which ingenuity dictate or law allow to inv. him in inconsistencies, but so far as I could see, without success...

A couple of years later, the captain marked his tenth year on the force with a case combining the swashbuckling drama of his late 1850s maritime adventures with the painstaking evidence collection of more serious investigations. By the spring of 1863, the legal and ethical issues surrounding Archy Lee's personal struggle had erupted into a violent national struggle. The United States had been locked in civil war for nearly two years, and as other detectives active at the time demonstrated, the conflict extended well beyond massed armies colliding in the southeastern states. The naval component of the Civil War was relatively minor, even at the time, and it has been largely forgotten since. The Confederacy never deployed more than a tiny official fleet. But its use of those ships and licensed privateers for commerce raiding made a remarkable impact all the same, even if was tangential to the course of the larger war; historian James Stokesbury remarked that in combination with other trends, the South's raiding "struck American merchant shipping a blow from which it never really recovered."

Some of the Confederacy's most effective raiders were commissioned from British shipyards—one reason why America's government had particular interest in Confederate activities in London—including the CSS *Alabama*, which ran wild for nearly two years. In March 1863, a port of San Francisco surveyor warned Isaiah Lees of a plot by local secessionists to profit by the *Alabama*'s example. The surveyor drew Lees's attention to the recent sale of the *Chapman*, a fast schooner, which he believed was intended for use as a rebel privateer. Lees, still slowed somewhat by a buggy accident a year earlier, assigned several men to keep an eye on the ship. In the early hours of March 14, they observed a number of men boarding and summoned Lees. When the *Chapman* cast off at dawn and began to leave port without declaring cargo, Lees was free to move openly and did so with his usual gusto; despite a bad leg he was first to enter the hold after police forces caught up with and boarded the *Chapman*. A moment after colleagues watched Lees's lantern sink into the dark hold, they heard his voice announce loudly that "There's 15 or 20 damned rebels down here, just under the hatch!"

After seeing the crew rounded up and dispatched to Alcatraz, along with their ringleader Asbury Harpending, Lees turned to the less dramatic but equally important business of completing a case against them. Like the would-be bank robbers of the El Dorado years before, the would-be privateers had concealed bulkier evidence crudely; cases stamped "machinery" were stuffed with weapons and ammunition. With potentially more inflammatory documentary evidence, however, Harpending's crew had done better. They had managed to destroy much of it—but not irrevocably. Though even Lees could not reconstitute papers from ash, in the haste of the police raid not everything had been burned. Lees also found scraps of paper and soggy, wadded clumps in the hold; evidently the *Chapman's* crew had resorted to tearing and even chewing up documents in hopes of completing their task faster, and if the result was distasteful, an officer of Captain Lees's experience was no longer especially squeamish. He collected everything and, over the course of months, re-assembled bills of lading and a host of other documents. By the time of the trial in October, Isaiah Lees once again provided the court with thorough details of exactly those things the defendants wished most to conceal. Harpending and the plot's other two leaders received 10-year sentences, along with fines of $10,000.

With his repeated, and repeatedly successful, roles in such sensational events, Lees had established a considerable reputation by the mid-1860s. He was not the only police officer to win notice from San Francisco's press. For a time, Lees and another rising officer named Burke earned attention with undercover raids on the city's criminal dens, and in the late 1850s Lees's name often appeared alongside that of his partner Henry Johnson. Then, for a brief few years, all San Francisco's detectives found a chronicler nearly as legendary as Scotland Yard's early champion Charles Dickens.

He may or may not have described San Francisco's summer as the coldest winter of his life, but Mark Twain was in a position to know, having spent more than one of them in the famously foggy city. At the time, his own fame lay in the future. His writing from the period is entertaining, naturally, but Samuel L. Clemens was still only an ordinary, struggling beat reporter. He was often reporting on court cases, where he most likely became familiar with Lees and other officers, and in time he found positive things to say about a number of them. One article in the *Territorial Enterprise* even approaches the enthusiasm of Dickens' "Detective Police Party" from 15 years before:

> Detective Rose can pick up a chicken's tail feather in Montgomery street and tell in a moment what roost it came from at the Mission [...] Detective Blitz can hunt down a transgressing hack-driver by some peculiarity in the style of his blasphemy. The forte of Lees and Ellis, is the unearthing of embezzlers and forgers. Each of these men are best in one particular line, but at the same time they are good in all.

The future chief cynic of Gilded Age America, however, was simply not cut out for the role of propagandist for the authorities, even when they were hard working public defenders. Twain generally had good things to say about Lees, including a July 1864 story in the *Daily Morning Call* about a theft which the bibliophile Lees must have particularly relished his role in defeating: he and officer Rose captured a burglar who had stolen a number of valuables from the home of a Colonel Hayes, including "four standard literary works – Byron's poems among the number." The closest Twain came to any swipe at Lees was early the following year when he mocked the police for excessive coddling of the captain after an injury. The rest of the force, including Lees's former partner Burke, who had risen to chief, were not let off so lightly. Eventually Twain's barbed criticism of the city's police ("Don't they parade up and down the sidewalk at a rate of a block an hour and make everybody dizzy with their frightful velocity?") made life in San Francisco increasingly awkward. In the end, he moved on to Calaveras County and the beginnings of literary fame.

Even in his most acerbic writing on the SFPD, Twain made a point of singling out Lees and Ellis for praise. After a rocky start, Lees had become a stalwart on the city's police force; Burke, Johnson, Ellis and other names came and went, but Lees continued to earn respect, year in and year out. In late 1859, Lees won promotion from captain of detectives to captain of police, after which only one post remained still ahead of him. And between Lees's consistently impressive record and the relatively brief tenures of controversial chiefs like Curtis and Burke, it must have seemed only a matter of time before the papers began reporting on "Chief Lees." So it proved, but not until after a much longer delay than Lees might ever have guessed. After rising from patrolman to captain of police while still not quite 30 years old, Isaiah Lees was to see his climb through the ranks stubbornly halt for nearly four decades. In May 1862, Lees added the title of Deputy U.S. Marshal to that of captain of police, but otherwise his career had reached a plateau, and there it remained.

Even as the city grew and transformed around him, and the occasional reforms, reorganizations and scenery shuffling continued at the police department, Captain of Police Isaiah Lees resembled an unchanging landmark. The situation must have been at least somewhat frustrating, particularly after such rapid early promotion. Yet Lees does seem to have been generally content with his lot, and in some sense it may even have been a blessing. Lees eventually went on to do a very credible job as an administrator, but his greatest gifts were as a *detective*, taking to the field personally to study witnesses and evidence close at hand. Other celebrated sleuths, after rising to prominence, spent much of their careers directing affairs from a more remote position; some times they continued to make significant contributions to the profession's history and other times the job of administrator simply complicated or even marred a great career. In Lees's case, it seems that elevation to the role of chief at a much earlier date would have been merely a waste of great talent. Other men could and did manage San Francisco's police competently. It's doubtful that anyone else could have compiled Lees's record of personal triumphs in solving one memorable crime after another for decades. Upon promotion to captain of police, Lees had already established himself as a detective of note, but the far greater part of his eventual legend had yet to be written.

Like most who achieved greatness in his field, Lees took an interest in the potential for science to aid in the art of detection. Much of his own approach was simple and straightforward; though he employed disguises on some of his early raids alongside Burke, he had little use for them after advancing to the role of detective. Lees asked questions, examined evidence, and used logic to fit together his findings. As his biographer writes, "he was the quintessential detective; the tireless investigator who carefully assembled his clues until they made sense. No miracle worker or Sherlock Holmes, Lees always worked very hard to solve a crime." Perhaps for that reason, Lees had no sentimentality about tradition in what was, after all, still a new specialty anyway. If science and technology could help discover more evidence, or reveal more from it, he was more than willing to try it out. In addition to introducing photography to San Francisco law enforcement at his own expense, Lees included in his library works directly related to criminology and others more tangential, but possibly still important. In looking back at Lees's career, upon his retirement, the *San Francisco Chronicle* listed among his virtues how "As Captain of Detectives Lees went deeply into the study of photography, microscopy and the kindred sciences which would be useful in the detection of forgeries."

Both this self-guided study, as well as his by then well-established facility in court, were impressively displayed in an 1870 forgery case. The affair began with a conversation with banker George Hickox, of Hickox & Spear, which makes for a diverting tale in itself. The *Chronicle* reported a colorful encounter, beginning when "a nervous, go-ahead-like-a-locomotive man rushed plumb against" Lees. The captain attempted to delay Hickox for a moment, to deliver a warning about a possible check fraud. But the banker was desperately anxious to follow a hot tip, and per the *Chronicle* was "just bursting with excitement, and involuntarily danced and gave little squeaks." When Lees finally managed to deliver his warning about someone cashing a large check drawn on Treadwell & Co., Hickox's "auburn whiskers had wilted, and he said 'He's been around to our place an hour ago and said he would return in an hour for the bills.'"

Hickox's estimate of the timing was spot-on, and when the two men had hurried back to his bank, matters became more serious. John Spear had just paid out more than $14,000 in greenbacks on just the kind of check that rumors had led Lees to expect. A visit to Treadwell & Co. provided further confirmation; the check was legitimate, but the name and amount had been chemically erased and then replaced with other figures. Lees knew something of the processes and material involved in this technique, and thus had some idea of what to look for. The bank was able to provide him an adequate description of whom to look for. With that, Lees was off to stake out the first steamer bound for Sacramento. More men were dispatched to cover other potential routes out of the city, but Lees suspected this would be the con man's likeliest destination. He was right, and upon deciding that a man named George Howard was his quarry, Lees stopped to greet him. Asked his business, Lees replied dramatically but very honestly "I am Captain Lees, and I am red-hot after that forgery of yours."

Despite insisting that he had only $70 with him, Howard had almost exactly one-third the amount of the stolen funds in his bag. Lees reasonably concluded that two others had been in on the fraud, and after he arrested Howard, other detectives tracked down Lewis and George Brotherton as likely accomplices based on Howard's known circles. Per the *Chronicle*, "Both men had large amounts of cash," but even more importantly "Brushes and a vial of white powder were particular evidence." Given the many witnesses to his role, tying Howard to the crime was no great challenge, and he pleaded guilty; the case against the Brothertons was initially much weaker. The only potentially solid links to the forgery were the brushes and powder found on them at their arrest. So Lees set himself to explaining their significance as plainly and conclusively as possible.

In court, Lees and a chemist he recruited provided the jury with a live demonstration in the basics of chemical forgery. They showed how the Brothertons' powder, chlorate of potash and carbonate of soda, could be made into a solution and used to remove ink from a check. Going further, Lees then produced expert testimony to explain how this would also eat away the surface coating, or sizing, of paper used for checks, before showing how rice could be boiled to make an effective patch for the sizing. Rice just such as that which police had found along with the Brothertons' powder and brushes. The whole demonstration was fascinating to onlookers, and as it happened those who missed out had the chance to catch it again later, as multiple appeals, three trials and an escape from prison kept Lees involved in the case until 1872. In the end, though, the prosecution's case stood and the Brothertons were returned to prison with their accomplice Howard, where they served 14 years.

In 1871, San Francisco deployed approximately one police officer for every 1,500 people—nearly one-third the proportionate size of forces in London or New York. If the City by the Bay was a good deal smaller, it had more than its share of big city problems. In addition to ordinary, run-of-the-mill criminals like thieves and counterfeiters, there were the occasional rioting mobs as well as near-feral youth gangs and the growing power of the "tongs," which maintained a tight grip on much of the city's drug trade, prostitution, gambling and other rackets. Crime kept the San Francisco police busy year in and year out. But there were high and low points within the larger trend. Within the space of a few years, Lees worked three remarkable cases, beginning with a complicated municipal corruption matter in 1874.

Captain Lees may have been grateful for a chance to restore some of the shine to his reputation, after another conflict over Spanish treasure had tarnished it in the first years of the decade. After locating Buenaventura Pereda, the suspected thief of $28,000 from Spanish army barracks in Cuba, Lees and his chief convinced him to surrender most of the funds. Lees then banked the money for safekeeping while he arranged its return and, of course, an appropriate reward. But a new controversy interrupted his plan upon Pereda acquiring legal counsel and recanting his surrender of the money. This time, unlike the wrangling over the silver from the *Cornelia*, the local press was also critical of Lees's actions if not his motivations. The *Bulletin* allowed that "It is but justice to say that Officer Lees has an untarnished character for integrity," but the combined legal and press jabs may have stung, all the same. Meanwhile, Pereda was suing Lees for all of the contested money plus $100,000 for damages. Lees responded by going over to the offensive against Pereda, finding multiple witnesses who had been in Cuba and could confirm his initial confession to stealing the money. Pereda then tried to withdraw his lawsuit, but the court declined to let him back out so easily, and eventually all of the money was returned to the Spanish government. If Lees received any reward for his efforts, though, it must have seemed dearly earned.

Thereafter, Lees seems to have dealt with "disputed funds" through less personal and more official means, at least when any significant amounts were at stake. His abilities could be employed better, and less controversially, in foiling others whose unauthorized appropriations left no doubts as to their motives. In 1874, the city's mayor approached Lees personally to investigate several assessor's office employees who had begun living well beyond what their official salaries could have explained, dining regularly at the city's finest hotels and showing off diamond stickpins at the race track while placing conspicuously large bets. The mayor's trust in Lees testifies to the esteem he commanded even after the ugly fight over the Spanish cash. Particularly as Lees would have to work entirely alone: as corruption might extend outside just the high-living deputy assessors, Lees would have to investigate the assessor's office without the help or even awareness of anyone inside.

Any fraud likely involved falsified or faked poll tax receipts, and Lees had to employ roundabout means just to acquire a sample of the office's official documents for comparison. Later, he significantly extended a trip back east, on which he had been dispatched to pursue a forger (who finally eluded Lees by the effective if drastic means of self-poison), to Chicago, Philadelphia and Montréal after receiving word that one of the deputies had set out for the French Canadian city to make "property arrangements." Lees found him visiting engraving and printing operations instead, and managed to surreptitiously acquire a printing plate for the counterfeit receipts, which he had learned to distinguish from the real article. When the deputies were finally brought to trial that October, Lees was the main witness, and much of his testimony consisted of demonstrating the minute differences between real and forged receipts. Even in the *Chronicle*, it sounded like relatively dry fare, but it was effective: "All deputies received richly-deserved terms in San Quentin."

Any want of excitement was, moreover, made up over the next few years as Lees played starring roles in two celebrated local dramas. Lees's recovery of the *Elaine*, painted by locally born artist Toby Rosenthal, was a relatively minor affair in terms of detective work, but in terms of fanfare it was a high point of his career. The *Elaine*'s 1875 exhibition at a Kearny Street gallery drew huge crowds prior to its April 13 disappearance; afterward, even larger crowds assembled to gape at the empty frame and indulge in weeping and other Victorian melodrama.

Lees observed a number of clues at the scene, but in the end, cracking the case proved largely a combination of one good description of the "suspicious looking characters" loitering outside, the evening before the theft, plus the familiarity with known criminals that skilled detectives develop. Lees recognized one of the descriptions as William "Cutface" Donahue and promptly found a photo in one of his mug shot books, which the witness confirmed. The *Chronicle*'s account of the subsequent events makes rich reading, with near misses, carts racing through the streets at dawn, and a knock at a door answered with the muzzle of an antique blunderbuss. After Lees's identification of Donahue the recovery of the *Elaine* was, all the same, largely a matter of competence rather than brilliance. Occasionally the extraordinary response to a minor feat brings acclaim to the right person, though, and such was the case with Lees and the *Elaine*. The largest crowds yet flooded the Kearny Street gallery to view the restored painting and, at its side, a gilt-framed portrait of its savior. In general, Lees seemed quite content to be respected but otherwise left to go about his business, but he was truly the man of the hour after getting back the *Elaine*.

It was well that he savored the moment of glory, as more difficult times were ahead. Violent riots two years later saw every last law and public safety employee in San Francisco called up to maintain order, Captain Lees included. Though entering his late 40s he was still as durable as he was discerning, and that too was well, not only for battling the riots but for an even more sensational and grueling challenge that began later the same year. "The Great Duncan Hunt" was a frustrating manhunt for Joe Duncan, a fugitive banker. Typically, Lees himself had played a part in discovering the frauds for which Duncan was wanted, but finding him afterward proved the larger challenge by every measure. The Duncan Hunt became one of those cases that seems to defy a normal news cycle and only attracts greater and more intense attention the longer that it drags on; having wrapped up the Tichborne Claimant affair a few years before, Jack Whicher might well have sympathized with

Lees, particularly as the Great Duncan Hunt also generated controversy and criticism. The San Francisco police spared no effort to find Duncan. Lees and others worked around the clock for days on end, and years afterward Lees blamed the case for ruining more than one officer's health. "[That case] killed a couple of my men and broke down a number more," he insisted. Yet as weeks and then months went by, the exceptional efforts may have simply intensified public frustration with the missing results.

In February, weary and much abused police finally got their man. Once again, Lees led the getting. His close observation of Duncan's son, Willie, and a friend of his might seem like an obvious step. But popular rumors all held that the elder Duncan had long fled the city and was hiding someplace far from San Francisco, perhaps Michigan. Lees knew from experience that the peninsular city was quite difficult to slip out of unobserved, however, if police were on the alert. He discounted the rumors and believed that the wanted banker was still somewhere close despite months without a sighting. And perhaps, had he been given to guessing, Lees might even have guessed part of the address, as his surveillance of Willie led the detective once more to Kearny Street. Twenty years before, he had begun his police career there as a patrolmen, and heard the sounds that led to a dramatic find at the El Dorado; more recently he had returned the *Elaine* there after its theft. Now he followed Willie Duncan to a meeting with another man, whom Lees also knew, and when Lees's instincts told him to follow the second man, he led the captain to a Kearny Street boarding house. Lees managed to follow the man inside and see him enter a room with obvious, though inadequate, caution.

That was enough for Captain Lees. He proceeded swiftly on the conviction that Duncan had been found, and that night he returned to the Kearny Street house in force. Certain of his conclusion, Lees was taking no chances: multiple units were covering every possible exit while Lees led a raid on the house personally. He was obviously wound tight. When one officer stumbled on the way up a darkened stairwell, Lees hissed "Who's that? If anyone makes any more noise, I'll kill him!" And when the mysterious door was finally opened on a thin, pale figure with several weeks' beard, Lees made it clear that Joe Duncan's game of hide-and-seek was firmly at an end. The feeble protest that "You can't come in here" was met with a blunt warning that any movement would lose Mr. Duncan the top of his head.

The *Chronicle's* praise was lavish, promptly putting all criticism of the police's search for Duncan in the past to declare that "Captain Lees, whose persistence and skill finally triumphed over all difficulties, will add greatly to the credit of his office and to his reputation as a detective, which is already world-wide." If "world-wide" overstated matters slightly, it was not entirely inaccurate, either. Later that year, Lees finally took a break after his efforts, for a long-dreamed-of vacation in Europe. A theme of detection wove through his travels. On the way east, he stopped in Cincinnati to identify a forger who had been captured there, after Lees lost the man's trail amidst the press of seeking Duncan. The rest of the voyage, taken with daughter Ella because Mrs. Lees's asthma proscribed such extensive travel, was a break from work, but not from policing. Though Lees had finally become an American citizen a decade earlier, he was warmly welcomed back to the nation of his birth by Scotland Yard, as well as by the Sûreté during a visit to Paris. And when Lees and Ella returned home at last that autumn, even there they were met by a brass band and speeches extolling Captain Lees's virtues. San Francisco was not to be outdone in appreciation for its much admired detective.

Within a couple of years, local recognition of Lees also included "rank with Vidocq and Macé," which the *Marin County Journal* awarded him after he closed a murder case that had defeated the local sheriff. Still, not everything Lees touched was a success. Some years later he tried to help out a friend who was acting as lawyer in a high profile divorce case against Senator William Sharon. The divorce was bitterly contested, and at one point Lees was fooled by phony evidence, resulting in considerable embarrassment when the error went public. Lees was left disgusted by the whole tawdry mess and decided to cut his losses, probably concluding that, unlike the flap over the *Cornelia*, there simply was no clear-cut crime for him to prove and thereby vindicate himself.

There were better uses for Lees's energies. After his return from Europe he mostly settled back into as much of a routine as being San Francisco's captain of police ever allowed. Through the 1880s, Lees focused on his job with relatively few distractions, whether from treasure hunting expeditions, department reorganizations or press hysteria. Such periods did little to build claims to greatness, but Lees was probably just as content to enjoy some time at home with Jane and his books rather than working day and night to solve sensational crimes. His reputation was, by then, firmly established; in 1893 the police, press and public cheered his 40th anniversary in the department.

The green recruit in his early twenties had been replaced by a veteran past 60. The city he policed had changed remarkably in that span, and on the outside Lees had been altered as well; in his later years Lees's dark hair turned silver, and his lean features took on a somewhat puffy appearance. But inside he had lost none of his interest, or insight, or toughness. At one point in his 50s, Lees fought to subdue a desperate, cornered thief who allowed afterward that "Lees was a tough old man." And if his body suffered little from time's passage, his mind only gained as his store of experience grew larger. Lees had every intention of remaining on the job to celebrate a 50th anniversary in the new century. It would put him into rare company indeed; even the long-lived Vidocq had not been active in policing for a full 50 years. The French sleuth had remained impressively active even into old age, unlike other greats who faded into retirement, but there, too, Isaiah Lees was about to give him a considerable run for his money. The fifth and final decade of Lees's detective career arguably surpassed all of the rest, at least in remarkable crimes, including a number of sinister murders that were among the darkest he ever confronted.

A few months after his 40th anniversary on the force, Lees was able to enjoy a relatively pleasant exercise in pure puzzle solving, deciphering a coded journal taken from a captured bank robber. Upon breaking the code, Lees discovered that the bandit had given a false name. This was no surprise by itself, as even with photography and the very beginnings of systematized fingerprinting under way, such deceptions were still common. But this prisoner was not. He was in fact William Fredericks, the man who armed a violent breakout from Folsom prison and killed the Nevada County sheriff. Discovering Fredericks in his jail through codebreaking must have been wonderfully satisfying for Captain Lees, both intellectually and professionally.

Bringing a different murderer to justice, later the same year, proved a far more demanding matter. In late December 1894, Luther Weber received a traumatic shock upon opening his family's Sacramento grocery store. Blood was dripping from the ceiling, above which his parents made their home. The scene upstairs only confirmed his worst fears, as both Mr. and Mrs. Weber lay dead from a brutal assault. The local police found evidence suggesting a burglary gone wrong, and two culprits, but nothing pointing to their identity. They notified the region's other departments of the details and asked for their vigilance, seemingly all the help anyone else could offer. But Captain Isaiah Lees of San Francisco decided to do more. A $1,000 reward probably encouraged this gesture of help. But Sacramento must have been glad to have it all the same. The veteran detective reviewed the known evidence, and provided one insight into bloody clothes found at the murder scene, most likely left by the killer in exchange for clothes taken in the robbery. Lees examined them and declared "It's the work of a couple of foreigners. Do you note this cloth? That's foreign material. These are no common tramps or yegmen."

Otherwise, though, the trip to Sacramento was a bust despite canvassing the local inns and immigrant quarters. A gold watch discovered in San Francisco's own jail on New Year's Day and bearing the inscription "To M. Weber, from mother" proved even more frustrating; Luther Weber confirmed it as a gift Mrs. Weber had received from her own mother, but the previous night's disorderly drunks had all been tossed out before a custodian found the watch. The names in the prison register suggested various possibilities, but all proved dead ends. For a second time, Lees had discovered a wanted murderer in his own jail, but this time too late.

It was June when the investigation finally started moving again, and then only along a winding course of middlemen and second-hand stories. Eventually, these led Lees to a Russian immigrant named Ivan Kovalev, one of 10 convicts who had escaped a Russian prison some years before and, after an American ship saved them at sea, had been brought to San Francisco and allowed to remain as "political prisoners." Unfortunately, even the harsh regime of czarist Russia may have been too lenient in Kovalev's case. After much investigation into the Russian and his accomplices, Lees ultimately concluded that Kovalev had not only butchered the Webers, but later on fatally stabbed his "friend" and accomplice in the Webers' murder, a man named Tscherbakov, to ensure his silence. If Kovalev's intellect had rivaled his brutality (and not been frequently dulled by alcohol, besides) he might even have gotten away with the crimes. But at last Lees cornered the elusive killer, and Kovalev was hanged a little over a year after the Webers' murders.

The detective was denied any of the posted rewards, despite his efforts, as they had all been made in the line of duty. Times, it seemed, were changing. Lees probably resented this costly new ramification of "duty," but he continued to pursue his own as diligently as ever. During the long gap in the Weber murder investigation, another crime closer to home shocked San Francisco and demanded the efforts of its captain of police once more. It also gave the city's highly competitive and sensationalist newspapers their biggest crime story since the Great Duncan Hunt, as the discovery of slain young women at blood-spattered crime scenes tends to do. Particularly when that discovery is made within a church. When the murderer was finally convicted after what the press inevitably labeled "the trial of the century," attendance at the execution was restricted to recipients of black bordered invitations, which were nonetheless swiftly reproduced by counterfeiters.

For Captain Lees, the Emmanuel Baptist Church investigation was much more a matter of simple diligence than one of sensational discoveries. The lead suspect may have been a quiet young momma's boy, but Lees quickly found his instincts pointing squarely at Theodore Durrant, and eventually, through his usual thorough efforts, found the evidence to prove it. The detective found a shop where Durrant had tried to pawn one of the girls' rings, and a friend whom Durrant had asked for notes on a lecture that he was allegedly attending at the time of the girl's murder. Most important, Lees eventually forged a nearly unbreakable chain of witnesses to Durrant's accompanying one of the victims in the hours before her death and leading right up to the crime scene. The evidence was effective; after the trial, jurors eventually admitted that a guilty verdict and recommendation for hanging had both been unanimous, on the first ballot, and that they actually lingered over cigars to give an appearance of longer deliberation. Captain Lees's biggest difficulty with the Durrant trial may have been the erratic juror, Horace Smyth, who threatened to derail the proceedings with outbursts including a threat to "fill them full of lead" if any of the sheriff's deputies angered him. Even this risk was contained, however, and Lees saw another remorseless killer brought to justice. Secrest notes that

> Isaiah received much good press for his work in the case—full-page articles relating highlights of his long career and praising his detective skills. But he was sixty-five years old and the [Durrant] investigation and trial had worn him out. Throughout the trial he had been working on other cases.

Perhaps a change is indeed as good as a rest, as a diversion from blood-soaked murder investigations seemed to revive the wearied detective. In early 1896, a representative of the local Nevada Bank paid Lees a call with the kind of puzzle that he might exercise his brain on without wishing to forget about it when he went home. A bank draft placed in Lees's hands had made it through two clearinghouses without any suspicion that it was false, and only when auditors were balancing books at the end of the previous year did they discover that $12 had become $22,000. The bank traced the paper back to an Arthur H. Dean, who had established himself as a friendly, reliable client before cashing the check for sacks of gold on December 18. Lees recognized a well-known pattern and knew even before looking into it that Dean was long gone.

One of his first steps in the investigation was to contact the American Bankers Association's detective agency, the Pinkertons, remarking that "we'll need them on the eastern side of this thing." By the 1890s, the Chicago-based agency operated coast-to-coast, and Lees had already enjoyed fruitful cooperation with its late founder's sons, William and Robert. His recovery of stolen Spanish gold, which led to so much trouble, began in response to an alert from the Pinkerton agency. Rather more happily, in 1891 Lees made a novel discovery while interviewing a suspect in a theft from the San Francisco Express: noticing an odd bulge in the man's trouser leg, Lees split the seam and found a stack of crisp new bills. His work in that case won much more positive comment, including a telegram from Robert Pinkerton to say "Hurrah! It's a great victory and the greatest blow struck [against] train robbery in years."

In the case now before him, Lees found an even greater test for his intuition. Although "Arthur Dean" might be an alias, the man was real enough and police had no trouble finding witnesses to describe him. The problem was that the descriptions from bank employees differed from the people at the *Chronicle* building where his abandoned office was located, which differed from the people who rented him a typewriter, etc., etc. Even if Dean had not altered the check by himself, he had clearly altered his own appearance, and in a number of ways. Lees saw a challenge here, and determined to confront it.

As a departmental secretary, Otto Heyneman worked closely with Lees in his later years, and his recollections provide many of the details from cases of that era. In this instance, he remembers how Lees "got up and locked his door, issuing peremptory orders that no one was to disturb him..."

> Two hours he spent over those puzzling, varying descriptions, each one vitally different from the next one, and after a long, tedious research, he made one composite description which was a marvel in its absolute correctness of every feature of Dean as I later knew him...

Lees's synthetic description, in combination with the Pinkertons' extensive network, eventually paid off. On the last day of February, a St. Paul bank clerk recognized "G.W. Woods" as Dean, and notified the Pinkertons, who quickly apprehended him. He was soon turned over to Lees, still defiant and laughing at his captor, insisting that "I'll rot here before you'll get anything out of me." Lees did indeed want something from Dean: information on the man who had forged the check. Such a convincing forgery could only be produced by a man of a rare and dangerous skill. For Lees, the case was woefully incomplete without that man, and he was determined to get him. Yet he sensed that Dean's bluster was not empty, and that he would be a difficult man to crack.

Lees had never been a believer in third-degree methods, anyway, but in this case he took a completely opposite approach. The special treatment and liberties granted to Dean were so astonishing that the *Chronicle* was indignant, but Lees persisted, and in combination with marathon interviews he finally wore down his boastful captive. In May, Dean gave up Charles Becker, internationally wanted forger known as "The Scratch." By this point, William Pinkerton was personally involved in the case alongside Lees in San Francisco, and he moved rapidly to capitalize on their opportunity. Pinkerton agents seized Becker in New Jersey, along with a forger's kit, which he tossed into a river while attempting to flee; this and the testimony secured by Lees produced a life sentence at trial. Though this was later shortened on appeal, Lees was triumphant. The *Chronicle*, having been won back around by the success of his tactics, noted happily that "Captain Lees looked ten years younger after the verdict was announced."

By that point, the removal of "The Scratch" and his meticulously crafted forgeries from circulation was probably indeed a welcome break from other cases. Even as telegraph wires had flashed his composite description of Dean across the nation, Lees's attention had been pulled from that investigation by another entanglement with greed, lies and murder. The case tested the captain's resolve all the further because no one else believed it was anything of the kind. To the contrary, everyone but Lees saw a crime *prevented* by the loyal and brave actions of butler Frank Miller. The servant freely admitted shooting the man found dead at the home of Julius Franklin, whom Miller served. According to Miller's account, the unknown man and two others had broken into the house in the early morning. Miller claimed that he then surprised them, receiving minor wounds in a struggle with the armed member of the party before shooting him in self-defense, upon which the other two intruders fled. Miller had reported a similar defense of the Franklin home one year before, for which he was handsomely rewarded; Mr. Franklin and most others were ready to see this new incident as further evidence of a commendable, stalwart gentleman.

Lees would have none of it. By the 1890s, his long experience alone gave him an intuitive sense of familiar patterns in many crimes; untangling the details kept his mind busy, but it took much more than brazen lies to mislead him. He had been hearing those for a long time, and in listening to Miller's account his thoughts may have briefly drifted back more than 40 years to the similar tale offered by Jose Forni. As an amateur detective, Lees had found an explanation quite different from self-defense, then, and as an old hand he was hardly going to be satisfied with it, now.

Yet for all of his knowledge and repeated commendations, Lees met with nothing but skepticism and doubt in attempting to debunk Miller's heroics. Though ranked "with Vidocq and Macé" he still had to prove his cases with evidence, and sometimes even that was not enough. Lees began finding evidence suggesting another version of events quickly, during his examination of the Franklin home, although much of it was an odd assortment that only Lees perceived as relevant. Searching Miller's bedroom, Lees pulled a newspaper from a stack by the bed and flipped through it, then told Heyneman to mark it "Exhibit A." His subordinate's response was to "guess the old man has gone dippy," per his later recollection. The captain's scrutiny of tiny bugs on Miller's bed sheets and subsequent check of the alleged burglar's body for similar vermin probably seemed equally eccentric. Challenges to Miller's story and the extent of his injuries, which the butler finally admitted as very minor, may have seemed like more promising lines of inquiry, as might Lees's observation that the home's phone and alarm wires had been tampered with in out-of-the-way locations. Yet they might also have seemed like a stubborn old man unwilling to admit that he was wrong.

That suspicion may have been at the back of the self-defense verdict eventually pronounced by the coroner's jury. The alternative advanced by Lees was apparently deemed too farfetched, for all of its clever connections between a variety of curious evidence. Ever thorough, Lees had found the dead man's identity and then tracked down people who knew him, just as he had with Jose Rodriguez. In this case the corpse was that of Billy Murray, a drifter, and other local tramps not only remembered Murray, but Miller as well. According to them, Miller had come around recently with offers of a chance to earn a little money and some new clothes. They had declined, but Lees suggested that Billy Murray had not, to his cost. Lees argued that Miller had given the tramp his bed, in which the detective later found traces of the same fleas and other vermin that infested Murray's body, along with clean clothes; the search of Franklin's home had eventually turned up a bundle of old, dirty clothes wrapped in the exact newspaper pages missing from "Exhibit A." The butler probably then roused Murray early the following morning, Lees continued, and led him to the door before shooting him and then scratching himself, perhaps overdoing it slightly in the darkness. Franklin's sizable reward to him after a similar story, a year earlier, provided a plausible motive.

The theory advanced by Lees might almost be reproached as cliché in our era, though in 1896 "the butler did it" hadn't yet become a staple of detective story satires. All the same, the coroner's jury dismissed the story as unconvincing, and perhaps dismissed Lees. Yet if they believed him to be a stubborn old man, Lees went on to prove them entirely correct in that belief, while proving them wrong in everything else. Miller's account of his past had struck the detective as too vague, so Lees continued digging into that; in time he found that the butler was actually not "Miller" but Hoefler, and the son of a man alive and well back east, contrary to Miller/Hoefler's story. To this discovery, Lees added testimony from more local tramps and evidence of other lies by the "heroic" butler, and gradually his defenders began to give in. At the last, even Julius Franklin declared "I am thoroughly satisfied that Captain Lees is correct... about Miller. I have become so disgusted with him that I don't want to see him anymore." Franklin got his wish when Hoefler skipped town just before the police were ready to arrest him, though several months later, Lees received word from Santa Barbara that the fugitive had been arrested there for attempted kidnapping; he eventually received five years in San Quentin.

Even with its frustrations and mixed outcome, with its strong parallels to his first murder investigation the case of "Frank Miller" would make a fitting bookend for the detective career of Captain Lees. In a sense it was, too, or at any rate was one of the last mysteries he resolved before that career ended in the way Lees most wanted it to end: with the commencement of the career of Chief Lees. After more than a third of a century as captain of police, Isaiah Lees was sworn in as San Francisco's chief of police on April 7, 1897. It was a long-awaited promotion greeted with essentially unanimous approval, though its lateness in arriving must have spoiled the new chief's enjoyment somewhat. Not least because it meant he would be unable to share the occasion with Jane. Lees himself seemed hale as ever, at 66, but Jane had been troubled by ill health for years, and that January her body had finally given out. Lees might have been forgiven for feeling bitter about the timing. Chief Pat Crowley had actually announced plans to retire in early 1896, then placed them on hold for another year until the passage of legislation providing for increased pensions. Lees could hardly begrudge another's desire to squeeze a bit more money out of the job, just as he himself had done many times, however. And the two oldtimers in fact had enormous respect for one another; the *Chronicle* described a teary-eyed scene as Lees bid the old chief farewell.

But the pragmatic Lees had no intention of his tenure as chief being merely a sentimental, brief victory lap before his own retirement. In his first annual report, Lees noted that since taking the reins "I have found in the Police Department of San Francisco what I had known for many years before, the best material coupled with the poorest equipment, of any department with which I am acquainted." He made every effort to change this, lobbying for the introduction and expansion of new resources with enthusiasm that might more typically characterize a new recruit than the senior officer on the force. Lees advocated for more police boxes, automobiles to replace horse drawn patrol wagons, a bicycle patrol, and "a steam launch for the harbor patrol." He also took full opportunity of the construction of a new city hall to make the most of the department's future home, working with the architect to plan a fully equipped, modern photography studio on site and situate it for the best possible lighting.

In other ways Chief Lees seems less progressive, and perhaps even something of a killjoy from a modern perspective. He was ruthless in his determination to stamp out gambling in every form. Local judges had, by contrast, largely given up on trying "poolsellers," given juries' reluctance to convict, and refused to sign arrest warrants that would only clog up the system to no purpose. Lees considered this wholly unsatisfactory and came up with a work-around that allowed officers to make arrests without warrant, using a loophole that was at least technically legal. He didn't even bother with that degree of legal nicety in his efforts to shut down another "gambling" activity, meanwhile; in his efforts to keep the city's women out of "bucket shops" Lees almost gave substance to the comments of a defense attorney whose rhetorical flourish had once compared him to the Russian Czar. As the chief saw it, the women who patronized these brokerages to speculate on stocks and commodities did no more than, per the *Chronicle*, "daily squander their own and their husbands' money." In response, Lees stationed officers outside each one to take down clients' names and addresses and warn the women that they could be arrested for vagrancy if they returned. Lees acknowledged that he was taking extraordinary measures but defended them as necessary to enforce public sentiment that the literal writ of law did not reflect.

This was hardly Lees's finest hour, though on the whole his tenure as chief was characterized by the professionalism and intelligence that were his trademark. When controversy did eventually engulf his administration, moreover, it was not over his policy toward bucket shops. Lees should be best remembered for his detective career anyway, regardless of the pros and cons of his years as chief, and that career had one last great chapter in "the celebrated Botkin case." The poisoning of Mrs. John Dunning and Mrs. J.D. Deane of Dover had in addition to its eventual San Francisco connection many of the hallmarks of those crimes which lend a distinctive, sinister overtone to Lees's case book. The lethal poison's delivery in a daintily wrapped box of candy, complete with a note reading "With love to yourself and baby, Mrs. C," suggests an eerily perverse malice, in some ways surpassing even the most ruthless and calculating murderers Lees had known over the course of five decades.

The investigation that resulted from the package's San Francisco postmark was also every bit as methodical, thorough, and patient as Lees's work had always been. Though promoted to chief, Lees led the inquiries in the case personally, and frequently from the field. He questioned confectioners' shop clerks, combed dry goods stores and interrogated druggists, taking note of details as seemingly trivial as the pattern of handkerchiefs and printing method of price tags. Despite the noise and sensationalism about the case, Lees left little room for doubt that Mrs. Cordelia Botkin had poisoned Mrs. Dunning, with whose husband she was carrying on an affair, as well as Dunning's friend who had the bad fortune to share the deadly gift. The *Chronicle*, which had already recorded so many of Lees's successes, still declared that "Seldom, if ever before, has so strong a case been made out against a person charged with murder..."

It was enough, in the end, although repeated appeals dragged out Botkin's defense until 1904, when she was finally sentenced to life in San Quentin. By that time, Chief Lees was no longer around to see his last great case conclude successfully. On January 2, 1900, Lees retired just a few years shy of his hoped for half-century, amid controversy largely drummed up by William Randolph Hearst's *Examiner*. The *Examiner* had attacked the department over allegations of corruption, though these were contested by other papers, and the *Examiner*'s editors were widely suspected of seeking an excuse to place their own favored candidate in the chief's office. Throughout a long career, Lees rode out a roller coaster of departmental politics and vindicated himself repeatedly in the face of doubt and criticism. But when Mayor James Phelan, also supported by the *Examiner*, appointed new police commissioners, Lees took the occasion to step aside, perhaps as much because his era was passing as anything else. With obvious regret, he announced that "For twenty-two years I have been connected with the present Board of Police Commissioners and I felt that when the men with whom I had so long been associated were not reappointed I, in all manliness, should go down with the ship."

Lees's decision raised him above the bitter arguments and finger-pointing that ensued among the *Examiner*, the department, and the mayor's office. The ex-chief, in contrast, could bask in the glow of retirement tributes including a lavish spread published in the *Chronicle*. He could even continue his work, which may ironically have been the result of retiring that he enjoyed most. Lees never formally opened a private detective agency, observing that he had no wish to challenge the Pinkertons with whom he had long enjoyed excellent relations. But he frequently visited City Hall and assisted as a consultant on investigations, particularly that of Mrs. Botkin; a 1901 story headlined "Lees Again in Harness" noted Lees organizing the police's case in one of the poisoner's endless appeals.

*

As endings for great detective careers go, that of Isaiah Lees is probably one of the best. Lees died just shy of his 72nd birthday on December 20, 1902, following an abscess of the ear complicated by diabetes. And, though he passed away peacefully, in bed at home with his children at his side, in another sense he "died with his boots on," having continued his life's work into his last months and with a final case still in progress, which eventually joined his long record of success two years later. Though by no means a millionaire, as some had speculated, Lees died very well off, leaving his surviving son and daughter an estate of dozens of city lots, mining shares, and personal property including his treasured library, which was valued at $3,000.

Lees also left a legacy as one of the earliest, best and longest-serving in his profession. William Pinkerton, well on his way to a status as dean of the detective profession, called Lees "The greatest criminal catcher the West ever knew." Within a span of just of five years, tributes had poured from his adopted city three times: at his promotion to chief, his retirement, and finally his death. Though Lees had requested only "a simple Masonic ceremony" the pageantry for his funeral was probably the most elaborate of all, with crowds lining the city's streets to see the casket pass by.

Afterward, Isaiah Lees faded relatively quickly from memory all the same. That disappearance was undoubtedly hastened by the great earthquake that leveled much of San Francisco within a few years of his death; in many ways the city he had known and protected was gone and relegated to the past along with Lees himself. Today, a visitor to San Francisco would struggle to find any traces of either one. There are no public buildings named for Isaiah Lees. A search of the *Chronicle*'s online archives dating to 1995 surprisingly produces one result, but only for a list of fall books, which includes Secrest's biography; the fact that Lees was once a celebrated San Franciscan is not even mentioned. If his part in the city's history were pointed out to a modern resident, Lees would likely seem a steam age anachronism in the San Francisco of foodies and entrepreneurs, anyway. The city of today's notion of a famous old forty-niner is probably Joe Montana.

Such, of course, is the nature of history, particularly for detectives. And Lees, who both arrived in San Francisco with dreams of a quick fortune himself and saw enormous change just in his lifetime, would probably be neither surprised nor upset at subsequent generations' forgetting, even and especially in his city. Like his fellow Englishman, Whicher, Lees was ultimately a professional and more concerned with doing his job well than with creating a lasting legacy. Both men could look back with satisfaction at their reputations in their own time, Lees in particular, and to whatever extent it might have mattered could claim, today, that they fared no worse in the long run than others who were much more driven by celebrity. Times simply changed, and the world moved on; a few would yet mount astonishing challenges to the trend of history, but the rise and subsequent evaporation of Isaiah Lees as a famous figure stands in well for that of the very concept of real-life great detectives.

CHAPTER SIX
WILLIAM AND ROBERT PINKERTON

"One day we are in a little country village in
Maine or Canada, the following month in Havana.
There never seems to be an end to man's
criminal enterprises."

(Personal correspondence of Robert Pinkerton)

IN HIS OLD AGE, William Pinkerton scorned the notion of the detective
hero. A large, curmudgeonly figure who had known the battlefields of
the Civil War as a youth and lived to see the new world that followed
the Great War in Europe, Pinkerton held forth on a diverse range of topics,
but crime and crime fighting had always been his chief interest. He insisted
that the latter was a practical, even dull matter entirely unrelated to the
sensational adventures of dime novels, pulp magazines and, more recently,
Hollywood films. Journalists were always ready to lend an ear to such pro-
nouncements, whatever their own thoughts. The boss of Pinkerton's National
Detective Agency may have been a bit of a grump but he was an engaging
grump, always good for an interesting quote. Moreover, Pinkerton himself
was an interesting individual, a famous figure who had become almost a
national institution.

Though he would have denied any such claim or brushed it aside as exaggeration, there was also deep irony in William Pinkerton casting scorn on the
idea of detectives as dramatic adventurers, because his own life was one of the
greatest examples. In their day, William and his younger brother Robert had
contended with criminals and crimes whose scope rivaled that of any detective

career before or since, including their famous father's. Allan Pinkerton had built and directed a National Detective Agency, but his sons were genuinely national, and even international, detectives in person. While still teenagers they were engaged on Civil War spy missions deep into Confederate territory; by the time they were young men they were chasing down badmen in Havana, or the dusty plains of the Old West, or the capitals of Europe. Officially, William was based in Chicago and Robert in New York, but in practice both were at-large detectives on a scale that few, if any, have ever matched. If the elder brother, in particular, later bristled at ideas of great detective epics, it may have been because in some ways they were all too realistic.

As detectives, the Pinkerton sons were distinct from their notable peers, and not only for their geographic range. Of their points of difference, foremost may be the fact that, unusually, they did not enter the profession by chance. Unlike Vidocq, Lees, and their own father, they never had any career other than that of detective. Even Whicher and Pollaky had started out from other areas of police work before formally taking up the identity of detective. In contrast, by the time William and Robert were old enough to begin learning a trade, their father had operated a more enduring reproduction of Vidocq's private detective bureau for more than a dozen years. And for Allan Pinkerton, there was never any serious question that his boys would do anything but follow in his footsteps.

Neither young man seemed to mind their paternally imposed career path. Both argued with their stern father, at times, but more out of an eagerness to take over the agency than a reluctance. Indeed, while it's true in some sense to say that the Pinkerton sons were handed an established detective agency rather than having to build their own, it's also likely that both would have scoffed at the idea that anything was "handed to them" at all, particularly during the long frustrating years when they were desperate to loosen the reins from their father's tight grip. In 1879, Robert even came as close to the outright rebellion of which Allan was forever accusing them as either of the brothers ever did. The 31-year-old threatened not only to strike out on his own if he could not have a larger role in the family business, but to change his name as well, prompting an inevitable explosion by his father before eventual cooling off and reconciliation.

It's possible that Robert was never entirely serious, and merely blowing off steam, of course. The fact that he, rather than the older William, went the furthest in challenging their father is nonetheless an interesting snapshot of the relationship between the two, itself another point of distinction among the great detectives. From boyhood until Robert's death in middle age, the two were nearly a matched set, and it's impossible to describe the career of one without including that of the other. They ran the agency in tandem, avoiding what might have seemed inevitable rivalry. They pursued separate investigations with nearly indistinguishable style and frequently picked up or handed off cases between themselves, like twins finishing one another's sentences. In photos they appear similar in appearance, style, and even expression, with burly frames and faces often jutting forward as though daring the world to stir up trouble on their watch. Both seemed even in middle age somewhat like overgrown boys, too, or perhaps like boys playing earnestly at being serious men; though active field operatives, whose embrace of their work's rough-and-tumble aspects often calls to mind a boy's adventure story, they shared William's later pretense of stodginess. In letters, they addressed one another as "Dear Sir," and rarely addressed anything besides work at all. The family's biographer, James Horan, wrote in *The Pinkertons* that "Wives and children were never mentioned in their letters, only crime, criminals, and business."

Of those three topics, William's and Robert's relative interests marked one of the few noticeable differences between them. Robert's enthusiasm was more for the latter aspect of their job. He, it seems, had inherited their father's instinct for capitalist empire building. William's energies, by contrast, were always guided a bit more by the same fascination with crime that must, if on a subtle level, have led Allan Pinkerton to begin nosing into counterfeiting gangs and other mysteries in the first place. Unlike his brother, William made crime his only real business. He tried the University of Notre Dame for a year and did some course work at a business college. But his real education took place in the Chicago underworld. In his own work on the Pinkertons and their agency, Frank Morn remarks that "Mike McDonald's saloon, The Store, became William Pinkerton's university, and many lifelong friendships were made with professional criminals. Soon he became a walking rogues' gallery."

Robert and his greater interest in profitable, predictable business strategy held more sway over the brothers' partnership through the early part of their careers, just as Robert went the furthest in challenging their father. William probably took the lead in case work, however, including just the sort of lively episode he would later dismiss as nonsense. In early 1868, Allan dispatched his elder son to investigate a robbery of the Harrison County, Iowa, Treasury, which he believed might be tied to the Reno gang that the Pinkertons had recently challenged in Seymour, Indiana. Allan advised William to begin by looking for a "disreputable place" owned by someone from Seymour.

Having an enduring instinct for such dens picked up during his informal apprenticeship, William readily discovered a saloon run by a man who was not only from Seymour, but an ex-counterfeiter, to boot. William just as readily recognized the place as a curious haunt for a leading local citizen, and "pillar of the Methodist Church," named Michael Rogers. Upon alerting his father to this surprising patron, Allan wired back that police files hinted at a questionable past. William proceeded to investigate Rogers and found further cause for suspicion. The man's seemingly innocuous payment of his taxes struck the detective as significant, based on its timing very shortly before the robbery; to William's crime-focused mind this suggested someone "casing" the building for accomplices. A less distrustful person might reasonably have seen nothing other than innocent coincidence. But when William subsequently observed Rogers welcoming Reno gang members, as guests, it was enough to satisfy such doubts and secure an arrest warrant.

Backed up by other Pinkerton agents, William led a dawn raid on Rogers's home. He personally bashed in the door, surprising Frank Reno himself in the middle of breakfast with two known counterfeiters. William then capped off the victory with one more dramatic discovery. During the subsequent search, some smoke rising from the kitchen stove drew William over to investigate; lifting up the lid he was just in time to rescue $14,000 taken during another robbery. He may have been awfully suspicious for a 21-year-old, and had an unhealthy fascination with the criminal mind besides, but in the detective business, those things paid.

The Pinkertons chased a great many more train robbery gangs in the decades that followed. The pursuit of one, from a few years after William's solo outing, provides a good illustration of the brotherly tag team approach that typified many of their larger investigations. William and Robert had good reason to combine their resources in confronting what was clearly a serious crime. Five outlaws had held up a train near Moscow, Kentucky, shooting a Southern Express Company messenger in the lungs before emptying his safe. The man's wound proved fatal, though he managed to gasp out a description of two of the bandits before dying. Searching for plausible suspects who fit the descriptions, the Pinkerton brothers then spent weeks stomping through the rough local back country. Gradually they heard enough stories of two brothers known for working the opposite side of the law, Levi and Hillary Farrington, to select these as their men; Levi, in particular, was unlikely to be confused for another, as a giant of a man known for his crack marksmanship besides. The Farringtons' associates William and George Barton, and William Taylor, had probably rounded out the gang.

At this point, progress in the investigation slowed for a time. The Pinkertons even tracked down the Farringtons' taciturn, rifle-bearing mother at her Tennessee farmhouse, but she would only state the obvious, that her sons had ridden off. Robert returned to New York to attend other business, and William carried on the search alone. He did not wait long for a new lead. Upon robbers again targeting the Southern Express Company on the very same line, near Union City in Tennessee, William knew where to direct his quest.

From Union City, he found hints of a trail through the hardscrabble farm country and back into Kentucky to the far western town of Hickman. There, his inquiries about a party of five strangers elicited word of a recently opened general store at the even more remote outpost of Lester's Landing; unsurprisingly the store seemed to entertain few if any customers, but the owners appeared to be prospering. After locating the proprietors' cabin in the swampy country around Lester's Landing, William proceeded to mount another Wild West style raid. Backed up by two hired guards, William and a former Memphis policeman named Pat Connell let themselves into the darkened cabin.

Just as they suspected, some of the gang members were indeed present. Unfortunately, they included Levi, who recognized Connell and put a bullet into him, touching off a firefight. Amid the confusion, William began shouting instructions to an imaginary posse, to confuse his opponents; whether the ruse helped or not, the Pinkertons' actual numbers proved enough, and the raid captured everyone except Levi. He had escaped during the skirmish, while his brother Hillary had not been among the party. The Pinkertons would take up their pursuit again soon enough, though in the fight's immediate aftermath William had his hands full with four prisoners, a search to conduct, and an injured colleague; he personally pried the slug out of Connell's wound by candlelight.

Examining the cabin afterward, William turned up a curious scrap of paper. The trail of clues that followed led him and his team eventually to Missouri and the rented home of a farmer and distant Farrington relation, named Duram. It proved a harder target than the Lester's Landing cabin, however. The Pinkertons were joined by a genuine posse this time, but their opponents saw them approaching, and the farm grounds offered little cover from the Farringtons' fire. A call to surrender met with rejection, punctuated by rifle fire, and the two parties then traded shots for nearly an hour. The raid had become a deadlocked siege.

Stymied in any direct approach, William's solution was ingenious. Taking stock of the situation, he noted that the house sat on gradually sloping ground, and that the owner was among the posse. William arranged to buy the house from him, along with a wagonload of hay from a neighboring farm. He and a few other men slowly rolled the wagon behind the house—trying their best to avoid occasional potshots from inside—until it was poised at the top of the sloping grounds. William then made it clear that, if the house was not evacuated, it would promptly become the target of a wagon full of burning hay serving in the role of a land-based fireship. Negotiations continued for some while, but William Pinkerton had checked Hillary Farrington. He eventually emerged along with George Barton and various other relations, plus an armful of pistols and rifles. After taking these into custody, William found a further arsenal still inside the farmhouse and couldn't help asking Farrington about the decision to surrender; Hillary replied that he simply couldn't bring himself to see cousin Kate Duram's piano incinerated.

William had performed admirably in leading pursuit of the Farrington gang alone. Neither he nor his brother ever wavered from their spirit of team-work, however, and he readily passed along everything Hillary Farrington had told of his brother Levi's movements. It was thus Robert who would secure the gang's remaining members. His business in New York concluded, the younger Pinkerton had little trouble finding Levi, upon tracing him to Farmingon, Illinois; in addition to the outlaw's conspicuous stature he had, according to the local sheriff's warning, "whupped the whole town in the last few weeks." Allan Pinkerton had never been intimidated by physical violence, and obvi-ously William had no hesitation about two-fisted crime fighting. Robert was no different, although in finally subduing Levi Farrington, after a bruising fight, the detective did pragmatically engage the help of another Pinkerton agent, a pistol turned impromptu club, and an extra large pair of handcuffs, which proved necessary to actually close around the huge bandit's wrists.

Perhaps it was with this in mind that Robert employed a less athletic, but probably wiser approach in capturing the last member of the gang still at large, William Taylor. With the indefatigable Connell at his side, Robert caught up with Taylor on a duck hunting expedition. Unlike his partners-in-crime back at Lester's Landing, Taylor did not recognize either lawman and accepted their claim to be fellow hunters, as well as Robert's friendly offer of whiskey. Taylor sat down his rifle and gratefully tipped back the flask for a long drink, only to find upon lowering his head again that his new friends were pointing his own rifle and another gun at him.

Other detectives had also pursued cases over long distances, by this time. Isaiah Lees in a few instances, as well as the elder Pinkerton. Yet William and Robert's father made a single one-way trip across the Atlantic Ocean and, though he ranged through much of the United States in the course of his career, never personally returned to Europe. By the younger Pinkertons' late teens, "Paddington" Pollaky was active across a territory at least as large and a much greater number of nations; nonetheless, he, too, was essentially a one-continent detective. William and Robert Pinkerton outstripped them all. Whether on horseback, by rail, across oceans on steamships, or even hacking their way through jungles on foot a time or two, they harried wanted fugitives with all the energy of Allan in his prime combined with the growing means of a prospering detective agency and an industrializing world.

In his pursuit of a South Dakota state treasurer who disappeared with $300,000 of public funds, Robert followed a path through the American West, to Florida, to Havana, and finally to Vera Cruz, Mexico, where he arrested the fugitive and recovered the money. It was probably this adventure that prompted his letter observing that "One day we are in a little country village in Maine or Canada, the following month in Havana," but the case was by no means unique. On another occasion a similar fugitive, this time carrying the deposits of his New York bank, led Robert all the way to Honduras. Despite a yellow fever epidemic, Pinkerton followed his quarry's trail into the Central American jungle, again securing both man and money, though he was seriously ill for months after. William was no homebody, either. In one memorable case he achieved a satisfying transoceanic two-for-one against the Bidwell brothers—who had gone on the lam with a cool million dollars' worth of the Bank of England's funds—beginning with the arrest of Austin Bidwell in Havana. Then, in his own words, "Suspecting that there would be mail for him in the Havana Post Office, I called there and obtained a letter from his brother, showing that he was located in Edinburgh, Scotland, as a doctor. This was cabled to the London Police and resulted in his arrest the following day."

Both of the Pinkertons were eventually in regular contact with European police forces, not only by transatlantic cable, but many times in person. They had nothing like the polylingual fluency of Ignatius Pollaky, but their resources far exceeded those of his Paddington Green inquiry office. More importantly, William and Robert Pinkerton were entering the prime of their careers just as Pollaky retired. Horan remarks that

By 1900, William and Robert were familiar in London, Paris, Havana, Rome, and Constantinople. Foreign governments asked for their advice in reorganizing police departments, and there were always letters from Scotland Yard or the Sûreté, seeking assistance in apprehending international thieves.

A fellow American was the greatest of those international thieves, however, in the opinion of William Pinkerton, and of Horan who devotes considerable space in his Pinkerton biography to "the Napoleon of Crime." Adam Worth seemed to fascinate friends and foes, alike. More than any other, he illustrates the curious attitude of gentlemanly respect and even admiration that William had for his opponents, or at least their more intellectual "elite." Oddly enough, the feeling was often mutual, including in the case of Worth; several years after they began sparring, William received a peculiar tribute from the elusive criminal upon encountering him at a London pub. William and a Scotland Yard Superintendent named Shore were checking up on some of the American expatriate criminals' known haunts, and after exchanging a few pleasantries, Worth "told Shore he didn't know anybody but a lot of three-card monte men and cheap pickpockets, and he could thank God Almighty the Pinkertons were his friends or he would never have gotten above the ordinary street pickpocket detective."

Worth could afford such (very mixed) generosity, having personally eluded arrest. The Pinkertons roped a number of his associates, performing some impressive detective work in the process. But the mastermind seemed to remain forever out of reach. In 1868, Allan Pinkerton dispatched his right-hand man George Bangs along with Robert on what proved to be the prologue of an epic struggle with the Worth gang. The six-figure train robbery was, certainly, the scale of crime Worth specialized in, although slugging an express company guard hardly fit the reputation of a gentleman criminal. Robert proved his own capacity for well-founded suspicion in breaking the story of that guard, John Putnam, who was found after the robbery, seemingly unconscious and with froth around his mouth. Putnam insisted that he had simply fallen asleep, through carelessness, and then presumably been clubbed by the robbers whom he never saw. The only clues at the site—several rough cuts around the express car door and a few scraps of soap—offered no obvious help. Yet Robert had a hunch, and in pressing Putnam on his story he prompted the guard to get carried away. When Putnam referred to a specific area of the Bronx which the train entered just before the robbery, Robert demanded to know how he could have known that detail if he was asleep at the time, inside a windowless car. Putnam cracked, confirming Robert's suspicions about both his collaboration with the thieves and the unexplained bits of soap; the guard had made the "froth" from soap lather.

With the statements of Putnam and another railroad employee who had seen two men leap from the train with heavy bags, Robert and Bangs were able to narrow their investigation to a pair of Americans living it up in Toronto, Ike Marsh and Charley Bullard. They secured the men's arrest, and, upon searching their hotel room, much of the stolen money; the search also turned up a jagged-edged knife that matched the cuts found in the express car.

At that point, however, the Pinkertons' encouraging progress stalled out, as their latest opponents began to prove themselves considerably more resourceful than the Renos or Farringtons. Friends dug Bullard and Marsh out of the White Plains, New York, jail. Together, the robbery and jailbreak greatly boosted their reputation, and they soon welcomed the friendship of their profession's leading figure, Adam Worth. In combination with Worth, they planned and accomplished a new, dramatic coup: taking nearly half a million dollars in cash and securities from Boston's Boylston National Bank.

Robert and other agents promptly began canvassing the area for witnesses and circulating descriptions along with rogues' gallery photos, and while relatively pedestrian methodology it was enough to set his opponents on edge. Bullard protested that "Those damn detectives will get onto us in a week," and even Worth had little desire to test the assertion. Instead, he proceeded with negotiations to "work back" the stolen bonds through intermediaries, for a percentage of their value; such offers were by no means unusual at the time, and, in this case, the bank's management shared Worth's desire to cut his losses. They accepted, and dispensed with the services of the Pinkertons.

"Those damn detectives" had made things uncomfortably hot for the Worth gang, briefly, but could do little more besides pass their information to police forces and watch, as Worth and company sailed for Europe.

Cases like this point to both the great advantage and the great disadvantage of the Pinkertons' private for-profit detective agency relative to public forces of the day. By the 1860s they had grown to a scale that far exceeded the reach of any other law enforcement organization, and could pursue crime far beyond limited local jurisdictions. Occasionally, public police forces might sponsor a man pursuing a long-distance investigation, as Isaiah Lees did a time or two, but those were rare exceptions during a nearly 50-year career otherwise fixed in one city. For Robert and William Pinkerton, by contrast, such pursuits were practically routine. Yet they were only possible, in general, if a client was paying for them. Banks, railroads and even governments regularly did so, finding the Pinkertons' fees preferable to the sums that even a single ambitious thief could cost them. Occasionally, however, a smart and pragmatic operator like Worth could exploit this vulnerability to halt pursuit, at least temporarily, while he moved on to start fresh elsewhere.

This strategy was not entirely foolproof, as another gang learned in 1876, following a bank robbery that must have astonished even Adam Worth. In January of that year, another Massachusetts bank, the National Bank of Northampton, lost fully $1.25 million in cash and securities to an unknown team of thieves. The astonishing crime set a new record, which remained unsurpassed for 75 years. It also kept Robert Pinkerton preoccupied, on and off, into the next decade.

The Pinkertons were only brought into the case months after the robbery. Fortunately there was rather more, and more conventional, evidence available than in the express car theft Robert had cracked several years earlier: masks, overalls, linen "dusters," and iron sledges. The testimony of the bank cashier, who had been taken captive from his home and forced to reveal the vault combinations, offered an even more promising clue. One of the gang's leaders had constantly shrugged his shoulders, and eventually this same tic was able to jog the memories of numerous witnesses between Northampton and Springfield, where it seemed that the gang had purchased their gear and planned the crime.

Once more, though, the major breakthrough on the case resulted from identifying an inside accomplice more vulnerable to pressure than his unknown comrades. In long conversations with the cashier, Whittelsey, Robert found mounting reasons to suspect an employee, though not of the National Bank of Northampton. William Edson was a bank safe expert working for Herring and Co., an industry leader. According to Whittelsey, Edson had become a regular visitor to the Northampton bank. He had also filed the current vault keys—suggesting to Robert an opportunity to make a duplicate set—and suggested that all of the combinations be entrusted to just one senior employee for security. In retrospect, Edson's security "improvements" had proven deeply flawed, and Robert had a strong sense that this was not unintentional.

By November, surveillance of Edson along with continued inquiries into the shrugging man had produced likely candidates for all of the gang's membership. As the Pinkertons grew closer, the gang grew more nervous, and they opened negotiations to work back the securities as Worth had done in Boston. Unfortunately for the Springfield gang, this proven approach was thwarted by major errors on their part. They probably waited too long, for one thing, and by the time they offered to return the securities for a mere $150,000 the Pinkertons could counter with progress which the Northampton bank found more appealing; the bank refused the gang's offer as too high. The gang compounded that error by relying far too much on Edson, for far too long. The crooked safe expert was even conducting the negotiations, and while Edson used an intermediary, the bank and its detectives had secured that man as an ally, in addition to having Edson himself under constant surveillance. When Edson began to show signs of strain, Robert arranged to make sure that the next round in negotiations made no progress and then approached Edson personally. The big, imposing detective invited the nervous conspirator back to a private office and laid out the state of the case, calmly and confidently, in the process confirming Edson's fears that he was being watched. The tactic worked. Blurting out "By God, I'll tell you the whole story, Pinkerton," Edson proceeded to spend hours doing just that.

The shrugging "Hustling Bob" Scott and his partner Jim Dunlap were soon rounded up, followed by arrests of Billy Connors, Red Leary and Shang Draper. Yet as Worth's gang had demonstrated, detectives might be thwarted by more than one method. Buying off the Pinkertons' client had failed the Springfield gang, but a jailbreak did not. And no shovels were necessary; as Robert phrased it, in language perhaps chosen to avoid any open feud between the agency and public police, "They used the golden key," i.e. bribery. Scott and Dunlap, held separately, were unable to avoid trial. In court— no doubt determined to prevent the remaining prisoners from escaping as well—Robert overwhelmed their defense with a barrage of evidence that Isaiah Lees would have admired. In addition to the many witnesses who clearly recalled "Hustling Bob," he had a physician confirm that hair found on some of the discarded clothes matched Dunlap's; plus a variety of documents along with the still relatively new innovation of a handwriting expert to tie Dunlap to them. It was more than enough, and in 1877 the pair received 20-year prison sentences.

The rest of the Springfield gang remained at large, including Red Leary, who had retrieved the greater part of the stolen securities. Despite the red hair that provided his nickname and proportions recalling the giant Levi Farrington of earlier years, Leary proved remarkably elusive. Eventually it was Leary's seeming immunity to imprisonment, itself, which suggested a hope of closing the case. Even as Leary "had dodged numerous traps from Paris to Constantinople," in Horan's wording, Jim Dunlap had been sitting in a prison cell. Robert had no doubt that Dunlap was tired of the situation, and suspected that meanwhile Leary himself might be growing tired of life on the run. Robert persuaded Dunlap to get in touch with Leary about giving himself up in exchange for a deal.

Just what followed varies depending on who tells the story. It's likely that, whatever else happened, Leary was keeping his options open. In light of which Robert Pinkerton's tale of a night chase through the snowy streets of Brooklyn, leaping from a moving sleigh and finally taking Leary captive after a desperate brawl, isn't entirely implausible. The subsequent story in *The*

New York Times, however, noted multiple reasons for skepticism and added drily that "The story of Leary's capture, as related by Pinkerton and his men, partakes somewhat of the nature of a dime novel romance." Yet a near siege of the Jefferson Market Court by friends of Leary, a few days later, seems less easily fabricated. On balance, the evidence suggests that Leary's cooperation with detectives was indeed less than complete.

In the end Leary did fold, aided by a "leaked" warning from Dunlap that he would appear as a witness against his old partner unless the stolen securities were returned. Upon word from Red, Mrs. Leary collected the long concealed money, and finally the great bank heist was resolved—or nearly so. Robert placed his support behind Dunlap's appeals for parole in repayment for the convict's help, and in late 1892, he was finally freed. Even then Robert could not quite close the books on the case, however. Dunlap's attempts at legitimate work met with endless bad luck, and for years Robert was subjected to occasional pleas for help, as well as calls from "Hustling Bob" Scott's sister Mary, whose smothering infatuation for Dunlap drove him into hiding more than once. It was only when the reformed bank robber made a botched attempt at a comeback that Robert, and Dunlap, could at last have some peace.

William was far from idle during these years, if nonetheless entirely content to leave the Northampton bank robbery and its numberless loose ends entirely to his brother. Along with more routine business, he secured the arrest and conviction of the memorable "Diamond Swallower" Charles Woodward in 1878, in spite of the thief's disposal of the only stolen item on his person via his trademark method. In 1886, he broke up a ring of thieves targeting the Chicago stock yards, and solved another robbery of the repeatedly victimized Adams Express Company, persevering through four months of tedious work before uncovering the mastermind in the humble guise of a Chicago coal man. Other captures resulted from much more rapid action, by contrast, sometimes to the astonishment of those around the detective. William once vanished from a London tailor's in the midst of having his measurements taken, dashing out the door without a word of explanation. Hours later he returned, offered his profound apologies, and explained that while glancing

William and Robert Pinkerton
Pinkerton's National Detective Agency Records, Library of Congress, Washington, D.C.

out the shop window he had seen an internationally wanted forger; after trailing him to his lodgings, William notified Scotland Yard, whose capture of the forger led to further arrests and preempted a major robbery.

Both Pinkertons could and did dazzle observers with this kind of casual, instant recall of criminal dossiers at a mere glance. A few years before fingerprinting became common practice, an assistant handed Robert a photo of a man arrested in Syracuse, New York, for a robbery in which he and an accomplice had killed a young police officer. The man in the photo had given his name as McCarthy, but police hoped the Pinkertons might recognize him as a known offender. Robert handed the photo back and said "Tell Syracuse this is Dink Wilson who held up the St. Louis and San Francisco line in 1891 with Marion Hedgepeth. From his description the other man in the killing could be his brother, Charles Wilson." Following the quick dispatch of the Wilsons' files, the Syracuse police arrested Charles, and went on to secure convictions for the pair.

In this and most ways, William and Robert remained closely aligned as they aged. They adopted the same facial hair, which Horan vividly describes as "thick black Corsican bandit moustaches." They shared the same broad build, and both gradually filled out as managing the agency began to limit their time spent on drawn-out manhunts. As their father grudgingly eased into retirement, they extended their seamless partnership from the field to the office, then continued to work together in remarkable harmony after Allan's death placed full responsibility for the business's direction completely in their hands in 1884. For the most part, the National Detective Agency needed little in the way of major rethinking, of course. The business was profitable; good relations prevailed with clients and much of the Western world's police. William and Robert added more staff and new offices, essentially continuing the expansionist strategy that their father had pursued throughout the agency's history. They also closed down one branch: that which employed women. In this matter they were rather more conservative than their father, though again agreed between themselves.

If there was any significant point of disagreement between William and Robert, it was entirely in emphasis, and even in this their attitudes mostly proved complementary rather than contradictory. Robert could obviously match his older brother's instinct and knowledge about crime and criminals, and readily take on train robbers, safe-crackers and other high-drama investigations. Yet what was a lifelong passion, for William, was more of a job for Robert. The younger Pinkerton was ever the more business-focused, and might well have brought every bit as much energy to manufacturing widgets as to battling crime. He had grown up in the latter profession, and so made it his business instead, but crime fighting was still a business to him rather than a calling.

The contrast with the rest of his family was subtle but significant. Allan Pinkerton had first introduced the uniformed guards division, but for him they always remained essentially a convenient and profitable offshoot of the agency's main work; Robert, by contrast, saw this market as a reliable, more businesslike source of revenue with considerable untapped potential. William continued to share their father's vision of the agency, but at the same time saw no real need to oppose his brother's ambitions. He simply focused his attentions on the considerable demand for detective work, and gave his assent to Robert's management and expansion of the guard service. This arrangement worked very well until 1892, when the safe, reliable and predictable security guard business suddenly and disastrously ceased being any of these things.

*

The profession of detective has never been immune from controversy. From Vidocq to the present day, scandal has been a basic risk of the trade. But no detective's work has ever gone so wrong, or met with so great a firestorm, as did the Pinkerton guards' actions at Homestead. To much of the public, the distinction was academic at the time; private investigators and private security staff were widely considered interchangeable, and both were referred to as "detectives" and often even as "Pinkertons," regardless of their employer. The guards at Homestead, nonetheless, really *were* Pinkerton employees. And whether or not they were "detectives," and regardless of the extent to which they were acting on behalf of the client rather than William and Robert, "Pinkertons" had been at the center of a shocking, deadly catastrophe.

The bare outline of events at the southwestern Pennsylvania steel town is fairly simple, and in most ways similar to other labor actions of the era. In mid-1892, negotiations between union workers and Carnegie Steel broke down, and union and nonunion workers both went on strike. Other nonunion "scab" laborers were nonetheless ready to take their places on Carnegie's terms, but strikers stood firmly in the way of any such move. After months at a standoff, Carnegie management sent in Pinkerton guards to break up the union pickets, and violence erupted. None of this was unusual in turn-of-the-century labor relations, but at Homestead this grim but typical scenario turned especially bloody. At least nine of the strikers died in exchanges of gunfire with the Pinkerton men, while the guards were eventually overwhelmed and beaten mercilessly; three of their number died from the violence at Homestead, and many more on both sides were left maimed. Ultimately, Pennsylvania's governor dispatched the National Guard to take control, and in the long run Carnegie defeated the strike, though at a stunning cost.

The Homestead Strike immediately became a national trauma. Entire books have been devoted to arguments over its full significance, which continue to this day. For Pinkerton's National Detective Agency as well as for William and Robert Pinkerton, the significance is probably rather simpler, if by no means minor. Homestead was the disastrous end result of a business decision that, if made for sound business reasons, ultimately proved wrong for both business and humanitarian reasons alike. Intentionally or otherwise the Pinkertons took sides in a frequently violent struggle between capital and labor. They may or may not have done so eagerly; ahead of a Senate hearing William claimed that "We held off until the last moment on this business, but our company having done Carnegie's work for years, they insisted that we supply the watchmen." They certainly did not want the actual outcome that resulted; the Pinkertons will always have their diehard foes who see father and sons alike as villainous enforcers for the robber-baron aristocracy, but this goes too far. None of the Pinkerton dynasty was particularly sympathetic to union demands, even those taken for granted today, but none of them were pure champions of reactionary opinion, either. And all were, personally, honest men who proved many times their belief in fairness and justice. Even if they disagreed with many in the detailed interpretation of those beliefs, they were not cheats. To see either Allan's direction of efforts against the Molly Maguires or the Pinkertons' involvement at Homestead, 16 years later, as plots to destroy organized labor is to indulge in both caricature and conspiracy theory.

Yet the guards at Homestead were nonetheless an armed intervention in the battle between labor unions and corporate ownership, firmly on the side of the latter. One for which the men whose surname matched the guards' nickname of "Pinkerton" bore ultimate accountability. As strong believers in personal responsibility, the Pinkerton brothers could hardly claim that Carnegie had genuinely "forced" them to supply armed guards. If they did so reluctantly at Homestead, it was still their decision, and consistent with a policy that they had pursued for years; in other testimony William himself noted that "Our employés have been opposed in all parts of the country to over 125,000 strikers within the last twenty-six years." They had no doubt hoped and intended that these men would serve only as a neutral force in the conflict, "protecting private property and the lives of non-union laborers," but this was simply unrealistic. Particularly given not only the nature of that conflict—"in nearly every instance our watchmen have been assaulted, stoned, and abused"—but the nature of those watchmen as well. To the Pinkerton management, the detectives and guards conflated by the public were not only different in role but different in quality. Detective agents were highly trained, long-term professionals. Guards, on the other hand, were members of a larger force, often expanded on short notice using "seedy characters with short, volatile tempers" according to Frank Morn's study. Whatever they intended, the Pinkertons were sending large numbers of poorly vetted enforcers into volatile, often desperate situations. They should have foreseen the outcome of this policy, they pursued it anyway, and they paid a penalty for it, if obviously a mild one compared with the lost lives on both sides.

Next to this, everything else that can be said of the Pinkertons and Homestead is merely detail. William's subsequent defense of the practice ranged from melodramatic, e.g. a claim that if businesses cannot employ private guards in the face of strikes then "we reach the point of anarchy and communism," to interesting, e.g. his point that private security forces restrict the cost of defending a corporation's grounds to its owners, while replacing them with state militia would pass that expense to the taxpaying public. But in the end there was no adequate defense for a bad policy that, even if it benefitted someone, had on balance proven far more costly for the National Detective Agency and its owners than could pass even a truly heartless accounting.

William and Robert Pinkerton were not heartless, so much as thoughtless and irresponsible in certain areas. And the lessons of Homestead helped correct that. The best and wisest response they made to the lost lives, and resulting outrage, was to change the policy that had invited them. The Pinkertons did not close or sell their guard service division, or even abandon "strike work" entirely. But they greatly reduced their presence at strikes and introduced further precautions that they should have given thought to long before, including paying some attention to a union's openness or opposition to private security measures at a given strike. The reputation of the Pinkertons would never really recover among America's labor movement, but the agency removed itself from the role of active foe, and was able to carry on with its other, still generally applauded, work.

The changed focus of the agency after Homestead meant a shift in prominence from Robert to William. To some extent this may have been more by default than by any change in relations, as the market Robert had focused on was now approached with hesitancy instead of aggressive growth, and William's specialty of detective work assumed relatively greater importance. Yet biographers recognize a more personal ascendancy of William Pinkerton after Homestead. He shared the responsibility for dispatching guards to the strike, of course, and if he made a small attempt to shift it toward Carnegie, he never publicly disavowed the guards as his brother's men rather than his own. Security services had nonetheless been Robert's enthusiasm rather than that of William, who saw detection as the true mission of the National Detective Agency. It's therefore plausible to imagine the events of 1892 leading to a subtly more confident William and a less assertive Robert. Morn suggests that, at the resultant congressional hearings, Robert was still frequently interrupting or qualifying his brother's statements. But from the press accounts, it seems that William was already taking over the role of public spokesman for the agency. Whether it was established so soon after Homestead or not, it was a role that he performed more and more frequently in the years that followed, as he gradually shifted out of field work.

He was not quite ready to retire from the chase personally, however, any more than his brother. The Pinkertons were still only in their mid-40s as they began adjusting their own and their agency's practices in the wake of catastrophe. Robert had already found a small niche for himself in security arrangements for horse racing. The sport of kings was a rare diversion from his otherwise business-fixated life, or something like it; Robert sold his own stable after a few years because it took too much time from work, but taking charge of track security allowed him to pursue the hobby without actually taking a break from his job. When his ambitions for the uniformed guards division foundered, he probably found catching pickpockets and cheats at the tracks a fair alternative outlet for his time and energy.

At the end of Robert's life, *The New York Times* noted that he "had charge of the police work at all the New York race tracks as well as in Washington and New Orleans." His role was not restricted to a purely advisory one, either; the *Times* also recalled him frequently playing the role of a very discreet "bouncer," personally advising known crooks to return home in the most polite language possible to avoid a scene, while relying on his reputation and sturdy physical presence to get the real message through. The man who had wrestled toughs like Levi Farrington and Red Leary was still a formidable sentry. Not everyone was so easily deterred, all the same; after an occasionally comical "war" to defeat a New York gambling syndicate's varied attempts to flash the results from races without paying track owners, the syndicate's tactics turned more serious and they sponsored a few attempts on their adversary's life. Robert's would-be assassins had no more luck than their predecessors had against his father, however. When one vengeful crook pulled a gun on him in the middle of a fancy restaurant, Robert doubled the man over with a fist into his gut, shoved him over a table, then handed the dazed ruffian over to local police.

William, meanwhile, was able to exercise his brain in one more train robbery investigation, which might almost serve as a model case for the Pinkertons' detective methods under his watch. The victim was entirely appropriate for a standardized, "sample" Pinkerton case as well, being once again the Adams Express Company. (At times, one suspects that bandits were consulting an alphabetized directory of railroad firms and proceeding against the first express company listed.) In striking a train near Calumet, Illinois, in the fall of 1893, thieves emptied the express car safe of $70,000. They also allowed Chicago-based William to arrive on the scene in short order, which he did, finding the train still stopped before an improvised log barricade. The engineer told William how he and his crew had stopped the train and stepped out to remove the logs, when three masked men revealed themselves. The bandits herded everyone into the engine's cab at gunpoint, then forced the express car messenger to open the safe. They hastily stuffed its contents into a bag, leapt down, and then vanished into the brushy, rural country which then still surrounded Calumet.

With relatively little to go on despite reaching the scene of the crime in almost record time, William turned to the basics and began canvassing the area. In *The Pinkertons*, James Horan describes William in the 1890s as "a huge, brooding, moustached giant symbol of America's lawmen" and his methods as "plodding" and "methodical." And yet, Horan declares, William Pinkerton was somehow "brilliant" as a detective all the same. Brilliant may not be the right word, exactly. But William was a smart and effective sleuth. If his methods were often plodding, they were the product of both experience as well as some measure of theory, in fairness. William had spent a good deal of his life tramping around sparsely settled areas and knew that in contrast to the city's anonymity, a rural setting made any strange person or event both more obvious and more memorable. The Calumet robbery shortly yielded a perfect example. Inquiring at a farm one morning, the lady of the house offered William both breakfast and information about just such a small novelty: hours before the train hold-up, she had taken notice of the curious sight of "a strange red buggy with red wheels and a horse blanketed to its fetlocks" tied to a tree. The observant woman supplied directions to the tree in question, as well, and an appreciative William was promptly on his way.

Brilliant or not, the Pinkertons were never entirely reliant on plodding means like questioning local residents one by one. They were quite capable of very respectable observation and deduction when there were clues to observe. And the spot to which William now gave his attention offered at least two: several strands of horse hair were still caught on the tree that the farm wife had described, and the impressions of horseshoes were visible on the ground. To the untrained eye, neither would seem to do more than loosely confirm what William already knew. But the ultimate Pinkerton detective, "The Eye" himself, could call on long experience in both a general sense and, in this case, a specific one. If William's interests surpassed Robert's in some subjects and lagged them in others, they still almost invariably overlapped, and William, too, had become an aficionado of the ponies. Thus he could see more than just bits of horsehair and a few horseshoe prints; the latter, in particular, he immediately recognized as a racehorse's rather than work shoes. Within hours, inquiries after "a pacer shod with racing plates" led him to a local man named Jack Kehoe. A saloon keeper who owned just such a horse, as well as a red buggy.

With this discovery, it was back once more to making inquiries, only now they were far more specific. William had little difficulty piecing together the movements of the all too conspicuous red buggy and established that a friend of Kehoe named Jack King had driven it out of town the morning of the holdup and returned late that evening. Conversation with a local brothel owner added the information that her business had recently hosted a late night meeting between Kehoe, King, and a man named Dominick Hogan. As the express messenger "forced" to open the safe for the train robbers was also named Dominick Hogan, this was a juicy morsel, though at the same time perhaps not an entirely shocking discovery. The Pinkertons had many other clients beside the Adams Express Company, and no doubt solved many crimes that lacked any inside collaborator. Yet the latter does seem to have been a common enough feature that an otherwise textbook investigation would have been incomplete without one.

By the same token, past experience had also shown the value of talking to as many railroad employees working near a robbery as possible. Other agents had pursued this routine line of inquiry while William was discovering the trail of the red buggy. Perusing their reports, he was particularly interested by the actions of a former employee named George LaLiberty. On the day of the robbery, his former colleagues had allowed the fireman to "bum" a ride along an earlier stretch of the train's route. At the depot where he disembarked, a baggage handler confirmed to William that when LaLiberty also sought to check a trunk for free, "rough words" had followed, and that he suspected that LaLiberty had thrown something behind a pile of packages while unobserved for a moment. William decided to explore the curiously stingy LaLiberty's involvement further, and had agents clear out the depot's entire baggage room. After shifting boxes, bags, and trunks, they found a crude mask made from an old coat lining back in a corner. William believed he had enough to warrant conversation with Mr. LaLiberty himself, and likely enough to rattle loose an honest word or two if handled correctly.

This too had proven reliable many times over—as had the fact that even if there was honor among thieves, it was not absolute. LaLiberty, whether genuinely sidelined by his partners or simply electing to cut his losses and seek a portion of sympathy, confessed to involvement in the robbery while blaming the others for cheating him. He confirmed Kehoe, King, Hogan and a fifth man named Edward as taking part, and explained that the stolen money had been hauled west to a hiding place, near Marquette, by means of Kehoe's fast horse and well traveled red buggy. Pinkerton agents swiftly rounded up money and men. William was able to report good news to the Adams company a mere 72 hours after the theft, and with LaLiberty's testimony tying together the material evidence the other conspirators all received five-year sentences in short order. While the case would hardly make for a novel even with considerable padding, in every other way it made for a considerable improvement on the endless pursuit of the Maroneys that William's father had led in the first case for Adams, more than 30 years before.

William and Robert Pinkerton both remained active detectives through much of the 1890s, but between approaching middle age and the demands of running the agency they were less and less often out leading posses through the western plains or spending weeks on international manhunts. There was still plenty of crime to pursue in and around the cities they called home. The robbery at Calumet had, of course, been little more than a day trip for William. And in the middle of that decade the diabolical murderer H.H. Holmes struck in the agency's home city of Chicago, itself, where Pinkerton agents lent crucial assistance to city police in bringing the infamous butcher to justice.

The Pinkertons continued to travel, but mostly by train rather than on foot or horseback. Robert was managing security for many of the country's major race tracks and, as noted, often representing the Pinkertons in person. In 1896, William worked side-by-side with San Francisco's great detective Isaiah Lees in cracking the Nevada Bank forgery ring as part of the ongoing work for the American Bankers' Association and its clients. The following year he personally led a security detail of 40 detectives for President William McKinley's inauguration, noting wryly that only the opportunity to look for thieves or anarchists could explain his taking time for such pageantry: "I will be there myself. It is not often that I care to go to an inauguration ball." (America's government was, alas, still only bothering about presidential security in occasional high profile circumstances and ignoring the more ordinary settings in which one assassin had slain Lincoln, and another would do the same to McKinley early in his second term.)

Toward the end of the 1890s, William closed a very old case, stretching back more than 20 years, without leaving his office or even really investigating.

In 1876, the famous *Duchess of Devonshire*, painted by Thomas Gainsborough, had vanished from a London exhibition. The theft was every bit as astonishing as that of the *Elaine* only one year before, and on a much larger scale. Like Captain Isaiah Lees, William Pinkerton took very little time in establishing a prime suspect for the crime; in William's view "there was only one man with nerve enough to pull off a crime such as this." He was in no doubt that this was the work of the Napoleon of Crime himself, Adam Worth. The real puzzle in William's mind was not who, but *why*. The *Duchess* was not only valuable but a prominent masterpiece. Worth might have had the nerve to steal it, but no one would have the nerve to fence it. William could not imagine what anyone could have done with the stolen *Duchess*, and unlike the previous year's great art theft there was no quick recovery this time; Pinkerton, as well as London's own eminent detectives of the day and the rest of the world, remained in the dark as years and then decades went by. Until one day, out of the blue, William received a message from Adam Worth. Even more extraordinary than this was the fact that, while couched in the most discreet language, Worth's message made it clear that he had the *Duchess* and was interested in returning it. William readily if warily accepted, and began a novel series of private meetings between the two old adversaries.

The memories on both sides stretched far back, further even than the theft of the painting. Robert Pinkerton had been the first to clash with Worth's gang, after the robberies of the late 1860s, which ended in what was at best a draw. But William, with his naturalist's fascination for the criminal kingdom, had taken up the matter when Worth resurfaced in Paris and the Pinkertons had persuaded another burgled bank to sponsor some further investigation. Robert may have had other work, or may simply have had no interest in an excursion that seemed a poor use of time; extradition treaties of the day did not, it seemed, cover the crime of bank robbery. William went instead. The still-young detective was only too eager to match himself against such a canny organization. So eager, in fact, that he disobeyed a direct order from his father for the first time in his professional life.

At the time, Allan was still keeping operations on a tight leash as usual, and proceeding cautiously, even though their client was growing restless.

Allan wanted to place an additional man, a trusted underworld informant, on the job, and ordered William to stay put and wait. William couldn't do it, though. In observing Worth's Paris circle from a distance, he had recognized a man named Chapman who was wanted for forgery, and, unlike bank robbery, this was an extraditable offense. When Chapman separated from the rest of the gang for a trip to Brussels, William deserted his official assignment and followed him, first to Belgium and then to London. Unfortunately, the gang's own sources tipped them off to the extradition paperwork in time, and Chapman joined his friends Bullard, Marsh and Worth himself in eluding the Pinkertons' grasp. Which may only have made them all the more intriguing to William. Before finally returning home to face his father, without even an arrest to deflect his outrage, William determined to have at least one close look at the gang's leader for himself. So after returning to Paris, one night he marched directly into the American Bar, which Worth operated, and collared its owner for a brief, somewhat awkward chat.

It may have been William's boldness, along with the Pinkertons' various dogged, if always just-avoided, pursuits of his operations, that led to Worth's praise of William at Scotland Yard's expense in another bar, some years later. After that, the Pinkertons and Worth rarely crossed paths until the day Worth strode onto William's home turf, a generation later. The detective and the master thief had both changed; age had lined and grayed both men, though William was heavier while Worth was already worryingly thin and beginning to feel the illness that would prove to be tuberculosis. The setting for this more conciliatory meeting between middle-aged men was appropriately more private than the bars where they had feinted at one another in younger days; Horan describes William's office "filled with pictures of dogs and horses and the memorabilia of Pinkerton's active life. It looked like a gentleman's study, where he could relax with friends." And if neither Pinkerton nor Worth would have quite called the other "friend," they now behaved like friends all the same. Their long meetings were much less interrogation or negotiation than conversation, mostly reminiscence about days gone by.

In the end they did arrange the *Duchess*'s return also, probably for a discreet and relatively modest ransom. Worth confessed that, as William had surmised, he had not dared either sell or exhibit the painting, and merely kept it rolled up in storage for 22 years. Coming from the tired and ailing Worth, it must have seemed by itself a rather poignant concession to the detective who had so long appeared the loser of their contests. William seemed content, under the circumstances, to let bygones be bygones. Others were less generous; when word of the painting's surrender reached William's occasional colleague Isaiah Lees, the recently retired chief of police insisted that "This talk of Worth having reformed is all bosh." Officially, the return of stolen property was the important point, however, and there William had done his job. Lees himself had once showered the con artist Arthur Dean with kindness and friendship, after all, in order to advance a case. In truth, though, William's friendship and even concern for Worth was no ploy, and had it been it probably would have insulted the shrewd Worth.

In truth, each man simply liked and respected the other as one who had spent his life in the same business, if on opposite sides, and done so with skill and even decency. William and Robert were both known for playing fair with their adversaries, seeing a crook as a person and offering him a square deal, even as they worked hard to put him behind bars. Worth, for his part, was a thief but a sophisticated, reasonable one who had used finesse and negotiation, rather than charge into violent showdowns. William appreciated this, and also probably just admired Worth's success in a field he had studied for most of his life. He would dismiss the notion of the amazing detective, but, strangely, William Pinkerton did believe in the amazing criminal. Or at least he did while they existed. In 1902, not long after Worth's death, William was quoted at some length in *The New York Times* for a story headed "Crime's Aristocrats Gone." As he saw it, silk glove artists had been replaced by more brutish men, and methods. "We have no great burglars or forgers in the United States today," he declared with obvious regret. Though not mentioned by name, few were in any doubt as to one particular gentleman crook he must have had in mind.

By the early years of the new century, William was addressing the public more and more often, as a spokesman for Pinkerton's, and for law enforcement, generally. Robert, by contrast, was largely absent from the limelight and the field, both, which may have contented him. Unlike his brother he had always been more interested in running a detective business than in performing or talking about detective work. On the other hand, it's possible that in time the brothers' roles might have shifted once again, and that Robert might have reassumed prominence by directing the solution of a headline crime or through some other coup.

He did not get the chance. Though only in his 50s, Robert had begun suffering heart trouble by 1904, which could also help explain his reduced public profile. He turned to the fashionable therapy of hot springs baths, and after visiting the spa at Bad Nauheim, Germany, returned home feeling renewed. Three years later he was on his way to Germany once more, aboard the liner *Bremen*. His health had taken another turn for the worse, and his detective's intuition may even have warned him that his time was growing short; before departing, he reportedly pressed his fine watch on a baffled friend. He set out hoping to postpone the end, all the same, but gave out before he could give the restorative waters a second try. Robert Pinkerton died at sea on August 12, 1907, of what papers attributed to "fatty degeneration of the heart."

The response to Robert's death at 58 may have exceeded that for any detective before or since, including the other members of his family. The tributes rivaled those paid by San Francisco to its own Isaiah Lees five years earlier, but now they issued from cities throughout America and Europe. Newspapers filled columns with praise of Robert's exploits as a crimefighter and his effectiveness as guardian of the nation's racing; the Stewards of the Jockey Club adopted formal resolutions of regret and testified that "not once in all the years has there been a successful theft." Enormous floral displays from the Stewards and countless other groups required "three large vans" to carry them all. The black mark of Homestead was largely forgotten, amidst the sentiment of the occasion. Even opponents joined in the praise for a giant in his field, with one old bank robber tracked down by a reporter testifying that "He was a square one."

Robert's estate, valued at three million dollars, was shared among heirs who included his successor at the agency, another Allan Pinkerton. Somehow, during a life spent at offices, crime scenes, race tracks, and on long chases through the remote frontiers of civilization, Robert had found time to marry and father three children, though all are nearly invisible in the accounts of his life. His wife Ann Hughes and their two daughters remained so, afterward; the exception was his son, typically identified as Allan II to limit confusion resulting from his family's stern economy with given names. Born in 1876, Allan II had graduated from Harvard at age 20 and promptly gone to work for the family business just as Robert and William had a generation before. Upon his father's death, he was exactly the age that Robert had been when his own father's stroke had first dropped responsibility onto his and William's shoulders. And, just like Robert and William, Allan II felt both ready and impatient to have a real say in decision making, and frustrated by the older generation's apparent hostility to any new ideas. Meanwhile, his Uncle William found the tables turned, and wondered why this young upstart had so little appreciation for the wisdom of experience.

Allan II also carried on the tradition of serving his country in wartime, though his military service was more conventional and also more costly than his father's, uncle's, or grandfather's. When America joined World War I, Allan II joined the new army gathering in Europe. During the relatively brief American involvement, he served on the staff of General Pershing, and, later, put his detective experience to work overseeing criminal investigations for the army's provost marshal general. But he also suffered exposure to poison gas, which caused lasting damage to his health—later impaired even further by tuberculosis—and never entirely recovered. Thus, the National Detective Agency largely remained in the hands of his durable uncle William, even into the years of Prohibition.

Since their boyhood together more than half a century before, the life of William Pinkerton had played out in parallel with and been almost unimaginable without his brother, Robert. They were, outside of fiction, very possibly the ultimate detective partnership. Then one day there was only William, though this sudden isolation's full significance to him is largely unknown. If William felt any lasting, existential grief at his brother's absence he kept it to himself; he expressed sadness at the passing of Adam Worth and his peers more than once over the years but seemed to deal with the loss of Robert mainly by carrying on as before. From one perspective, that may not be so very odd. Both had been so alike throughout their lives that the absence of Robert didn't really change William's relationship or involvement with any other part of his life. Even though Robert never lived to age 70 himself, the world had a ready and close approximation of what he would have thought, said, and looked like if he had.

In most ways other than his unusual longevity, William never departed greatly from the traditions of the brother and father who preceded him, or changed much at all, really. He grew somewhat more crusty, occasionally somewhat grumpy. Back in 1897, he had already reacted tetchily to a newspaper story about his pocket being picked in Denver; he not only fumed to the *Times* and insisted that nothing of the sort had happened, but even ordered his attorneys to pursue a lawsuit for damages. A dozen years later, effectively in sole charge of maintaining the storied National Detective Agency's place as *the* private detective agency, he was upset again over a new and more serious threat to that reputation.

Competing detective firms were not new. Many ex-police officers lacked the late Isaiah Lees's reluctance to enter competition with Pinkerton's, even though the agency's relations with police had long remained friendly. Most of these rivals remained tiny mom-and-pop establishments, however. If there were a few more of them and they were getting a bit more ambitious during the first decade of the 20th century, they probably should have remained a mild annoyance at most, even for a gruff, aging William Pinkerton. And very possibly they would have, had it not been for another William, who gave Pinkerton fits with both their considerable differences and, truth be told, their considerable resemblance.

William J. Burns shared a first name with William Pinkerton, and a variety of other characteristics, as well, though neither would have willingly admitted it. The former Secret Service operative also resembled William's father, Allan, at least in the outline of his career. Burns, too, had pursued a relatively conventional occupation for a time, before a few smallish opportunities to try his hand at detection, followed by successful years as a government agent against counterfeiting and other frauds and, finally, striking out to found his own private detective agency. Yet Burns differed from the Pinkertons completely in terms of his personality and style. If William and Robert had a subtle quality of boys trying to be serious adults, Burns had the decidedly unsubtle quality of a boy with both a thirst for adventure and a shameless exuberance in pursuing it. The dramatic moments and remarkable feats of Burns's investigations were, arguably, no more frequent or spectacular than those of William and Robert in their younger days. The great difference was that Burns unabashedly reveled in them. He found a rapt audience in the nation's press, moreover, and if in his later years William Pinkerton became more outspoken himself at the same time as he became more dismissive of the romantic "detective hero," it's likely that both were in part responses to Burns.

On top of his accolades from the press, Burns provided a more substantive reason for William's resentment when, in 1909, he won away the Pinkertons' longtime client, the American Bankers Association. Which had to be particularly alarming, as Burns's agency was at the time less than a year old. Suddenly, William Pinkerton had a rival not only for attention but for real business.

With time, the loss of the ABA, though serious enough, would prove the biggest direct coup that Burns ever scored against the National Detective Agency; Burns's agency never again equaled that first triumph. It was, moreover, realistically the product of disagreements between the Pinkertons and their client going back a number of years, most of them coming down to a matter of money. The Pinkertons had enjoyed something of a monopoly while no other agency operated at a scale required by a client like the ABA, and had probably grown somewhat arrogant in their relations with an effectively captive customer. From their perspective, it was foolish to abandon pursuit of Butch Cassidy and the Sundance Kid simply because they had removed to Argentina. As demonstrated on multiple occasions, however, from the perspective of bankers, there was no sense whatsoever in spending money to harass criminals who had fled the continent. Disagreements like these became ongoing sore points. Meanwhile, a particularly impatient ABA officer named L.W. Gammon aggravated the conflict while setting the stage for its surprise resolution. Gammon knew Burns from his days working for the Treasury

Department, and he may well have pitched Burns on a deal to replace the Pinkertons, rather than the other way around. Whatever the sequence of events, they reached an agreement for a lower rate and delivered a shock to the 63-year-old Pinkerton.

In some ways, the news must have been a relief all the same, given the deteriorating relations with Gammon. And in business terms, William Pinkerton's response was constructive, immediate, and fitting: Gammon had very nearly created his own detective agency to replace Pinkerton's, so William created his own organization to replace the ABA. The Pinkerton Bank and Bankers' Protective Unit was by no means an immediate replacement for the lost revenue, but it helped, and sent an unmistakable message that the National Detective Agency was not going to roll over. In other ways, though, William mostly just stewed. Burns eagerly and publicly disparaged his rivals; as with most of Burns's antics, William considered this vulgar and tried to elevate himself to a more serious plateau. At one point he claimed in a letter that "We have reached a stage where we pay no attention to him," though this was far from the reality. While less obvious than Burns, William Pinkerton kept the rival agency in his sights and took the occasional shot, not all of them entirely sporting.

More consistently with his idea of responding to Burns's taunts with dignity and professionalism, William sought to position himself as a more serious spokesman for the detective field. He would not mention Burns, and could try to project lofty indifference to him with some degree of credibility, since the role of public expert was not a new or sudden departure. William had detailed with regret the changing methods in burglary years earlier (remarking also on the subculture of hoboes, who seem to have been a peculiar fixation). In 1905, he read a paper on the relatively sophisticated methods still prevailing, among forgery gangs, to a convention of the International Chiefs of Police to which he and Robert had both been welcomed. His efforts to speak out on criminology probably had a new energy and purpose, though, once Burns took to the national stage.

Whatever his motive in promoting them, William's ideas on crime, criminals and society were often at least interesting, as well as rather thoughtful and progressive for a wealthy, well-connected old tycoon. Addressing another conference in 1912, William spent some time on his familiar eulogy for the old-time "Silk Hat and Kid Glove Professional Criminal" as well as anecdotes about where a few individual examples had gone over the years. But he was not entirely concerned with nostalgia. He also spoke at some length on the theme of rehabilitation, and his conviction that even longtime crooks could reform, but must have opportunities. He made it clear that he was advocating a message with direct practical relevance to his audience: "I ask our police chiefs to take into consideration the man coming out of prison and give him some encouragement."

This was a belief which all the Pinkertons had endorsed, and had also attempted to practice themselves. William offered his conference audience the example of one old reprobate, whom his father had attempted many times to help turn over a new leaf, always without success; years afterward William himself had met the man who, he subsequently confirmed, had finally gone straight after all. In 1907, Robert, perhaps indeed sensing the conclusion to his life, had sent William a letter in which he looked back on his career and avowed that he had always been glad to help those lawbreakers "who are sincere in their desire to reform, and help themselves." Believing Jim Dunlap sincere, if luckless, Robert had never closed his door on the fellow no matter how wearying his repeated pleas became. William carried on the family tradition, and Adam Worth was hardly the only crook to meet with friendship and sympathy from his former adversary. When another bank robber less adept than Worth finally won parole he received help from William in getting set up as a salesman, as well as a number of letters asking about he how was getting along. William often inquired after crooks he had helped send away years before, many times providing a bit of seed money as well; per his own words, "I always like to help these old fellows and put them on their feet."

By William's later years, these personal efforts might have been ascribed to an old man feeling sentimental. But he continued to speak out for assistance on a broader basis, as well. In 1911, William had returned to London with a selection of the agency's detectives to keep an eye out for American pickpockets and con men targeting the crowds during George V's coronation; afterward, Scotland Yard praised his work and William returned the favor by commending their approach to rehabilitation. In America, he believed, convicted criminals were too often released with little aid or direction to anything but going right back to their old ways, while "in England, they help a man all they can to do the right thing."

Britain also came in for a more general if more peevish tribute because, in William's view, "Here men do not give out sensational stories for self-advertisement, which in America are so often fictitious." Suggestions to the contrary aside, he was obviously still brooding over the fame of William Burns. His continued annoyance shows through in remarks such as this, and his repeatedly expressed contempt for "sensational stories" of detection, specifically:

Detective tales may be diverting, but police news of any kind should be kept to the bare facts... So I have refused to write them, and I would be glad if others did the same.

Gumshoe detectives are usually just plain rot. Detective work is only using good common sense and nothing else.

Our work is not filled with mysteries. It is serious and straightforward, when it is successful. There is no such thing as a deduction. It is both ridiculous and impossible.

Unsurprisingly, Hollywood also came in for a kicking in William's later years, for the way that the popular new entertainment industry "glamorized" crime. Yet for every stuffy conservative pronouncement—most of which only made Burns seem even more refreshing by contrast—William could surprise with an endorsement of progressive thinking. In addition to helping criminals reform after they had been caught and served their time, he called for more resources to deter crime in the first place, through "education and more education." In particular, the jowled, heavyset conservative businessman in his old-fashioned clothes proposed that government should fund scholarships for children of the crowded urban poor. And he declared Prohibition the cause of "the national crime wave" in 1920, well before wider sentiment reversed on the measure. He supported various innovative thinking in terms of more direct approaches to crime fighting as well. During his coronation visit to London, William studied Scotland Yard's use of fingerprinting, with the specific hope of returning to America with evidence to support the method's widespread adoption. He also campaigned for a coordinated, national intelligence service following the outbreak of World War I, though like other useful ideas advanced by the Pinkertons (such as a full-time security detail for the president) this did not spur a real government response until long afterward.

William Pinkerton had no last great case as a detective. Though he long outlived his younger brother, and, unlike their father, remained in relatively robust health until the end of his life, he still effectively retired from hands-on investigating at middle age just as they had. He was an active director of the National Detective Agency's work, yet there were relatively few headline investigations in which he even played an oversight role. Whether due to Homestead, or to the extinction of great criminals, or to Burns, the Pinkerton agency's work for one reason or another became exactly the sort of routine, unexciting business that William insisted real detection was like. When his work did make the news in later years, it was more often for what were essentially security jobs as at McKinley's inauguration and the coronation of George V; William was managing trained detectives rather than rough-edged guards, but a drift back toward his brother Robert's vision still represents a mild irony during William's years of solo leadership.

William remained well known, but more for being a prominent public figure and an elder statesman of detection than for active detective work. Appropriately, then, his long second career and life both came to an end while he was on the road to address another series of conferences. William Pinkerton died December 11, 1923, in his room at the Hotel Biltmore in Los Angeles, "of ailments incident to his age, 78 years" per the vague yet adequate pronouncement of *The New York Times*. Their full coverage of William's death was more extensive, and the news received wide international notice; nonetheless, it was not quite the same outpouring that had met Robert Pinkerton's death 16 years earlier. Time had, realistically, moved on to some extent. Though William had remained familiar and respected, his dramatic personal triumphs were much further in the past at the time of his death. People's memories had probably faded, as had more than a few of the people themselves. William had outlived many of the major figures from his own life: his brother Robert, his respected colleague Lees and his admired opponent Worth; William had married, too, but his wife had been gone for nearly 30 years. According to Charles Hermann's *Recollections of Life and Doings in Chicago*, "When William Pinkerton died in 1923, it was estimated that most of the mourners were from the underworld."

Which, if true, is both fitting and unsurprising. Criminals accounted for the greater part of the people he worked with, and neither William nor Robert ever made much time for lives outside work. In that sense, the circumstances of William's death were also fitting in one other way, as both he and his brother were far from home at the time. William out in America's West, Robert on his way overseas; the Pinkerton brothers died still the at-large, international detectives they had been in life. Their own most active years had aligned with the brilliant, legendary high noon for both Pinkerton's National Detective Agency and the detective profession, generally. At the end of their lives, it was a respectful nod to that era that they should expire while on the same kind of long journeys that had characterized their heyday, itself effectively finished. William's deprecation of astonishing detective exploits may have been both grumpy and a little ironic, but it was also realistic. Even as the public was celebrating Burns as it had no detective before, William Pinkerton knew that the time for such adventurousness was ending.

Thus, one last time and probably not a little sadly, he and his brother Robert were united in seeing that the agency and the entire industry's future would lie in quiet, predictable security work rather than in unraveling daring and mysterious crimes. In the long run, the agency's disastrous policy at Homestead was succeeded by a move away from carelessness, from controversy and from headlines, but not from proactive but dull security services. Robert's son Allan II outlived his uncle William by only seven years, and while his own son upheld the legacy of the first Allan in a genetic sense until the 1960s, by then the pioneering enterprise that had established the very term "private eye" was long since history. Today, Pinkerton Government Services could hardly be further from that founding spirit, and advertises "government compliance" as its salient offering. Somewhat more poetically, one might recall William Pinkerton's remark after the death of Adam Worth, and repurpose it instead: "We have no great detectives or manhunters in the Pinkerton agency today."

CHAPTER SEVEN

WILLIAM BURNS

"Surely! There is no mystery
about it, you understand."

W HEN THE NEW YORK TIMES assessed William Burns's resolution of the baffling Monroe note counterfeiting case and compared it to the work of a celebrated fictional detective, Burns must have liked the idea. The connection seems to have held lasting appeal for him. Years later, at the peak of his own fame, Burns even befriended the detective's creator, Sir Arthur Conan Doyle. Their association reveals much about a complicated, contradictory man.

Like much of the life and career of that man, the story of Burns and Doyle cannot be understood without first making reference to the Pinkertons. The author of countless beloved fictional mysteries, Arthur Conan Doyle had a lifelong interest in real-world crime, as well, and through his fame and success was able to meet and correspond with some of criminology's leading figures. One of these was the co-owner and eventual sole director of America's great National Detective Agency, the internationally traveled William Pinkerton. The two Victorians' shared interests made them fast friends, and on one occasion gave them much to discuss when they also shared a long ocean voyage.

Yet that same cruise eventually led the shipmates' friendship to a rocky shoal. Upon the publication of Doyle's novel *The Valley of Fear*, first serialized in 1914, William Pinkerton "raised the roof" in the wording of James Horan's history. The story incorporated a lengthy fictionalization of the Molly Maguires case that Pinkerton's late father had directed decades earlier, and William felt the author had taken advantage of information shared in confidence between friends. In fact, Doyle never concealed *Valley of Fear*'s origins in the Pinkerton agency's infiltration of the "Mollies," and his primary sources were almost certainly public accounts including that of Allan Pinkerton himself, rather than private conversation with his son. But William felt Doyle should at least have asked his approval, first. Officially, he accepted the author's sincere apologies, but their friendship was never the same; when in later years the Pinkerton chief scowled at detective-hero tales, it may not have been solely in response to Burns.

That said, William Burns was involved in the situation and not merely in a general sense. The accounts of a variety of sources all leave a similar impression of Burns almost literally swooping in to capitalize on the rift between Pinkerton and Doyle. Burns had already been making overtures to Doyle by that point; it may well have been a 1913 conversation with Burns that began Doyle thinking about the Molly Maguires case and led directly to *The Valley of Fear*, in fact, rather than any of Doyle's exchanges with Pinkerton. And while Burns can hardly have planned the eventual result, he seemed entirely shameless in exploiting it. With a chance of not only matching his rival but, suddenly, of trumping him as well, Burns buddied up to Arthur Conan Doyle more eagerly than ever. He also did so as visibly as possible, not only arranging (and getting much mileage out of) photos with Doyle, but even working out an appearance for the author in a film serial directed by another of the gregarious sleuth's friends. A born performer himself, Burns no doubt enjoyed all of this aside from the boost to his own profile relative to Pinkerton's. But that was by no means unwelcome. In *Front Page Detective: William J. Burns and the Detective Profession 1880-1930*, William R. Hunt observes that "Every move of Burns annoyed William Pinkerton. He was sure that Burns courted the friendship of Arthur Conan Doyle in the hope that the author would refer to him as 'America's Sherlock Holmes'—which he did."

Yet for all his showmanship, there was always far more to Burns than critics like Pinkerton would acknowledge. Burns's interest in Doyle may have been a product of vanity, but Doyle's interest in Burns was certainly not. The author was an insightful judge of people and had little reason to flatter Burns with exaggeration. He seems genuinely to have found the energetic detective impressive; talkative, and somewhat brash, but at the same time a charismatic, interesting and formidable operator. His description of a man possessing "the easy and polished manners of a diplomat over something else which can be polished—granite" must have delighted Burns's ego, but it was undoubtedly Doyle's real impression as well. The real-life celebrity detective's friendship with the detective story author thus touches on the best and the worst aspects of William Burns. On one hand: charisma, intelligence, and skill worthy of his fame. On the other, however, shallowness, juvenile exhibitionism and, particularly in the friendship's end years afterward, an egotism not always matched by ethics.

For all of his later dramas and controversies, the origins of William Burns were remarkably conventional, compared with many of his peers. William John Burns was born in Baltimore to Irish immigrants Michael and Bridget Burns in October 1861. A short time later, the Burns family went out west— but not especially far, resettling in Zanesville, Ohio. Mike Burns was a tailor, and had no interest in sodbusting frontier life or in much of anything daring or unusual.

It was a perspective he tried to impart to his son, Bill, but to little avail. The freckly, towheaded boy had a much different type of character, enjoying puzzles, stories and any excitement he could hunt up, or make up. If that posed a challenge in Zanesville, it was just the first of many challenges that through-out his life would only encourage him. As did his father, in one entirely inad-vertent way. After moving from Zanesville to Columbus in 1873, Mike Burns took a break from tailoring to serve as police commissioner. Though brief, that tenure as commissioner led to his teenaged son taking a keen interest in the city's police. The lively boy won not only friendship but respect, after his discovery that victims of a burglary ring were in each instance away on travels which the newspaper society pages had announced beforehand.

Mr. and Mrs. Burns entertained some hope that their son's interest in crime might lead to something respectable, in turn, and away from William's delight in acting and theatre. A career in law sounded promising. Eventually they got something of a compromise between the two, but first, Burns's path to the role of celebrity detective took a minor detour. After a brief business course, he went to work alongside his father at the tailoring shop. It wasn't a law office, but the elder Burns was content, proudly renaming the business "Burns and Son." The 23-year-old son, however, was quickly bored and longing for some distraction to liven things up.

He soon got his wish in an unlikely form: county electoral paperwork. It seemed that some of the vote counts from the most recent election simply didn't add up. Upon closer inspection, in fact, they proved to be forgeries. Franklin County prosecutor Cyrus Huling wanted to know whose—and he approached William Burns with the job.

That choice may seem like a non sequitur, but in context, the approach to Burns wasn't quite as odd as it first appears. Even into the late 19th century, the formal practices of American police and detectives had advanced little beyond what met Scotland Yard's Jonathan Whicher more than 60 years earlier. Instinct and very informal, on-the-job training taught new recruits what worked, or else it didn't; having hung around detectives and interested himself in their work as a youth, Burns's qualifications weren't tremendously less than those of some actual, serving policemen. An outsider may even have been preferable for one reason or another, in this instance. It's possible that Huling turned to Burns partly from concern about collusion, although, given the low odds of Columbus city detectives being part of a minor election fraud, it's more likely that they were simply reluctant to take the job and enter a political minefield. For Burns, though, this sort of hazard usually proved more of a lure than a deterrent. Thus, bored with needles and thread, he agreed to see what he could learn.

Burns liked to claim that "There is no such thing as mystery if you will only use a little common sense." Unlike William Pinkerton, Burns was probably winking at you when he said it. Nonetheless his investigations did generally proceed from reasonable speculation. In evaluating the falsified vote tally sheets, Burns began with a few basic facts. First, the clerk who discovered the boosted vote counts for local Democratic candidates testified that it was skilled work; the simulation of his own handwriting was so close he could only be sure of the difference because the forgery used a slightly different ink. Second, the Republican success in the election had been a complete surprise. From this, Burns reasoned that the attempt at subverting it had been improvised at the last minute, rather than anything planned ahead of time. With these points in mind, he asked himself: where would someone find a safecracker (to get the tally sheets in the first place) and a skilled forger in a hurry?

Finding a specific answer required, as it usually does, a combination of patience, alertness, and a bit of luck. If the Irish-American Burns's ready discovery of that luck—through socializing at a tavern no less—was stereotypical, it too was not entirely without an element of logic. The Ohio Penitentiary was a dependable place to find forgers and cracksmen, after all. So Burns became a regular at a tavern frequented by the prison guards and, irrepressibly outgoing, was soon not just listening but joining in their conversations. He eventually accumulated a number of clues as well as strong support for his theory that the fraud was no master plan. On one occasion, the guards made very matter-of-fact reference to an inmate named Tom Campbell claiming that he had falsified the recent election's results. They considered it a great joke because Campbell was committed to the prison hospital's "crazy ward" at the time, yet Burns was naturally intrigued. He laughed along, and said it sounded like Campbell belonged there, too, at which another guard replied "That's what Doc Montgomery said." More laughter followed, then the conversation drifted to other topics. But one participant still had Campbell and "Doc" Montgomery on his mind. There they would remain as Burns followed up with more discreet inquiries, later, and found that the prison doctor was defeated county prosecutor Robert Montgomery's brother.

With that, Burns had a real investigation, and during the weeks that followed he proceeded to work out much of his subsequent repertoire. He immersed himself in the yeoman's task of examining the prison's records; discovered and tracked down other parties to the caper, in one instance while on an extended visit to his future rivals' home of Chicago; and, with just enough facts to make it convincing, bluffed a suspect for all he was worth. This last gambit produced a confession, in combination with a deal to talk, as it would do many more times.

The larger outcome of the investigation was a mixed verdict. After two years and three grand juries, an eventual trial ended without result when two "highly suspect" jurors held out for acquittal. This disappointing result held more lessons for the aspiring detective's future, but far more important from Burns's immediate perspective were the personal rewards of his effort. He had taken on a puzzle, found a solution, and won plaudits and praise for his performance. Hunt's biography speculates temptingly about what his subject might have made of the generous reviews: "maybe he had fooled his father after all and become an actor."

Burns unquestionably loved the celebrity he won as a detective. If any in his profession ever enjoyed more fame, none ever enjoyed fame more, with the possible exception of Vidocq, and even there the margin must be narrow. Between his promising first outing in Franklin County and his next real head-line case, however, Burns persevered through nearly a decade of hard slog for little money and even less glory. When an audience finally took notice once again, he played up to them, shamelessly, but dismissals of Burns as a shallow attention seeker overlook an impressive capacity for plain, dogged hard work.

His initial success convinced Burns to leave tailoring and make detection his career. The job proved something much less glamorous than the hobby had been. Burns became a struggling "gumshoe," at the very bottom of the profession's hierarchy. For a time, the extended court proceedings back in Columbus may have kept the memory of his first case fresh. If Burns sustained a faith in further greatness through all the lean years that followed, though, his positive attitude must have been astonishing. It certainly received no outside encouragement. His father openly disapproved of quitting the shop for this new fancy. Anna Maria Ressler, whom Burns wed shortly before launching his new career, largely kept her opinion to herself but it was scarcely more optimistic.

Other than Burns himself, perhaps the only person who really believed in him was Tom Furlong. The owner of his own modest St. Louis detective agency, Furlong provided a good deal of freelance work to Burns along with a degree of mentorship that would constitute most of his training as a detective, beyond hard-won experience. The work was mostly quotidian: chasing around the Midwest after bad check writers and other minor frauds, or seeking missing husbands for abandoned wives (even as his own spouse might have sympathized with them).

No accounts survive of how Burns connected with Furlong, or why he went to work for the small, Midwestern agency rather than the much larger and relatively prestigious Pinkertons. The idea of William Burns becoming a valued agent of the man he would drive nearly to distraction, instead, is an interesting counterfactual, but if Burns ever sought employment with the Pinkertons, neither he nor they recalled it afterward. Instead, they were in competition from the very beginning of Burns's career, with the playing field heavily tilted in the Pinkertons' favor. William Pinkerton and his brother Robert had the resources, the name recognition, and most of the good clients. What was left over made slim pickings. Whether or not Burns consciously sought to take the privilege and position of William Pinkerton away for himself in later years, it's certain he had cause to resent the larger agency. Already, by the late 1880s, he was regularly damning them as crooks and liars. Burns actually won over a hostile source, during an arson investigation, in part by supporting the man's conviction that "Pinkertons" were all crooked, which Burns must have seconded with gusto before explaining how *he* was different from those many frauds.

This case and another arson investigation were very nearly the only genuinely interesting or exciting jobs of his first time out as a private detective. The later arson case was apparently so interesting that Burns continued it even after accepting a full-time government job; for a while he juggled both public and private work, as many a detective has done, moonlighting and even taking a period of leave to complete his last assignment from his old friend Tom Furlong. All the same, Burns must have had few real second thoughts about his decision after a few years of the down-at-heel PI's life. In 1889, he began a new phase of his detective career, which proved more demanding but also more interesting, more rewarding and far more glamorous. The Secret Service was about to gain a dazzling new star.

In his personal appearance, William Burns was far from dazzling. He has a faintly odd look about him in most portraits, as though photographed before he was quite ready and thus ever so slightly askew somehow. He looks almost befuddled. His expression conveys neither the roguish intelligence of Vidocq, nor the steely character of Lees or Allan Pinkerton, nor the bulldog assertiveness of Pinkerton's sons. Vidocq might have admired the puzzling variety of descriptions of his fellow extrovert's build, at least, which range from "short and stocky" to "athletic and trim," though some of this may be the result of observations at different points in Burns's life. When he signed up with the Secret Service, he was still only 28 and probably still tended more toward "athletic." Later in life the term "portly" may have become somewhat more fitting, though he was never notably obese, particularly by 21st century standards. In most ways his appearance was not notable at all, really; chroniclers consistently describe Burns's overall visual impression as almost remarkably unremarkable. At first glance, simply another dull businessman in gray suit and derby hat, perhaps a bank manager.

Spending any length of time in the man's actual presence would have left a considerably different impression. Compulsively outgoing, Burns would quickly press any observer into the role of an audience. Gene Caesar, whose work *The Incredible Detective: The Biography of William J. Burns* is itself a lively if almost breathlessly praiseful account, describes him as "quick and precise in his mannerisms, compelling in his geniality, and explosive in his rage." All of which is absent entirely from the surviving images of Burns—black and white still photos from a century ago. They offer no evidence of his apparently impressive charisma, energy, or intelligence. Nor of the one visual hint of a live-wire nature otherwise concealed beneath an unassuming exterior: his fiery red hair. Like Winston Churchill, another energetic and sometimes erratic redhead, even in his earliest photos Burns is left deceptively gray.

Examining his history, however, makes plain that Burns was never dull or gray. And as an agent of the Treasury, he was genuinely to shine, though it still took considerable work to achieve. One of the "General Orders" for Secret Service operatives proclaimed that "Each man must recognize that his service belongs to the government through 24 hours of every day," and distant postings for weeks or even months made clear that it was meant literally. In return for monopoly access to his time and attention, the Secret Service paid its new Assistant Operative exactly three dollars per day, raised to four after a year upon a promotion to Special Operative. Burns had already gotten used to meagre pay and absence from his family, though. His new career at least offered more exciting work, and exciting work could win back public attention.

First, Special Operative Burns had to put in five more years of learning the ropes, of working to prove himself, and of waiting for a real chance to do so. But after paying his dues, he began to receive something back, at last. In 1894, luck found William Burns again and this time she hugged him tight. When Secret Service chief William Hazen sent Burns to investigate the state of Mississippi's "monetary warrants," which bore a considerable resemblance to the national currency, reporters took an interest in the matter and followed Hazen's engaging new agent around. A few months later, Burns made more acquaintances among the press upon seizing counterfeiting equipment from a quack doctor who had sought to branch out into new frauds.

Steady progress continued through most of the 1890s with a trilogy of counterfeiting investigations. In 1895, Burns helped put away "Long Bill" Brockway and his gang by piecing together a homemade apron, found among counterfeiting equipment, with distinctively shaped scraps of oilcloth from Brockway's home. His success on that case earned him promotion to full Operative. The next year, Burns uncovered a Costa Rican connection between a vast counterfeiting operation and would-be revolutionaries, beginning from nothing more than a burlap cloth stamped "XX1634."

Cases like this with their countless opportunities for puzzle solving and role playing fascinated Burns, and his results won both notice from the press and approval from his employer. Yet Hazen's confidence in Burns only extended so far. When an impossibly perfect counterfeit $100 James Monroe note turned up in Philadelphia, in 1897, the Secret Service chief found his promising Operative theorizing too far. As something of a maverick genius himself, it was natural for Burns to imagine that some lone inventor had made a breakthrough in photo etching and to suggest an exhaustive study of the engraving industry to locate anyone capable of such work. Chief Hazen, by contrast, was a rather more conservative intellect. He dismissed his operative's fanciful notion and sent him off to pursue routine inquiries in Chicago. Hunt notes drily that "Burns was disgusted."

As the next several months revealed, however, he was not alone. Despite the successes Burns was producing, the Treasury was unimpressed with Hazen, and finally replaced him. (Ironically, his demotion may have been in part a result of ordering a protective detail for the First Family, which was then still an unauthorized misuse of Secret Service resources.) Hazen was out, and *Chicago Tribune* editor John Wilkie was in. It proved fantastic news for Burns. If Furlong helped him get started as a detective, Wilkie enabled Burns to complete his rise to stardom and remain there. Burns was nearly as old as his new chief, but for most of his adult life he looked a decade younger than his real age. More importantly, he had an ambitious young man's energy and impatience. Wilkie gave his agent rein to apply them, beginning with the Monroe note mystery. Burns's proposal was revived and approved.

Other Secret Service men immediately began looking up all of the nation's best engravers. Burns already had further ideas, meanwhile. With freedom to pursue them, he left the others to it and made for Philadelphia along with another operative named Billy McManus.

Philadelphia was the source of the first fake Monroe notes. It was also a leading center for printing and engraving dating back to Ben Franklin's time, as Burns knew well. He knew a good deal by now about the resources that counterfeiting required, in fact, and among these was muslin cloth. Just like the legitimate Bureau of Engraving and Printing, counterfeiters used heaps of the stuff, pressing their paper between wet sheets of it just before printing. So, Burns and McManus toured the city's dry goods stores. Many stores had filled large orders for muslin, but Burns pressed them all for anything memorable about the buyers, even trivial details, and eventually his persistence paid off.

One storekeeper recalled how a customer "kept winking, as if he had something in his eye." That "something," Burns realized, might be fine particles of metal or grinding dust, which often afflicted the eyes of engravers. Burns and McManus had no name for this winking fellow, but further deductions reinforced an impression of someone living or working in the area. Combing the large list provided by their colleagues, they found two men who, as it happened, had recently opened a printing and engraving shop nearby. Arthur Taylor was a skilled engraver but unremarkable within his field. Baldwin Bredell, however, was both an expert in steel engraving and "a reputed mechanical genius." A closer look at this pair was clearly in order.

Burns could be ingenious in devising complicated schemes, but he had the sense to try simple measures first. Unfortunately, the direct approach of a nighttime break-in was foiled by sturdy locks on the front door and even windows of the engravers' fourth-floor shop. Such extensive precautions only made Burns more suspicious, but actually bashing in a door or window was bending the rules too far, he decided. The alternative by which Burns finally gained access to the shop was almost an adventure by itself, involving a complicated piece of theatre staged for a young custodian—and aspiring acrobat—complete with costume. Yet, for all its novelty, the scheme seemed a strategic failure in spite of tactical success. Burns obtained keys to the shop, but searches came up empty handed. His much ballyhooed new thinking had arrived at a dead end and remained there; as weeks became months, Wilkie must have entertained second thoughts about backing the plan and even considered abandoning it, had not the endless surveillance made it clear that Taylor and Bredell *were* involved in something. Their shop conducted no legitimate business to all appearances, but both men lived well, and eventually agents even observed them spending some of the phony notes in Atlantic City. All the same, Operative Burns must have been feeling distinctly anxious as the investigation neared a one-year mark.

A few weeks before that unhappy anniversary, other operatives finally found some new information, though it merely revealed a larger operation rather than any direct evidence or other vulnerability. On a trip west to Lancaster,

Pennsylvania, Taylor and Bredell paid visits to a cigar manufacturer named Jacobs and a tobacco warehouse owner named Kendig; upon their return, Wilkie found that a sample box of Jacobs' cigars bore a fake revenue stamp. Burns soon made his own visit to Kendig's often deserted warehouse in hopes it might conceal the evidence he wanted so badly. Here again, locks proved no match for the combination of William Burns and a venturesome lad; hiring a young little leaguer for "a joke on a friend," this time Burns happily smashed in a window and made a quick search of the warehouse before leaving a baseball inside and a convincingly distraught boy outside to cover his tracks. The ruse worked, but once more his larger goal was frustrated. The warehouse contained stacks of the blue paper used for revenue stamps, and a partitioned-off corner, locked up tight. The latter was plainly intriguing—yet his trick had produced only a one-time pass rather than a key.

Burns still had a key to the Philadelphia shop, though, and the shop had its own secret room in the form of a locker. For more than a year, regular inspections of the shop had found this unlocked and empty. But recently, operatives had found the locker sealed up during their occasional daytime peeks into the shop, though still empty each night. Burns may have been tempted to take inspiration from the election fraud case that launched his career a dozen years before, and ask "Doc" Montgomery for the name of a good safe-cracker. Instead he turned back to simple, if slow, methods. Filing down blank keys in hopes of working out the right pattern through trial and error would take time, he knew. But what were weeks, or even months by this point? So Burns sat down and made key after key, then tried and discarded key after key, until one of them worked. Compared to the other ploys by which he defeated locks during the case, it was almost embarrassingly dull work. But the result more than made up for that shortcoming: a $100-note plate, not only bogus but still only half complete.

With solid evidence in hand at last, the Secret Service began rounding up all of the long-familiar players in the Monroe note conspiracy. Chief Wilkie hailed the outcome as "The most important capture in the history of the Secret Service," and Operative Burns as the man "by whose efforts the unearthing of the counterfeit conspiracy was largely accomplished." Any wavering in his faith was obviously banished, and Burns would soon enjoy the results of this new confidence. On the other side, in contrast, Taylor and Bredell fell out with one another and helped the prosecution secure 12-year sentences for each.

The remarkable Monroe note case had one last puzzle to offer. When Wilkie summoned Burns to look at a near perfect, but counterfeit, $20 bill, it must have felt as though their exhausting efforts to defeat Taylor and Bredell had all been for naught. Except that both men had been in custody for quite some time by then. The Secret Service was convinced that all of the pair's printing plates were accounted for as well. Neither acknowledging that the case had been left incomplete, nor confronting yet another counterfeiting operation of such skill so soon, held much appeal. Having praised Burns to the skies for his recent work, Wilkie could be forgiven for simply handing over responsibility for a potential loose end. He did just that and Burns was soon off to revisit the troublesome investigation.

He began by visiting Taylor and Bredell in prison. Burns was ready to lean hard on both men, but they readily told him all about the new counterfeits the instant he broached the subject. They had one more set of plates, they said, which they had managed to keep secret. And now friends of theirs were putting it to use. But they were more than willing to call it in and let Burns have it in exchange for a generous reduction in their sentences. Burns rebuffed this offer, and suspected the whole story; it didn't make sense that the two had been sitting on such a bargaining chip so long, including through their mutual falling out. Yet they seemed remarkably smug about something. Everything suggested to Burns that the $20 plates in question were more recent work, but he would need to prove it could be done at all before proving that it had.

Checking conditions at the prison, Burns found that Taylor's family and a "shady" Philadelphia lawyer had made many calls, and that visitor's area security was lamentably porous. Yet a search of the prisoners' cell revealed nothing. The only point of interest was a small alcove, which made the detective pause. He noted small notches on the sides where a curtain might have been fastened; Bredell had already proven a legitimate "mechanical genius," and it seemed just conceivable that the space could have been employed for photo engraving. The only problem was that the work would require a camera. In 1899, the revolutionary "box brownie" was still a year away, and existing cameras were still too bulky to smuggle past even perfunctory security, as well as too delicate to reliably reassemble from parts.

Burns kept wrestling with the problem, trying to imagine himself in the position of an inventive prisoner with ample time and motivation. Finally, all of his thinking about cameras jogged the memory of a school demonstration from his boyhood. In the 1860s, cameras were even more delicate and expensive, yet he and his classmates had nonetheless learned to build one of their own using the centuries-old technology of the pinhole camera. This wouldn't even require a lens, yet it just might be enough for Bredell to have resumed his trade from within prison walls. Burns decided that he had the key to the newly repaired partnership and set about trying to break it up again. He selected Taylor for the attempt, as his family were likely accomplices to any post-sentencing scheme, and launched into his usual combination of evidence, deduction, bluff, and threat. Taylor gave in, and revealed a plot even more fantastic than Burns had fully realized. He and Bredell had not only made the new plates inside prison but printed the resulting notes there as well, using a tiny press smuggled in and out by family members. The whole feat was so incredible that they subsequently tried to disown Taylor's admissions and insist that they were technically impossible. Burns knew otherwise, however, and proved it, perhaps silently thanking a Zanesville schoolteacher from 30 years before. Thanks to a very practical lesson in optics, two counterfeiters were staying in prison even longer, rather than leaving early.

The Pinkerton dynasty biographer Frank Morn describes Burns as "a nineteenth century private detective in the twentieth" century. And in terms of a freewheeling, audacious style, this description is apt. Yet in just as many ways, Burns was a remarkably modern figure, sharing much more in common with the professional urban investigator of the 20th century than with the pioneering lawman of the 19th.

By the time Burns was born in 1861, Pinkerton's National Detective

Agency was a decade old, and most major cities employed a few detectives. The profession was still a rough work in progress, but it was an established idea. The same can be said of the America in which Burns operated. The country was split asunder by war during his lifetime, but the Ohio toddler was far removed from the conflict. Unlike the Pinkertons, Lees, and even Pollaky in Europe, the Civil War played no role in Burns's career. By the time he began his detective career, the war was a part of history, along with the antebellum, frontier America in which it was fought. Out west, the loose-knit empire of the Comanches still contested the dominance of whites into the 1870s, and bandits on horseback still staged train hold-ups into the 1890s, but even hints of the 19th century pioneer America are almost entirely absent from the life and career of William Burns. Throughout both he was faced with relatively modern, urban problems in relatively modern, urban settings.

The future Star of the Secret Service was born and raised in settled communities. Much of his early career then played out in eastern cities. When he began traveling west, established urban life had always arrived before him, as had increasingly modern technology. The cities in which Burns would ply his trade were already connected by railroad and telegraph networks while he was a child, and electric lighting and the telephone system were joining them by the time he began practicing as a detective. Burns's cases played out in electrified city neighborhoods and industrial parks rather than gaslit parlors or torchlit rural crossings. His career features one further curiously modern feature in that it was not only urban, but largely bicoastal. Though raised in the Midwest and eventually to make it his official headquarters, nearly all of his notable investigations were based in either northeastern cities or on the West Coast. The Wright Brothers only made their first brief flight at Kitty Hawk in 1903, yet for William Burns, the interior of the country was already becoming "flyover country" by the turn of the century.

Appropriately, Operative Burns began the new century by crossing the country. While still employed by Washington, his third decade as a detective saw him not only shifting from the East Coast to the West, but also shifting by degrees from a Secret Service agent to an at-large investigator for hire.

The first of his western investigations was still directly concerned with the business of the Treasury, even if it represented a departure from counterfeiting cases; in June 1901, Wilkie assigned Burns to solve the theft of $30,000 from the San Francisco Mint. Once again, Burns focused on working out a way that *he* might have pulled off the crime had he wanted to, and after examining the seemingly impregnable mint security he found both gaps and a strong candidate for who had exploited them. Eventually, he assembled enough evidence to close another case. The assignments that occupied Burns for most of the rest of the decade, however, saw him "on loan" outside not only the Secret Service, but the Treasury and eventually the federal government itself.

A small, unofficial commission to investigate a threat on the British ambassador's life in 1899 proved the beginning of a subsequent trend, as government agencies found more frequent need to borrow the Treasury's best operatives. Despite the long tradition of Pinkerton's as America's "National Detective Agency," men in government probably felt an instinctive preference for working with other men in government, and with the rising profiles of the Secret Service and its man Burns they had an impressive option for doing so. Perhaps more surprising was the fact that Chief Wilkie was ready to accommodate them and managed to do so; his predecessor had been reassigned in part for employing Secret Service personnel for then unauthorized protection of the president's family, yet within several years Wilkie was lending out Burns and other operatives on a semi-permanent basis.

The change may have reflected larger changes in Washington. By late 1901, the assassination of William McKinley had not only exposed the restriction of Secret Service personnel to anti-counterfeiting work as shortsighted, in at least one particular regard, but had also catapulted Theodore Roosevelt to the presidency. Only a few years older than Burns, Roosevelt shared much of the detective's energy, pugnacity, and impatience with the strictures of convention. His vigorous presidency launched reform campaigns on a wide variety of issues including battles against corrupt vested interests. When similar purposes beckoned the Secret Service's star operative further and further from its official mission statement, the Roosevelt government thus backed up Burns and Wilkie with approval and encouragement.

William Burns

George Grantham Bain Collection, Library of Congress,
Prints & Photographs Division, Washington, D.C. [LC-USZ62-114556]

*

The first of Burns's great western battles against abuse of the public trust stemmed, in part, from efforts to achieve the opposite. In the late 19th century the enormous value of America's publicly owned lands was an irresistible target for commercial exploitation. The National Parks program, established in the 1890s and subsequently championed by Roosevelt, extended federal protection to large areas of wilderness, maintaining some of the country's natural splendor in perpetuity. Implementing that grand idea involved an enormous number of practical details, however: establishing boundaries, appraising land, and exchanging lands in one area for compensatory parcels in another. The sheer volume of transactions and number of people involved proved powerful invitations to fraud.

Similar opportunities presented by industrializing society, particularly its railroads and complex financial networks, had done much to establish the detective as a profession in the first place. Yet these new land frauds were much more entangled than the express company robberies tackled by Pinkertons, or the swindles thwarted by "Paddington" Pollaky. They were considerably different from anything Burns had encountered before, too. From his amateur examination of election fraud through the San Francisco Mint theft, he had essentially been seeking the trail that would lead him to one man, or at most a small group of conspirators, who were trying to keep themselves or their activities undetected; occasionally the trail was long and labyrinthine, but in some sense there was still a direct way to proceed. Yet in the western land fraud case, and the even larger San Francisco investigation that followed, nothing was direct. Burns confronted sprawling, loose networks of conspirators whose frauds were not so much concealed from sight as they were conducted out in the open but camouflaged by numbers, bureaucracy, and obscure detail. Instead of one trail to a solution, dozens of trails real and false combined into a dense maze.

Burns may nonetheless have been better suited than any other detective for tackling such conspiracy cases. He had a good intuition and ability for selecting one figure he might peel away from accomplices, and, perhaps just as important, he had a pugnacious, barge-ahead style; there was no real way to make progress against crimes of this scale aside from choosing a place to start and then doing so. Burns did that. When the Department of the Interior first began to examine complaints related to the countless federal land deals in progress, they rapidly concluded that the problem required specialist investigative ability and turned to the Secret Service, where Wilkie naturally turned to Burns. In Washington, Burns made inroads quickly by identifying a crooked Land Office clerk and securing a confession from him mostly through pure bluff and force of personality, then exposing a series of higher- and higher-up figures one after another by using each one's admissions as leverage against the next.

This approach continued to prove useful when Burns returned west. Beginning at the outermost edge of the western land fraud schemes with a minor timber company scout, Burns pursued a growing inquiry to a scale that ultimately dwarfed the initial Washington campaign. By the time he finally moved on to other affairs, the land fraud investigation lasted more than two years and involved more than 100 indictments, 34 trials, and 33 convictions. The most dramatic of these allowed Burns to sign his work with a characteristic flourish, as well, against no less an opponent than a United States Senator. Much of the prosecution case against Senator John H. Mitchell rested on records of payments made to him via his law firm. When the defense attempted to nullify this evidence with a contract recording that all of the firm's profits would accrue to Mitchell's partner, so long as Mitchell held public office, Burns pounced on the contract's date. First, calling on his long experience with fraudulent documents of all types, Burns observed that neither the paper nor the ink could have yet existed at the 1901 date shown on the contract. For good measure he then made note of three words consistently misspelled in the document, before producing the law firm's stenographer; a recent hire, the man denied either writing or back-dating the contract, yet when Burns asked him to transcribe a sentence that included words misspelled in the contract the stenographer misspelled every one, in the same way.

After winding up the land fraud investigation, Burns proceeded to a second West Coast corruption case in San Francisco. This time, Burns was tackling a more general system of graft involving railroad interests and city power brokers, rather than the timber bandits and relatively context-specific frauds of the northwest. Yet in many ways the San Francisco "sequel" to the land fraud campaign was essentially "more of the same," though not only "more" in the type of phenomena that were repeated but also in the sense of their being greater in scale than the earlier case's. More-ruthless villains, more-complicated schemes, a longer and more drawn out investigation further removed from the official duties of Secret Service Operative; greater publicity and also greater controversy.

From the perspective of later history, San Francisco's nationally notorious corruption and the equally well-publicized campaign to uproot it have been largely overshadowed by the earthquake and fire that transformed the city overnight, in April 1906. For those living at the time, the day-to-day perspective was considerably different, however. Already, even before the physical damage of the earthquake, San Francisco was a changed place in ways that would have appalled Isaiah Lees. The late chief of police had known cronyism, abuses of office, and yellow journalism, certainly. But in 1905, the entire city's government was effectively captured in an electoral coup; Mayor Matthew Schmitz and other Union Labor Party candidates were so unapologetically corrupt that local Republicans and Democrats had organized an allied front against them, but to their own surprise, as much as anyone's, the ULP won every seat on the city Board of Supervisors. They promptly moved to cash in, with an aggressiveness and efficiency that was startling even in an age where the political "spoils system" was accepted custom. Anything was for sale, legal or otherwise, while very little at all was permitted without a payoff. Money poured in from the usual rackets like booze, gambling and prostitution, but large and fundamentally legitimate businesses signed on as well, including railroad firms and utilities. Above and behind it all, meanwhile, a private citizen named Abe Ruef collected and distributed the payoffs, bribes and other graft, keeping the whole system working smoothly and off the books.

For all the enormous scale and brazenness of the syndicate's corruption, however, opposition was by no means unanimous. The "machine" political systems of 100 years ago were good at benefitting enough people not only to win power—San Francisco's was popularly elected after all—but hold onto it. The reform sentiments of America's progressive era met considerable opposition, both moneyed and popular. (A decade later, New York's Mayor John Hylan proudly announced upon taking office that "We have had all the reform we want in this city for some time to come.") In San Francisco, the reform campaign leadership assembled in early 1906 was impressive: the owner of the *Bulletin*, Fremont Older; a young local millionaire, Rudolph Spreckels; fire eating attorney Francis Heney, who had just successfully prosecuted many high profile corruption cases in Oregon; and, at Heney's insistence, his detective ally William Burns. Theodore Roosevelt was behind them, too, authorizing the extended loan of Burns to an investigation lacking any federal law element and therefore funded locally and, to a great extent, privately. Yet the reformers proved to need every resource they could muster in the face of powerful, well entrenched opponents as willing and able to fight it out in the court of public opinion as anywhere else.

Burns had a first taste of public controversy in the Northwest, as the federal interference with profitable local enterprises initially drew hostility and derision from *The Oregonian* and other voices. Eventually, mounting convictions won around the people and press, but in San Francisco the opposition was rather more determined on all fronts. In the media arena, Burns had to contend with none other than newspaper magnate William Randolph Hearst. Several years earlier, Hearst's *Examiner* had driven from office the veteran local detective Isaiah Lees, and he was hardly more intimidated by an upstart outsider. Initially, Hearst was supportive of the reform campaign. As the affair dragged on and made life uncomfortable for more and more well connected men, however, he changed sides and directed all the resources of his media empire against it. Even the comic strips were recruited; after *The Examiner* lured *Mutt and Jeff* creator Bud Fisher away from the *Chronicle* in 1907, Fisher began introducing parodies of leading figures in the reform effort including one "Hot Tobasco Burns [*sic*]."

The genuine Burns could appreciate a little light ribbing (and even bad puns), and not only laughed at Fisher's cartoons but invited the artist to his home a few times. Most of the contest over his investigation in California was nowhere near so gentlemanly, however, or so humorous. Burns had first set up a real home in San Francisco, with Annie and his children, in part because of ongoing threats against his family. During the years of his work in San Francisco, he not only brought his family out to be closer but arranged a constant guard for his wife and daughters. With good reason, too, as the consortium of railroad interests and government fixers opposing him played rough. Their no-holds-barred methods included not only threats and intimidation but kidnapping, bombs, attempted murder, and possibly more than that. At one point late in the proceedings, Burns's close ally Francis Heney was actually shot in the throat, while in court, no less. Heney only survived by the slimmest chance, and his assailant was subsequently found dead of a convenient suicide while in police custody.

Against this hardened, ruthless opposition, Burns employed every tool in his bag and a few new ones in order to open cracks in the syndicate. He bluffed, threatened, offered deals, managed a network of sources to keep him apprised of rumors, and circulated a few of his own. Taking a cue from Hearst, Burns employed the newspapers as a weapon, in one case even arranging for the supportive *Bulletin* to print up a dummy front page exposing a corrupt businessman whose testimony Burns wanted against other figures.

The most important and most taxing of all his improvisational efforts was, at least in his own view, overcoming the big boss Abe Ruef. A keystone figure in the whole edifice of San Francisco corruption, Ruef was also every bit as determined and as canny a manipulator as his opponent. The two men spent weeks fencing, seeking weaknesses in one another's defenses; Burns later swore that "I never devised in my life as I did to get a confession out of Ruef." Burns probably wasn't exaggerating, either, at least in describing the challenge. As some indication of the difficulty, his results were rather less dramatic: in return for testimony against the city's mayor, Burns ended up agreeing to near total immunity for Ruef, who then refused to cooperate at all in subsequent trials.

The mixed outcome of Burns's long, exhausting struggle against Abe Ruef resembles in miniature the entire campaign's conclusion, such as it was. By 1909, it had absorbed the borrowed Secret Service operative's time and energy, and reformist supporters' fortunes, for most of four years. Burns's family had moved repeatedly in response to threats against them, while Heney had actually been shot and various witnesses removed through fatal accidents; painstakingly prepared cases had ended in hung juries, and dissatisfaction was no longer limited to Hearst papers, as more of the public soured on the seemingly unending acrimony. Even the bulldog determination of Burns himself was reaching a limit. In the end, efforts sputtered out, still frustratingly incomplete.

The years of work were by no means entirely for naught. Burns and his colleagues had punched multiple holes in the enormous system of fraud and corruption. Even if they failed to pull it down completely, time proved that attitudes and customs had changed too much for rebuilding, even after the active reform campaign shut down.

Meanwhile, for Burns personally, the effort had produced a number of positive results even without a triumphant finish. While controversy and vocal opposition had made his job more difficult, they had also made him the focus of more attention than ever before, much of it praiseful despite the Hearst empire's considerable reach. Many journalists were captivated by Burns, personally, but also impressed by his efforts' embodiment of the era's spirit of progressive reform. Frequent *McClure's* correspondent Lincoln Steffens was particularly laudatory in his coverage of Burns, whom he compared with President Roosevelt as one of the country's great men.

Thanks to a series of magazine articles by Steffens and other writers, Burns came to genuinely national notice for the first time and as a crusader against fraud and corruption. To those who had previously owned the position of America's "National Detectives," the sudden publicity for Burns presented an annoyance, and much worse was to come. By the conclusion of his years in San Francisco, Burns had effectively set up his own private consulting firm. He had organized and directed a team of investigators, entirely independent of his official employers at the Secret Service, with his three sons George, Raymond and even high school student Sherman all taking up roles as valued and reliable right-hand men. He had established a network of connections in government at both ends of the country and a highly publicized reputation as an effective check on frauds of all kinds. He had his own agency in everything but name, in fact, and every reason to remedy that final remaining detail soon.

*

By 1909, William Burns was nearly 50 years old. And if he still had the appearance and energy of a younger man, he also had the ambition and bravado. Any return to his official, "normal" duties for the Secret Service was probably never even considered after nearly a decade of increasing independence. Conveniently, the luck that, in combination with patient work, had given Burns his first entry into detective work and then his first exposure to national celebrity was still with him. Fortune had not only provided him an opportunity to create a second and much more lucrative private practice, it had practically completed the process by itself. Under those circumstances, a man like Burns was more than game enough to make it official. In April 1909, he did so, launching the Burns and Sheridan Detective Agency in Chicago.

His partner William Sheridan left Burns's narrative almost as quickly and anonymously as he entered it, coincidentally recalling the founding of Allan Pinkerton's detective agency 60 years earlier. The soon renamed William J. Burns National Detective Agency also copied its famous predecessor in other, and much less accidental, ways. The choice of Chicago as a home city seems impossible to explain, given the city's distance from any of the locales where Burns had spent his life and career up to that point, except as a direct challenge to the Pinkertons. And his initial proclamation that his would be a "clean" agency, eschewing disreputable work like divorce cases or strikebreaking, not only recalled Allan Pinkerton's General Principles but also contrasted pointedly with the atrocious violence at the Homestead strike under his sons' watch.

In many ways, it should be noted, the Burns agency's mimicry of his largest rival was simply sound business practice, requiring no personal animosity to explain. The Pinkertons had a successful business model, which had nonetheless retained considerable monopoly power for decades; in Burns, someone finally came along with the ability, reputation and connections to build up a true competitor at the same national scale. Coming out of government employment and lacking any legacy costs, Burns could offer pricing to undercut the older agency, and in that light it's little surprise that he soon signed up longtime clients of the Pinkertons, as well. His inside connection with L.W. Gammon was probably necessary for the early coup of taking over security for the American Bankers Association, but more large clients followed in short order as the Burns agency rapidly scaled up in size and range. Within his first few years, Burns secured similar contracts with the National Retail Dry Goods Association and large hotel chains, and even began earning commissions from the railroad industry, the Pinkertons' mainstay.

Still, regardless of the economic logic, there can be no doubt Burns personally relished every opportunity to upstage the Pinkertons, whether as a businessman or a detective. After dramatically achieving the former in his first year back in private practice, he met with a genuinely explosive opportunity to accomplish the latter in his second.

On September 30, 1910, detective-entrepreneur William Burns was once again heading west to California, to Los Angeles specifically, for a conference of his new clients the American Bankers Association. Twenty-four hours later his destination was unchanged, but in every other detail his original plans were abandoned for a new and considerably more significant mission. As America was historically reminded not quite 91 years later, though, the sudden and violent destruction of a landmark building in the center of a major city can have such results.

In this instance, the *Los Angeles Times* building was the object of terror tactics. At 1 a.m. on October 1, a powerful explosion shook the entire building. The immediate damage soon caused the second floor to collapse, shattering gas mains and thereby adding considerable fuel to the fires. At least 100 employees were trapped within the burning building; ultimately 21 people died and nearly all of the others present received severe injuries. The *Times* reported on the grim events the next day:

> A mass of wreckage and twisted steel girders projecting from heaps of debris, and underneath it all the bodies of a score of dead employees, was all that was left at daylight this morning of the Times-Mirror Company's newspaper plant, at First Street and Broadway.
>
> The explosion occurred at 1 o'clock this morning and was followed

instantly by a fire that enveloped the whole structure in flames, completely wrecked the main three-story building and the adjoining six-story plant...

Such an attack, on the headquarters of a major newspaper no less, prompted a tsunami of alarm and controversy when combined with a dramatic figure like Burns and the volatile politics of the era. No one claimed responsibility for the *Times* bombing, but there was no shortage of suspects. This was the age of violent agitation by anarchists, labor groups, and communists, as well as violent reprisals by industrial interests and governments against anyone who challenged them—as Burns could personally testify based on his experiences in San Francisco. The *Times'* belligerently antilabor owner, Harrison Gray Otis, immediately fingered his union adversaries for the bombing and began demanding a violent crackdown on them. Mayor George Alexander, with a somewhat cooler head, felt similar urgency in solving the crime but rather less desire to start a war. He needed someone who was not only highly qualified, but would provide a reassuring reputation for investigative ability and for fairness, as well. The mayor promptly wired William Burns for help.

Burns's fresh reputation as a principled, progressive champion against the western syndicates made him an obvious choice. As did his official renunciation of strike work, and his more general denunciation of the main alternative option, the Pinkertons, whom labor groups still perceived as innately hostile a generation after Homestead. Upon meeting his honest, open-minded outside investigator, however, Mayor Alexander may have felt a sudden rush of vertigo as Burns wasted no time before declaring the bombing an act of the prominent Ironworkers union leader, John McNamara.

This kind of thing shouldn't have been so surprising, coming from Burns. Hunt writes that "Burns never learned to control his need for dramatic announcements, even at risk of annoying clients. It was, after all, one means of becoming a legend." The *Times* bombing was one of the best, and worst, examples; given not only the charged politics of the case but the reasons behind his own hiring, Burns obviously would have been well served to withhold his theories until after he had a case for once. But as usual, at least some sound reasoning lay behind his theatrical gestures, all the same.

The mutual antipathy between unions and the *Times'* owner was well established, after all, and two more bombs discovered on the morning of October 2 reinforced the appearance of someone targeting union opponents. One turned up at Otis's own home, and a second at that of an officer of the Merchants and Manufacturers Association. The latter, moreover, was disarmed intact. Upon arriving in Los Angeles, Burns had gone directly to examine the sites of all the bombings, successful and otherwise, and he found the intact bomb nearly identical in construction to a bomb recovered from a Peoria steel firm by Burns agents a few weeks earlier. In his mind, at least, the Ironworkers union was obviously behind the bomb attempt in Illinois, and therefore plainly behind the new campaign as well. Mayor Alexander probably found this reasoning highly speculative, but he left Burns on the case.

Meanwhile, as the only difference between the two bombs was the newer model's use of high-powered 80% dynamite in place of nitroglycerin, Burns ordered his men to begin checking records of 80% dynamite purchases. This was a powerful and unusual compound, and the few sales tended to stand out. Gradually, inquiries led to two known anarchists named David Caplan and Matthew Schmidt, along with hints of a third, more elusive figure going by the name of "J.B. Bryce." Then the men's trail seemed to break up in the Northwest, just as that of "J.W. McGraw" had after the attempted bombing in Peoria.

Avoiding W.J. Burns had never been easy, however. And thanks to large, steady clients like the American Bankers Association whose conference had been his original destination in Los Angeles, Burns now had a national network of agents at his command, including his two surviving sons. (George had died of tuberculosis soon after the San Francisco efforts' end, sadly.) After progress on the West Coast stalled out, Raymond Burns and other agents back in Illinois rediscovered their suspects' trail, identifying J.W. McGraw as Ortie McManigal of Chicago. Following McManigal on a trip to Wisconsin led to an accomplice, who signed his hotel register as "Frank Sullivan" but matched the description of J.B. Bryce perfectly. While shadowing the men in Wisconsin, the Burns agents took further advantage of this break by combining a couple of tricks from the Pinkertons' history, and improved camera technology: when Bryce and McManigal went deer hunting they encountered two other sportsmen who chatted amiably for a while, and then took a souvenir snapshot before parting company. In short order, copies of this memento were on the way to Los Angeles and William Burns.

At this point, the detective could claim respectable if unspectacular progress for his months of work. Showing the new photos to witnesses from the night of the explosion, agents in L.A. were able to connect Bryce with a man seen carrying a large case into the alley behind the *Times*. There was every reason to support the investigation further. Then, Burns encountered the first real setback in the history of his new agency when Los Angeles's mayor unceremoniously dropped him from the case. The move didn't come completely out of nowhere; aside from his initial brash prediction, which Burns had so far failed to substantiate, he had disagreed with Mayor Alexander over a demand for daily reports. This new requirement was largely the product of pressure on the mayor from others, particularly an attorney who had sparred with Burns in San Francisco and was now directing a special grand jury organized after the bombing. Having little love for Burns, he eagerly made noise about the pace of the detective's investigation as well as his secrecy. Burns insisted that circulating constant reports on every discovery would compromise the case, but the mayor, caught in the middle, had made it a condition of employment and when Burns refused, he was off the case.

Or rather, Burns was off the city's payroll. He and his agency remained on the case. Burns simply would not back down from a challenge once accepted; unlike the Pinkertons he refused to suspend such a compelling investigation for something so trivial as the lack of a paying client. He still ran a for-profit business with bills to pay, of course, but he convinced himself that he could recoup the costs eventually once he cracked the case. In a throwback to the early days of detection, he proceeded in the hope of claiming the considerable reward money posted for the crime.

Over the following year, as the expenses mounted, Burns kept up the surveillance of McManigal and his friend, both of whom remained on the move. While trailing Bryce in Cincinnati, agents finally made the discovery Burns had been waiting for since day one of the assignment: a visit to his mother revealed that the suspicious figure whom witnesses had placed at the crime scene hours before the explosion was actually one James McNamara. His better known brother was none other than the Ironworkers' Secretary-Treasurer John McNamara, Burns's favored candidate for the mastermind all along.

Though rarely lacking in confidence in himself or his solutions, Burns must have been electrified by the news. Yet the other side of his determination was a deep reservoir of patience, particularly when working on a case. He was accustomed to years-long investigations before finally pouncing, hopefully with such overwhelming evidence to overawe his quarry along with everyone else. So he waited, insistent on finding some more substantive connection linking not only McManigal and James McNamara, but John as well, to the crime. It was a risky decision—no one was paying for the hours of surveillance, and at one point the still-at-liberty McManigal planted another bomb at an iron works in Los Angeles. Fortunately no one was killed, but the fixation on John McNamara could well have had disastrous costs. Burns was used to risks, though, even reckless ones, and so far they had proved worth the reward.

They continued to in his latest gamble. In early April 1911, agents observed McManigal and James McNamara boarding a train once more, this time carrying large, heavy cases. In Boston upon hearing the news, Burns dispatched his son Raymond to take up the watch in Detroit. When the two suspects were unable to get a hotel room immediately, they reluctantly checked the bulky cases, at which point the Burns agency finally seized its opportunity. In company with police detectives from Chicago, Raymond had McManigal and McNamara arrested, though the Burns detectives continued keeping their cards close to their vest. They claimed that the arrest was not for bombing, but for a recent safe-cracking in Chicago; completely innocent of this crime, the pair offered little resistance to extradition to Illinois. Upon stepping out of the train in the Windy City, they were met by William Burns, ready to perform one of his trademark dramatic revelations. Burns revealed that the prisoners were actually to be charged for the *Times* bombing, and aside from whatever other evidence Burns had, both must have known that the cases full of guns and bomb parts that they had carried to Detroit hardly suggested innocence.

Having unveiled his evidence, Burns usually focused next on splitting off the member of a team most likely to give up his partners, but on this occasion he didn't even need to make an effort. Ortie McManigal immediately pleaded to speak with the detective in private and proceeded to spend hours volunteering everything Burns could want to know. Burns had planned to lean on McManigal anyway, as the subordinate and an outsider to the McNamaras' literal brotherhood, but even he must have been surprised by how readily the high-strung conspirator turned on everyone. Names and dates, the *Times* bombing and other jobs as well; McManigal gave up everything in his desperation for leniency.

As the long effort finally approached a payoff, Burns may have felt euphoria, or righteous vindication, or even apprehension about the remaining loose ends. Yet at least a little of his winking showman's bravado is plainly visible in the next step he took. Concerned that news of the arrests might tip off John McNamara before authorities could arrest him, as well, Burns casually dialed Mrs. McManigal's home. Skipping any pretense at identifying himself, Burns reported in clipped tones that James and Ortie had been picked up on a safe-cracking charge. Dropping vague references to orders and prearranged plans, he then said that Mrs. McManigal should contact "a certain party" about wiring funds to the pair, before hanging up. The deception, necessary or not, apparently did no harm. On April 21, Burns's own genuine plans went into motion with almost clockwork precision. Upon word from Los Angeles, local police arrested John McNamara in the middle of an Ironworkers executive board meeting in Indianapolis, while police and Burns agency detectives gathered up bomb parts, explosives and other evidence in a series of raids.

Out of the busy and varied career of William Burns, a number of cases offer claims as the greatest. The Monroe note mystery may demonstrate the most inventiveness, while the crusade in San Francisco may have shown the most resolve; a relatively minor murder investigation in Georgia in 1913 could be Burns's finest hour in terms of courage and integrity. But for all the attention he won over the years, positive and negative, nothing generated more headlines than the *Los Angeles Times* bombing.

At first, Burns was deluged with praise by newspapers. He soaked up the attention, giving long interviews to reporters and readily sharing stories about the investigation. Former president Theodore Roosevelt sent a personal telegram of congratulations and "gratitude for your signal service to American citizenship." Soon, however, a backlash erupted. Unions and socialist groups, though regularly denounced by many as a dangerous menace, were also enjoying what proved to be their greatest levels of support in American history. Labor activists and their allies rallied nationwide to defend the McNamaras and to vilify those they blamed for framing them. Chief among the appointed villains was a man who had spent nearly a decade battling *against* corporate predators and their corrupt allies in government.

Taking note of his castigation by nearly everyone in the space of just a few short years, Burns stormily declared "When I'm employed to find out who committed a crime, I go out and find him. I don't care a row of red apples who he is or where he is." While this skirted the fact that he had declared McNamara the culprit before even beginning the case, he had a point. The McNamaras' defenders didn't care. In addition to accusing him of a conspiracy against innocent men, a few extreme individuals sent death threats, while a propaganda film distributed as part of the campaign depicted Burns as a cruel, brutish enforcer.

Aided by such portrayals of the case, advocates for the McNamaras also raised considerable sums for their defense. That defense was led in court by none other than Clarence Darrow, whose most famous cases still lay in his future but who was already considered a brilliant lawyer. At trial, Darrow managed to goad Burns into appearing testy and uncooperative, though much of the good he may have done his clients was offset by a jury bribery scandal; Darrow escaped any official censure though even Burns's critical biographer, Hunt, asserts without qualification that Darrow was guilty. In fairness, of course, Hunt also argues that Burns broke the law repeatedly and "outrageously" in the bombing investigation, particularly in his handling of the arrests, for which he was charged with kidnapping and even sought by the police himself, though also avoiding any formal penalties. Hunt suggests that "The sad truth is that the ethical standard among lawyers and detectives of the day was remarkably low."

In the larger picture, neither jury bribing nor kidnapping, whether alleged or real, compared with the atrocity of the bombing campaign in Los Angeles and elsewhere. And on the first of December 1911, all of the side controversies as well as the main arguments were tossed aside when the McNamara brothers confessed and pleaded guilty. Their attorneys had advised them that the prosecution case was "impregnable," and they listened, though they would later condemn their lawyers for poor counsel. The words of *The New York Times* are representative of the country's reaction. In an editorial titled "Apologies Due a Detective" it declared Burns "the greatest detective certainly, and perhaps the only really great detective, the only detective of genius, whom this country has produced."

The great detective himself insisted afterward, with some credibility, that he had remained confident throughout the whole roller coaster affair. He was sure of his case, after all, and with enough persistence and determination that had almost invariably been enough throughout his career. By this point, being vilified affected Burns little more than similar accusations had affected Jonathan Whicher in the Tichborne Claimant case decades before, or, for that matter, more than losing his funding had affected Burns himself earlier in the bombing investigation. Burns may have spent as much as $14,000 pursuing the McNamaras (close to $350,000 adjusted for a century of inflation). In the end, he probably recouped nearly all of his financial outlay through collecting rewards associated with the case, just as he had felt confident that he would. Just as he had felt certain that McNamara was behind the bombing, and that he would prove it in time.

Following his triumph in Los Angeles, Burns wanted for almost nothing except enough time for all the opportunities opened to him. The Burns agency was in greater demand than ever, and so was William Burns personally. By 1911 his celebrity was such that New York saw a play based on his exploits, *The Argyle Case*, open on Broadway. Burns himself finally enjoyed a literal turn in the spotlight following the opening night performance, basking in the audience's applause; the dreams of his Ohio boyhood 40 years before had been realized at last. Two years later Burns published *The Masked War*, about the *Times* bombing investigation, and, while sensationalized, his first literary effort too was generally well received. Everywhere he went people were eager to meet the famous detective, to ask his opinions about issues of the day and listen to his stories. It seemed for a number of years that he simply could not fail whatever he tried.

Controversy and critics never vanished, entirely. Much of the labor movement never forgave Burns for his persecution of the McNamaras, even after their confession; in turn Burns seemed to discard some of his scruples about strike work and began readily accepting roles amid conflicts between ownership and labor. Meanwhile, in spite of labor's disapproval adding yet another similarity between them, Burns remained on hostile terms with his chief rival William Pinkerton. The show business gimmickry of Burns, along with the seemingly insatiable public appetite for it, set the older detective's teeth grinding. And while he had neither the inclination nor the nature for a real challenge to Burns in the realm of celebrity, Pinkerton did pursue active efforts against him. Just like Burns, Pinkerton considered his rival an unethical blot on the profession; Pinkerton, however, not only criticized Burns but arranged various formal charges against him as well. He objected to various of Burns's practices, particularly his eager use of new wiretapping methods, as well as some of his detectives who didn't have the clean backgrounds which the Pinkerton Agency demanded.

Burns certainly did operate outside of the rules on occasion; this hardly made him unique among detectives, but times were changing, and efforts among both detectives and government authorities were beginning to professionalize the industry with licensing and other standards. Yet if Burns's temperament always remained better suited to the older "Wild West" detection of Pinkerton's father or Isaiah Lees, his critics were still sometimes plainly in the wrong. Even the responsible, businesslike Pinkertons. In the tragic case of Mary Phagan, the competition between Burns and his rivals played out at unusually close range and the outcome proved a strong rebuttal to William Pinkerton's assertion of superior principles.

*

A watchman was the first to report the body of Mary Phagan, found beaten and strangled in the basement of the Atlanta pencil factory where she worked. The murder of an innocent young white girl in the Jim Crow south of 1913 swiftly aroused intense passions and intense prejudices. Immediately following news of the murder, city police rounded up several black men for questioning, but suspicion soon affixed itself to an "outsider" of another sort. The factory superintendent Leo Frank was the last person known to have seen Mary alive, the two having remained behind on the day of her death when other company employees left early to attend a parade. Leo Frank was also Jewish and, therefore, every bit as subject to widespread bigotry as the community's black populace. As Atlanta's police began questioning him and local newspapers competed to whip up hysteria over the murder, Frank decided to seek help from the independent detective force of the Pinkerton agency. They would approach the situation rationally and professionally, and prove what had really happened, or so he hoped.

Unfortunately for Frank, Pinkerton detective Harry Scott didn't care for his client any more than the city detectives did. Scott decided that their theory about Frank murdering the girl *was* what had really happened. He readily coordinated his own investigation with the local police, and in the process found a custodian named Jim Conley who claimed Frank had asked him for help in disposing of the murdered girl's body. Thanks in part to the Pinkertons' "help," Frank was found guilty.

As with the McNamaras, many observers believed Frank was being railroaded. Unlike the *Times* bombing case, though, Frank continued to maintain his innocence, and the condemned man's defenders looked to William Burns as a potential savior rather than villain. In March 1914, as the Georgia justice system prepared to set a date for Frank's execution, the northern "Save Leo Frank Committee" appealed to Burns for help. The careers of more than one of his predecessors offered reasons for Burns to decline: like Jonathan Whicher he was being asked to take up a murder investigation long after the crime, with local police likely to be unhelpful if not outright hostile, while the prospect of endangering his business interests in the South was one that Allan Pinkerton had known 70 years earlier. Yet neither man had backed out of daunting situations; nor did Burns. Ever since he was a child, the chance to overcome adversity and resistance only spurred William Burns to greater effort. The chance to show up the Pinkertons was a considerable further temptation. So the detective went down to Georgia, and he found plenty of adversity and resistance on offer. The police clearly disapproved of his involvement, and threatening letters poured in. By 1914, Burns was no stranger to these, or even entirely to real violence, though being assaulted in Marietta and narrowly escaping an angry lynch mob must have raised a gingery eyebrow or two.

It also convinced Burns that regardless of who had killed Mary Phagan, Leo Frank had gotten nothing like a fair hearing. Burns spent weeks in the tense, hostile community pursuing his own thorough investigation of the murder. At last he announced his conclusion, and named as Phagan's assailant the custodian and key witness against Frank, Jim Conley. Looking into Conley's background, Burns had found a woman named Annie Carter who claimed that Conley had boasted to her of the crime. Moreover, she had dozens of love notes in Conley's handwriting, which not only confirmed the man's interest in her but suggested an obsessive, disturbed individual. Unfortunately for Annie Carter, Conley was not the last man to take an unwelcome interest in her. After newspapers published her statements, Burns did his best to keep her under wraps and even moved her to New Orleans for a time, but the Georgia authorities found her and returned her to Atlanta for "questioning." While in custody she retracted her statements, and, with that, any hope for overturning Frank's conviction in court collapsed.

Cutting his losses was not a habit Burns practiced, however. He took his case to the press, lending his own reputation and fame to the protests by Frank's defenders, much as his new friend Arthur Conan Doyle had done for another persecuted outsider several years earlier. As in the matter of George Edalji, the evidence was persuasive, even if the criminal authorities found reasons to reject it. The case assembled by Burns ultimately convinced Georgia's Governor John Slaton to commute Frank's sentence from execution to life in prison, in a courageous move which Gene Caesar describes as "an act of political suicide." It was a minor victory, at most, yet resentment toward Frank had grown so intense that even this was intolerable. A lynch mob overruled the governor, carrying out the sentence of death anyway after removing Frank from prison, entirely undisturbed by the guards. Some historians including Hunt have speculated that "The Knights of Mary Phagan" subsequently cata-lyzed a resurgence in Ku Klux Klan violence. Whether there was any direct link or not, Burns did not forget the encounter with hatred and intolerance and demonstrated it some years later.

At the time, however, there was little he could do but speak out, one last time, against the injustice. An unusually somber Burns told reporters that "throughout the United States and even in Georgia the prepondering senti-ment of thoughtful and fairminded men is that an innocent man is slain." Within the larger picture, it was also a rare defeat, and one that might have prompted a measure of sympathy from William Pinkerton given his family's own efforts to defeat mob justice in years past. Yet the affair had also produced more publicity for the insufferable Burns, this time directly contrasting with the Pinkerton agency's dismal role earlier in the same case.

Along with the general approval, Burns's efforts on Frank's behalf had also won a few new enemies, meanwhile, and per the old adage William Pinkerton had potential friends among them. Burns and Pinkerton were both members of the International Association of Chiefs of Police, but most of the members served on public forces, and in the wake of the Phagan case Georgia's del-egates were furious. Pinkerton made common cause with them and managed to secure Burns's expulsion from the IACP in 1915. The organization denied afterward that the decision had any relation to the events in Atlanta, and there were legitimate grounds for criticizing Burns. A few years afterward, Burns himself got the wrong man in the "Holiday Crook" crimes, and it was the Pinkertons' turn to correct their rival's poor judgment. Nonetheless, the sharply contrasting attitudes seen in the Phagan case must weigh heavily in arguments between Pinkerton and Burns.

It did not end them, of course. Burns remained a lightning rod for criti-cism, justified and otherwise. His conduct in the land fraud case years earlier returned as the subject of new controversy in 1911, when the Taft adminis-tration pardoned one of the men convicted through Burns's efforts. In 1913,

South Carolina's governor announced he would pardon anyone convicted with evidence provided by Burns, largely in response to the detective's investigation of him on behalf of his opponent in the previous election. In 1916 a court actually found Burns guilty of a misdemeanor, for illegally entering a law office to copy letters and install surveillance equipment as part of work for J.P. Morgan & Co. This, in turn, aided one of many attempts at getting his detective's license suspended, though the suspension hearing's decision was overturned on appeal.

Nonetheless, even as Pinkerton and other detractors pursued various charges against Burns with occasional success, his reputation remained largely intact. For great numbers of people, Burns was still a stalwart opponent of fraud and injustice. In addition to corporate clients like Morgan or the Bankers Association, state and local governments throughout America turned to the Burns agency for help; as governor of New Jersey, Woodrow Wilson hired them to root out corruption in Atlantic City, in what proved a memorable episode. Through intermediaries, Burns organized a dummy company proposing a new concrete "boardwalk" and secured promises of support from various city council members in exchange for generous bribes. Their subsequent embarrassment was all the worse upon learning not only that they had been set up but that, furthermore, each of the bills they accepted from Burns had been marked with tiny pinholes; when held up in bright light each note revealed the word "GRAFT."

Mischief like this, if unsportsmanlike as well as unprofessional, demonstrate that Burns still had a good deal of enthusiasm as he entered middle age. After the bitter outcome of the Mary Phagan case, Burns and his agency both coasted on the reputation earned from earlier work, somewhat; the celebrity detective continued to make headlines but it was nearly as often for a controversy as for a coup. When America entered World War I, the Burns family contributed dutifully, though unspectacularly. Burns Agency security guards kept an eye on various munitions plants and shipping terminals, and detectives worked to thwart spies and saboteurs, though all in all, these efforts were humdrum compared to those of earlier years. Sherman Burns served in Europe and apparently enjoyed the luck of the Irish just like his father, returning home without a scratch. By 1920, he and his brother Raymond were managing much of the agency's business affairs; administration had never been of particular interest to their father anyway, and as Burns, now a grandfather, entered his sixties he might very reasonably have begun easing into a well earned and comfortable retirement. With official control over the agency and (unlike the Pinkerton dynasty) an easy partnership with his sons, Burns could have taken a personal hand in cases when they interested him and spent the rest of his time writing stories or charming live audiences. And in the absence of any further great challenge, even Burns may have been content to do just that.

He very likely would have been more content, and much better off generally, had he done so.

The genesis of America's Federal Bureau of Investigation was almost glacially slow. America's first great detective, Allan Pinkerton, had laid the groundwork for a national investigative service in the middle of the 19th century. In the decades that followed, his private agency occupied that role on an occasional contract basis, first under Allan and then his sons. As time went by, the federal government assumed some of those duties itself, but only gradually. During World War I, William Pinkerton lobbied repeatedly for a national intelligence service without any direct success.

Yet the feds were lurching in that direction. In 1908, Congress had banned "loaning" of Secret Service agents to the Department of Justice, so President Roosevelt authorized the Dept. of Justice to create its own small force. By 1923, this Bureau of Investigation had steadily swelled to more than 1,000 employees, and America finally had a large scale, national investigative agency to match those of Britain, France, and other Western governments. William Pinkerton must have heartily approved in broad outline. Yet he must have been completely appalled by the choice of its new director.

The appointment of William Burns as the fifth chief of what we now call the FBI, however, had plenty of reasons to recommend it. Burns was not only an admired national hero, in spite of regular controversies. He was also a genuinely brilliant investigator, and moreover a veteran *government* investigator. Washington knew Burns and he knew Washington—or at least believed he did. His background before signing up with the Secret Service or even becoming a detective at all was a point in his favor, as well, at any rate from the perspective of the "Ohio Gang" that held much of the power under the presidency of Warren G. Harding. Attorney General Harry Daugherty, who knew Burns personally from his early life in the Buckeye State, urged him to join up and take charge of the new Bureau.

Yet there were good reasons why Burns should have shared at least some of William Pinkerton's apprehensions of disaster. While Burns had few peers as a detective, administrative responsibility was as noted neither a strength nor a particular interest for him. He successfully directed teams on many investigations, but directing a sprawling young government agency was a demanding task, particularly for a man approaching the sunset of his career. In addition to the technical challenges, meanwhile, the job would involve political pitfalls of which Burns should have been particularly wary. On a personal level, Burns had a great gift for judging and manipulating people, but in the world of broader political concerns he was well out of his depth. He had always announced his opinions readily, with little regard for how they fit into any coherent alignment, either with one another or with those of others. As a famous private detective this made him interesting and newsworthy; as a prominent political appointee it was poison.

Much the same could be said of the administration he was being asked to serve. Historians generally regard the scandal-pocked Harding administration as the worst presidency in America's history. In fairness to Burns, mere months after Harding's inauguration this would have been difficult to foresee, even for a seasoned political observer. As for the rest, Burns had spent his entire career embracing challenge and risk, triumphing over doubters again and again. Even if he did perceive any peril in this new project, it only made it all the more enticing. So, as Gene Caesar notes in his biography, "on August 19, in what hindsight can call the worst mistake of his life, William J. Burns... accepted an appointment as Director of the federal Bureau of Investigation, which newsmen were already dubbing the FBI."

*

The Bureau's latest director could claim a few worthy achievements when he stepped down a few years later. He managed to complete American law enforcement's transition from the older and complicated Bertillon system of identification to fingerprinting and paved the way, not without opposition, for a national registry of fingerprint records. He also mounted a commendable campaign against the revived Ku Klux Klan. The forces of hatred and intolerance had been responsible for some of Burns's few, bitter defeats over his career, from an Indiana lynching that he investigated as a young PI but found that no local court would prosecute, to the dispiriting affair of Mary Phagan and Leo Frank. At last he had a chance to strike back, and did so unhesitatingly. Under Burns, the Bureau of Investigation harried Klan groups relentlessly and pushed them back toward fringe status.

Outside of these efforts, however, little else that followed Burns's acceptance of the Bureau post was positive. Never particularly concerned about privacy or civil liberties, Burns cast a wide net with surveillance of suspected labor radicals and spies, and sparred with the ACLU. At the same time he was also frustrated as an investigator, in what must have suggested a perfect opportunity to recapture his old magic: on September 16, 1920, a wagon-delivered bomb had detonated outside the office of J.P. Morgan on Wall Street, killing two dozen people and injuring hundreds. Burns continued to pursue the case for years, even after resigning from his agency to take charge of the Bureau. He probably took little notice of any formal separation between the two roles, admittedly, and as in his earlier great terrorism case may have borne much of the investigation's cost himself; Hunt speculates that "it is more likely that Burns had hired Burns to carry on the long investigation." Yet after two years of dogged effort, agents lost the prime suspect in eastern Europe, the main witness became unreliable, and the entire case slipped away from Burns's usually tenacious grip.

It's just possible that the resolute detective might have restored his dulled reputation in time, or at least left the Bureau with the legacy of having achieved credible progress. If he had only made better choices in the company he kept. Unfortunately, as Bureau chief he was a poor administrator in the employ of an even worse administrator, and after years of exposing fraud and corruption, Burns found himself serving one of the most corrupt presidencies in U.S. history. Worse, just like Harding, Burns failed personally to distance himself from scoundrels even long after he knew more than enough to recognize them.

For Burns, the association that proved fatal to his Bureau career was with one Gaston Means. Described as "an unctuous North Carolinian" by Laton McCartney in *The Teapot Dome Scandal*, Means is invariably depicted as a lying, underhanded and possibly unstable con artist by every author who mentions him. During World War I, Means not only worked for the Germans but did so while peddling information to the British as well. Reckless scams like this were Means's stock in trade, yet he somehow survived and even thrived for years by being not only slippery but genuinely useful to his employers, if neither reliable nor remotely loyal. Burns was neither the first nor the last to make use of Means's particular talent for the least savory aspects of intelligence operations. Unfortunately and unwisely, though, he may have been the most consistent.

The basic events of the Wheeler scandal, in which Burns finally had cause to rue his employment of Means, are complex but essentially straightforward and broadly agreed by all sources. In March 1924, Attorney General Daugherty pressed Burns to investigate Senator Burton Wheeler of Montana. Wheeler had recently become one of the loudest critics of the administration of President Coolidge, most of which, like Daugherty, had carried over from that of the late Harding. Daugherty claimed that Wheeler himself was using his office for illicit gain, helping private business associates win federal oil leases. Burns dispatched three agents to Montana, where they found evidence of closeness but no direct conflict of interest or corruption. Burns submitted a report, then directed his attention to other matters.

No one else was inclined to do anything of the kind, however; not Daugherty, not Wheeler, and certainly not Means. Ever eager to expand his web of connections, Means had by this time approached Daugherty in hopes of finding an additional patron. But whatever his other faults, Daugherty at least had the self-preservation instincts to rebuff all of Means's overtures and even ordered Burns to sever ties with him as well. Burns, whether convinced that Means was indispensable, or perhaps hoping to avoid his likely response to just such a brush-off, quietly ignored this order. This failed entirely to secure him against a vengeful Gaston Means.

Meanwhile, Senator Wheeler also had Daugherty in his sights. Particularly after a grand jury indicted him back home in Montana, barely a week after the pressure on Daugherty had finally forced his resignation; Daugherty denied any role in the indictment, but the oil lease deals figured prominently. The resourceful Means had already made contact with Wheeler and eagerly offered both encouragement and all of the information he could want about Daugherty.

During the Senate hearings that followed, Burns was inevitably called to testify, and questioned about the use of federal agents to investigate political opponents. Daugherty was likely counting on and expecting his old comrade to close ranks and deny as much as possible, but to his credit the veteran bluffer instead answered Senators' questioning truthfully. Burns's testimony thus directly contradicted statements Daugherty had already given. Unsurprisingly, the usually combative Burns was subdued; *The New York Times* described his appearance while testifying as "ashen-faced." Two weeks later, following additional details of Daugherty's political motivations in pointing the Bureau toward Wheeler, Burns acceded to the new attorney general's pointed request and turned in his resignation.

Such are the basic facts of the scandal that finished Burns at the Bureau of Investigation. Ninety years of scandals later, they seem to represent relatively minor offenses by themselves; Hunt, whose study generally disparages Caesar's biography, nonetheless reaches the same conclusion as the earlier author that "up to this point, Burns's only crime was bad judgment."

The larger issue of how to interpret "Wheelergate" and other scandals, in relation to the rest of Burns's life and career, is more elusive. The fiasco with Daugherty and Means was by no means an isolated blunder. Burns played fast and loose repeatedly throughout his career, and by the mid-1920s had been challenged for it more than once. In *The Teapot Dome Scandal: How Big Oil Bought the Harding White House and Tried to Steal the Country*, moreover,

Laton McCartney accuses Burns of active complicity in hushing up the Harding administration's crimes, corruption and debauchery. Yet even taken at face value, the Burns depicted by McCartney is still a puzzle left incomplete. *The Teapot Dome Scandal* makes no mention whatsoever of his long years battling graft and fraud, in which Burns placed himself and even his family at risk in return for a modest government salary, or his pursuit of cases like the *Times* bombing and Mary Phagan's murder, which plainly contradict an image of ruthless self-interest. Absent any explanation, the notion of Burns as "the [Ohio] gang's enforcer, its muscle," seems as much a one-dimensional caricature as the fiendish mastermind plotting against the innocent McNamara brothers in their silent propaganda film.

People do change over the course of a life. But there is actually very little explanation or evidence for Burns really changing his views or habits between his reign as hero and trials as villain. A thorough accounting of his life and career instead reveals a largely consistent William Burns, who in fact failed to adapt amid changing times and circumstances. Throughout his life, Burns was a talented man well aware of his own talent and convinced of the infallibility of his own judgment. He was a creative, artistic personality who found success not by following a system of rules but by learning how to manipulate them and other people—much like his most talented opponents. Unlike Baldwin Bredell or Abe Ruef, Burns pursued interests other than his own gain. The same could be said of the McNamaras—they certainly considered themselves heroes as much as did Burns—yet the detective differed in fighting his battles by means that weren't harmful or destructive. While he readily bluffed and schemed by every means imaginable, Burns probably made less use of violence or direct pressure than almost any detective of note. Instead, the society that employed him repeatedly praised his work as *constructive* and virtuous. It was thus all too easy for Burns to see himself and his methods in the right when his opponents were thieves, swindlers or murderers and, time after time, found guilty and sent to jail.

Yet Burns was not a sheriff dispensing justice in the Wild West. He was a detective working in a recognizably modern, urban and complex world, which became moreso throughout his career. When he began exploring the work of a detective it was an evolving profession, where improvisation and flexibility were not only useful but accepted as completely normal. Forty years after the Franklin County prosecutor casually turned an election fraud investigation over to a local tailor, however, Burns was operating in both a much wider world and a changed one, as well. Its complexities had already challenged him, many times: in both the political opposition and the legal challenges to his handling of the *Times* investigation, in the controversy over his use of wiretapping, in the conviction for the kind of illegal trespass that had been routine in his Secret Service days. Burns nonetheless barged ahead through it all, as fiercely determined as ever, and, through a combination of luck and the generally commendable results he achieved, could dismiss his critics and remain confident in himself as the hero who would win out.

At the Bureau of Investigation both of these factors failed him at last. Burns's good luck ran out at the same time that he was deep in a situation too complex, and compromised, for any clear contrast between heroes and villains to redeem his own fibs, cheats and disregard for the rules. Through it all, Burns continued to act honestly and uprightly as he had understood the concepts; he ran a Bureau of Investigation that persecuted violent rulebreakers but didn't always bother with the rules itself, and readily lent a hand when an old friend like Daugherty had a "special" assignment, yet when called on the carpet to account for himself Burns told the truth rather than cross the line into an outright fraud on legitimate authorities. Burns, it seems, just never entirely grasped the subtleties on which his looser, more instinctive idea of right and wrong tripped up.

One last scandal, a few years after he retired from the Bureau, probably sums up much of the rise and fall of William Burns. In 1927, Burns was tried for jury tampering during an assignment for the Sinclair oil empire. Going back to his first real outing as a detective nearly a half-century earlier, Burns had regularly been frustrated by rigged juries and tried to prevent it; though already challenged on them a time or two before, he considered his efforts nothing more than legitimate surveillance for the purpose of preventing tampering. The court nonetheless fined him and his son Sherman $1,000 each and issued a citation of contempt along with a 15-day jail sentence, though the latter two were overturned. Infuriated by the whole proceeding, Burns insisted throughout that "My men didn't do anything for Harry Sinclair that I haven't done for the federal government hundreds of times!" The fact that he had often broken rules for the federal government, yet might not consistently get away with it in all circumstances, never seemed to occur to the old detective.

The great triumphs of Burns's life belonged mainly to the late-Victorian and Edwardian eras, before World War I. Despite his persistence, there was no last great coup to redeem the troubled years that followed. After the scandal of his exit from the Bureau of Investigation, Arthur Conan Doyle quietly dropped his correspondence with Burns and avoided discussing him, as did more than a few others who had formerly admired the detective. Burns and his wife settled in Florida, living there until his death in April 1932.

In his last years of semiretirement, Burns wrote a few more stories of his earlier adventures though they, like the small number of fictional heroes directly inspired by him, have since been largely forgotten while his other "retirement projects" such as the work for Sinclair have lived on to tarnish his legacy. William Pinkerton, who died just months before Burns left the Bureau in disgrace, had proved right in his perception of a more predictable, bureaucratized, businesslike investigative profession, even if his rival could never see it. The consequences of that trend did, however, eventually produce one particular twist which might have united the two old foes one last time in groans of revulsion: at the turn of the 21st century, the successors of Pinkerton's and the Burns agency were joined together under common ownership, following purchase by the Swedish conglomerate Securitas AB.

CHAPTER EIGHT
ELLIS PARKER

"An officer never becomes any bigger than his
friends make him, and without friends he soon
strikes his level. To have the people's confidence,
this is the most valuable asset an officer can have."

IN THE LAST WEEKS of William Burns's life a shocking new crime, which
for notoriety eventually surpassed all of his own famous cases, baffled
American law enforcement. Age and ill health, though, meant the man
once hailed as "America's Sherlock Holmes" would have to miss out on it. And
so the Lindbergh baby kidnapping, one of the most enduringly famous cases
in the nation's history, came too late for any dramatic resolution by the once
equally famous man histories usually depict as the last of his kind.

Yet if the downfall of Burns did effectively mark the end of the great
detectives' time, one last survivor carried over into the new era that followed.
His career represents a last curtain call for the story of amazing real-life
sleuths, and, in certain curious ways, for the story of Burns. Like the older
detective, Ellis H. Parker was called America's answer to Arthur Conan
Doyle's champion of deduction. And like Burns certainly would have wished
to do, Parker eventually undertook a commission to solve the kidnapping that
every detective of his day was itching to investigate. All of this, moreover,
despite being merely a humble county detective near the end of a long career
spent entirely in a New Jersey small town.

Some clue to why not only Parker himself but others, including the state's governor and the director of the FBI, thought he might be somehow uniquely qualified for that highest of high profile mysteries is offered by a minor, unrelated case from the same period. The early 1933 assault on a San Francisco school by an armed man who killed a teacher in front of her class was at least as shocking as the Lindbergh kidnapping, even if much less reported. On the surface, it also should have been much less mysterious. The assailant's motivation was baffling—allegedly he was angered about the woman punishing one of his children—but his identity was known. But by the time local police arrived on the scene, Tom Coumas had vanished, and for all of their efforts they could find no clues to where he had gone. Desperate for some lead, the city's district attorney Gaurd Darrow decided to seek outside suggestions.

Rather than calling in one of the nation's prominent private investigative firms, Darrow turned to a veteran public detective—but aside from that his selection of Ellis Parker was, literally, very far afield. Yet that decision was neither random, nor even rare. In addition to being acquainted with Darrow from younger days, Parker was consulted many times during his career by law enforcement in other jurisdictions, other states, and occasionally even other countries. Several years earlier, *New Age* magazine had described Parker as the "most borrowed detective in international police history." After receiving Darrow's letter, he proceeded to examine the dead-end case and demonstrate why.

The Burlington County, New Jersey, detective spent months on his initial inquiries into Coumas. He conducted the entire unofficial investigation from his office in Mount Holly, 2,500 miles from the local San Francisco police, who remained at a loss throughout. Still, his apparent inability to achieve any better result eventually prompted occasional ribbing from Darrow. Parker endured these jabs quietly, and continued working, until eventually he was able to telegraph San Francisco with a more direct reply:

HAVE ESTABLISHED COUMAS MARRIED IN VANCOUVER,
WASHINGTON, NINETEEN FIFTEEN
COME EAST AND LEARN
ELLIS PARKER

It was vintage Parker. His pronouncement was the result of nothing more mysterious than thorough observation, basic deduction, and patient follow-up. Yet it was more than others, tasked with the same problem and considerably better positioned to solve it, had achieved. Parker, a simple county detective entirely willing to pursue such slow, diligent inquiries, recognized his own ability and quite enjoyed showing it off. He could certainly enjoy gently tweaking someone who foolishly dared doubt him, though his sense of humor worked both ways and he could enjoy a joke at his own expense as well.

His feat of deduction was still only partially complete, in this case, but he had confidence that he would find his man. He had made his initial break-through by considering the ages of the widowed Coumas's four children; as the elder was 15, Parker concluded that Coumas had most likely married at least 16 years earlier. A methodical series of exchanges with state marriage bureaus followed, seeking record of a Thomas Coumas marrying in the years 1914 – 16, and eventually bore fruit. After tracking his quarry that far the detective was then able to turn up more of Coumas's history, determining that he had emigrated from Greece and, after some further inquiries, that he had entered the United States in 1914 in Portland, Oregon. Records there supplied the key information of the wanted man's original name: Smyrno Smyrnogranis. Upon relaying this alternate identity to law enforcement agencies throughout the continent, Parker quickly received news from Mexican authorities who had known nothing of Coumas, but could report that Smyrnogranis had just recently taken ship to Greece. When he arrived, police were ready and waiting for him. As John Reisinger notes in *Master Detective: The Life and Crimes of Ellis H. Parker, America's Real-Life Sherlock Holmes*, "Ellis Parker had tracked down an international fugitive without leaving Burlington County."

Parker's career resembles a condensed version of the whole history of American detection, from the unofficial "borrowing" which recalls Burns at the Secret Service, all the way back through the early frontier justice of Allan Pinkerton. At first glance, this seems odd, given Parker's distance from pioneering detectives' world in time as well as in space. Born in 1871, he was just entering his teens when Pinkerton died in 1884; by the time he took the first steps toward his own detective career another durable public servant, Isaiah Lees, was less than a decade from the end of his own. And, unlike New Jersey's adopted son Lees, Parker spent his entire career in the civilized Northeast.

Yet Parker's territory was an odd little corner of the Northeast, almost detached from the urban hubs around it. Burlington County, New Jersey, sits about 70 miles from Lees's New York area hometown of Paterson, but it may as well have been a world away, even decades after Lees decamped for the West. In some ways this was and remains the nature of New Jersey, itself: a small state jutting into the urban centers of New York and Philadelphia at either end, but at the same time home to areas so undeveloped as to spawn the name "pine barrens," and legends of mysterious and perhaps supernatural creatures. This region of oddly rural landscapes between two of the nation's largest cities provided a uniquely atmospheric setting for one last larger than life detective career. Even in Parker's own lifetime the seeming timelost, frontier landscape of his early years drew notice. In 1930, reporter Henry Beck wrote a newspaper feature on Parker's youth as a country fiddler in Brindle Town, subtitled "Village Where Ellis Parker Fiddled Ghostly Place." By Beck's visit, the lively hamlet of 50 years before had largely receded into mist. Hinting at strange rumors, even "cults and queer people," he suggested that "there is an inexplicable weirdness to the sands and swamps of the pine towns, occupied and not occupied. Brindle Town with its memories is a ghostly place."

This may exaggerate, but the context of Parker's much retold origin does, all the same, seem curiously like a mislaid piece of the pioneering West from a generation or two earlier. By the year of his first detective case, in 1891, electric lighting, telephones and even automobiles were appearing in the cities where William Burns was battling counterfeiters as a Secret Service operative. Yet just beyond the outskirts of one of them, Ellis Parker was earning a living performing at barn dances as part of the "Brindle Town orchestra," along with two friends. (Beck notes that "Payment was for the most part in silver but often Ellis received five and ten cent cranberry tickets" for the produce of local cranberry bogs, instead.)

Born to a Quaker family on land now part of Fort Dix, Parker was by all accounts a talented fiddler and entirely content with rustic and bohemian existence. Even after the official commencement of his detective career, Parker continued performing with the "orchestra" for several more years. He had good reason—as was the case for other accidental detectives in the West of decades before, crime solving apparently remained more of a local, improvised matter in Burlington County into the 1890s. When 19-year-old Ellis left a dance late one night to find his father's horse and wagon gone, along with the fiddle he had set beside them while collecting his fee, he wasn't entirely without resources. But the resources available to him were certainly rough. Burlington County didn't even have a full-time sheriff, and the likeliest source of aid was in fact a private, organized vigilante society dating back to the Civil War. Known as "the Monmouth, Ocean, and Burlington County Detecting and Pursuing Association," the group's primary service was thwarting horse theft, still a serious threat to a man's livelihood in that era.

Parker's recruitment of the Association may have been little more than a precaution anyway, or perhaps a courtesy, as he had a suspect firmly in mind. When he and an Association member found horse, wagon and fiddle all together in that suspect's barn, the testimony of his instincts proved impressive enough that the Association flipped things around, recruiting *him*.

Under the circumstances, signing up Ellis Parker for the Pursuing Association was a promising idea, given that his main occupation as a fiddler gave him a broad familiarity with all the region's rural crossroads and backwoods outposts, as well as their inhabitants, and latest news. It was also fairly low risk, as the Association was only a loose, independent organization that paid its members no regular wage or salary. Any income was the product of rewards or bounties; an ineffective recruit would involve no direct cost. Parker proved commendably effective, however, both at uncovering crimes and at spreading word of that effectiveness. Whether a natural performer's instinct, or evidence of a growing enthusiasm for his accidental avocation, he kept local press informed of any interesting development in his work. The press consistently responded. Within a few years, the semi-professional detective had a modest reputation throughout Burlington County, and with it an offer of turning investigation into more than just a sideline.

Decades of evolution toward formal and professionalized law enforcement were finally, by 1894, making an impact even in the New Jersey pine country. An increasing and urbanizing population was gradually making the old informal ways inadequate, just as they had in much larger cities more than 70 years before. Since then, the major cities' responses had become widely copied institutions, and the Burlington County prosecutor's call for a full-time county detective met no particular controversy. Eckard P. Budd might have appeared to be courting one in selecting a 23-year-old fiddle player for the job, but if he was taking more risk than the Pursuing Association had, it was a calculated risk all the same. Parker had a promising reputation for tracking down wanted persons or catching them out in evasions. If the Pursuing Association saw a county detective as encroaching on their trade, hiring one of their own for the role could help deflect resentment. Finally, Parker may simply have been as qualified as anyone available. While he lacked formal training in criminology, that was still a rarity in much of the country, and particularly in Burlington County. And unlike any outside lawman Budd might have considered, Parker had a good store of local knowledge and connections, which had only increased since the Pursuing Association had recognized the same resource.

Thus, in the space of a few short years, a young man went from fiddling at country dances for cranberry tickets, to part-time pursuer of horse thieves, to Burlington County's chief (and only) detective. Which, at least in a narrow sense, is very nearly the entire career history of Ellis Parker. He continued moonlighting as a fiddler for a few more years before retiring from the Brindle Town orchestra. In time, he gradually acquired staff to supervise in his job for the county. But his official title and rank effectively remained the same, from the first day of his job to the last.

In large part, Parker's unusually brief résumé can be explained by his life-long residence in Burlington County, New Jersey. The region grew and changed through his long career, but always remained apart from the more complex hierarchies of big city life; even today the county seat of Mount Holly is home to fewer than 10,000 people. But Parker's career is also evidence of how the improvisational early days of detection, with fluid boundaries between government service and individual enterprise, had come and gone. By the beginning of the 20th century, communities large and small had divided up and codified responsibilities, and America's state and federal governments were gradually following along. The window of opportunity for a freewheeling career like that of William Burns was closing, as Burns himself discovered by the 1920s. Any further legends would need to be made without much scope for sliding back and forth among the most promising opportunities, and instead through patient, hard work over not only months or years, but decades.

This was just as well for the man whom everyone casually addressed as "Ellis," really. Though he shared some of the same affinity for headlines demonstrated by Burns, Parker was in many ways better suited for the steady, long-serving local role of an Isaiah Lees. Most of the great detectives had families, or at least married, but how much those families were a part of their lives varied greatly; like the man who shared his New Jersey upbringing as well as his eventual four-decades-plus career as detective, Parker was very much a family man rooted in the community he policed. After several years as Burlington County detective, he married a quiet girl named Cora Giberson, and settled down to a cozy domestic routine in Mount Holly. Much later, when Parker's long career itself became the subject of an occasional reporter's question, he would usually offer some kind of simple homespun explanation for his success, one such being "a good wife and a contented mind." In retrospect it may have been remarkably apt, as both an explanation for success, and a warning against disaster.

However much a supportive spouse and peace of mind can contribute to success as a detective, greatness requires something more. Noteworthy cases to solve must be counted an important part of that something, especially after much of the novelty of detection itself has long worn off. Fortunately for Detective Parker he did not want for memorable problems, even in the years before his reputation drew them to him from further afield. "An inexplicable weirdness" to the pine country east of Philadelphia may have contributed, but then again, maybe not; long enough service in any location will probably confront a detective with his or her share of bizarre discoveries. Lees could testify to this, and in time so could Parker, as both men unquestionably met with their full allotment of strange cases and perhaps a bit more.

Much of the work was, of course, still far from glamorous or novel. In *Master Detective*, Reisinger reports finding only limited and incomplete records from the earliest years of Parker's career, but his brief overview of crimes from the 1890s is probably representative of the proportions of unusual or grim disturbances to minor, everyday nuisances. In addition to the familiar work battling horse stealing and other theft, Parker investigated "rape, indecent exposure, throwing rocks at train windows, stealing cabbage, stealing a barrel of flowers, stealing an overcoat, blowing a safe, incest, and the attempted derailment of a Pennsylvania Railroad train." Like other detectives on local government's payroll, Parker's work involved far more petty and personally motivated crimes than spectacular robberies, counterfeiting schemes, or acts of terrorism. Of the crimes left to police detectives, the most complicated and fascinating were usually instances of the most serious as well: murder.

The first memorable crime from Parker's eventually weighty case book was a murder, though the most memorable aspect was largely tangential to the crime. What might be titled "The Case of the Left-Sided Man" began the first winter after the detective's marriage in 1901. Now largely subsumed by the sprawl extending outward from Philadelphia, Riverside, New Jersey was still a relatively rural town then. When Ellis Parker was summoned up to a chilly crime scene, it was to examine the murder of a Riverside farmer named Washington Hunter. Mrs. Hunter had found her husband brutally beaten and stabbed to death. In considering the unexplained assault, Parker had a couple of pieces of information. He knew most of the county's residents at least slightly, and so he had known Hunter just as many other people had. He knew that the late farmer was known for two things that had relevance to the crime. One, he was very prosperous for the region, and apparently the murderer had taken several thousand dollars from Hunter's home stash. Two, Hunter was a "left-sided man." His major organs were transposed left to right, due to a rare genetic condition more technically known as *Situs inversus*. As a result his heart was on the right side, rather than the left, and to Parker the concentration of wounds on Hunter's right side suggested either an assailant who knew the victim, or someone local who knew of him.

Investigation outside the Hunter home soon turned up clues pointing away from the latter. Footprints visible on the wet, snowy ground suggested a party of four men, but one set of prints made a path away from the house and the other strangers' tracks as well. This anomaly caught Parker's eye, and it eventually led him to other curious findings, one of which suggested a visitor from New York. The lone man's prints led into a nearby woods before emerging near a railroad junction, and a watchman Parker questioned could recall a man emerging hours earlier from the woods very clearly, mainly because the man had neither coat nor hat in spite of the cold. His quarry's lack of winter clothing and apparent attraction toward the railroad led Parker to speculate that he might be from New York—Parker knew that unlike southern New Jersey the Big Apple had recently experienced unseasonably warm weather—and possibly trying to get back there.

Pursuing this underdressed phantom required the ability to read clues in urban settings as well as the backwoods. Parker eventually completed visits or calls to railroad staff at Riverside station, a ticket auditor's office in Philadelphia, the New York City police, and the U.S. State Department, as well as further conversations with Mrs. Hunter once a picture of likely suspects developed. Based on descriptions Parker assembled of the "loner," as well as the companions who had accompanied him from New York, Mrs. Hunter suggested that one of them may have been Jim Young, who had briefly worked for her husband as a farm hand. New York police proved familiar with Young, and arrested him along with two associates who resembled men seen with him on the train south; one of these appeared to be the loner who had then returned north by himself. Parker's instincts continued to tell him that this man was the key to solving the case. As usual, they proved correct, though in a form nearly as odd as the left-sided condition that provided his first clue.

Railroad employees had told Parker how all four men spoke German with one another. But Otto Keller seemed somehow foreign, even among the others, even aside from his unexplained departure from the crime scene alone. Contacting the State Department on a hunch, Parker learned the surprising news that Keller was not only a German, but a member of the country's nobility. With this information, Parker had identified both the outsider to the crime and the leverage that could get him to talk: upon noting that the seriousness of the charges would require authorities to notify Keller's family back in Stuttgart so that they might arrange for his defense, the wayward scion of titled Germany confessed everything. He had fallen in with the others in New York, he told Parker. The night of the murder they had all gotten drunk, Keller considerably moreso than the rest. He joined them on what was supposed to be a prank on a pinchpenny farmer Young had worked for once, only to discover too late that Young had a much more sinister errand in mind. When Young and the others attacked Hunter, Keller had run off, then played along with reconciliation when they found him later out of fear that they might pursue blackmail against his family. As for the fourth member of the party, Keller explained to Parker, he had lost his own life in a barroom brawl by the time the police began searching for them.

Parker found Keller's testimony plausible; it was self-serving, but fit the facts. Eventually the court system agreed and the German's surviving companions were both sentenced to death. The detective who tracked them down attended the execution, where, as it turned out, the strange and arbitrarily violent Case of the Left-Sided Man had one more memorable twist. While being escorted to his fate, Young's accomplice Charles Braun suddenly broke loose, then grabbed an axe. He very nearly added another life to that of Hunter's, but for the man who had brought him to justice for that crime. Without hesitation Parker struck the desperate prisoner from behind, knocking him down and allowing guards to recapture him. It was a rare and no doubt satisfying instance of directly preventing a death, in a career much more often spent accounting for deaths afterward.

Physical heroics were rare in Parker's career. On the surface at least, his was generally a much more casual approach to battling crime. In fact "casual and unassuming" serves to describe much of Parker's method, manner, and appearance, as well. Contemporary articles repeatedly comment on how little he looked like a detective, or at any rate like the lean, smart-looking ideal of a detective that popular culture had invented. In reality, few detectives great or humble ever conformed to this fictional ideal, but several decades before *Columbo* journalists saw novel irony in a keen investigative mind in such a rumpled form. Parker was known to dispense with coat and tie as often as he could get away with it, even though he occupied an office of some seriousness as Burlington County Detective. He was short, stocky, and, through the later years of his career when most surviving photos were taken, almost completely bald. The sole resemblance between Ellis Parker and a stereotypical detective was his ever-present pipe. Otherwise, he looked more like a used car salesman than a legendary sleuth.

That appearance did nothing to compromise his effectiveness, though. Possibly it helped. While certainly of sturdy enough build to clobber an axe-wielding convict, Parker typically had a low-key, approachable demeanor in dealing with suspects, just as with most people. This didn't make him unique; nearly all the detectives who won real celebrity eschewed violent methods. Their favored approaches nonetheless varied, from brash to manipulative to almost mathematically straightforward. Parker liked to win over suspects as a friend, and someone who would understand their troubles and even try to help, as indeed he did. He supported capital punishment for the worst villains, and also commented repeatedly on the importance of intervening *before* antisocial behavior crossed the line into crime rather than after, yet he was typically forgiving and supportive to offenders all the same, even after he charmed them into giving themselves up.

Once he assisted a convicted burglar, out of jail and trying to reform, with odd jobs and even a room in his own basement. The offer of sharing a home that welcomed 15 children (of whom eight survived to adulthood) over the years might, admittedly, have been a subtle blend of kindhearted charity and prod toward becoming self-supporting with all deliberate speed. But over the years Parker did establish a legitimate reputation for square dealing. In combination with a reputation for deduction that convinced more than a few wanted men he would catch up them anyway, and might as well be accepted as an ally first, this paid dividends. In 1920, the young man wanted for a near-fatal shooting in nearby Beverly slipped away from local officers only to head straight for Mount Holly where he readily surrendered to Ellis Parker. As the brief item in the next day's paper noted, "County Detective Parker's personal magnetism solved another shooting case on Tuesday."

Not everyone was a scared 18-year-old boy, and not every shooting was an accident, or only near-fatal. Even if Parker shared some of the reassuring, small town folksiness of Andy Griffith, Burlington County was not quite a northern Mayberry, and nearby Camden, New Jersey, even less so. Just a few months after the incident in Beverly provided a relatively light diversion, Parker was called on to solve another crime that proved more serious and much, much more puzzling.

On October 16, duck hunters reported the unnerving discovery of a shallow grave in some woods north of Camden; as the corpse lay just inside the Burlington County line it fell to Detective Parker to investigate. Arriving to have a look, Parker found that once again he had known the victim. In this case, moreover, he had already known that William Paul was involved in some kind of mystery. A bank messenger, Paul had not been seen since October 5 when he set out for Philadelphia with a delivery of more than $80,000. Camden's Chief Detective Larry Doran had investigated the disappearance and found Paul belonged to a small, sordid group of mostly married men who gathered regularly to enjoy girls and booze at a site they called "The Lollipop Inn." But progress on the case had stalled, and remained that way until Ellis Parker found himself examining Paul's body on the leaf strewn forest floor.

Now he knew the missing man's ultimate fate. But Parker needed to establish what happened during the 11 days between Paul's disappearance and discovery. The timing was important, and unfortunately the verdict of the medical examiners only deepened the mystery. In the simplest and seemingly most logical scenario, someone had robbed and killed Paul on the 5th, then dumped his body in the woods where it remained until hunters stumbled upon the grave. But the MEs ruled this out as impossible. Paul's body was too well preserved, with still-visible bruises. These did suggest some sort of violent end, but judging by the overall condition of the body, that end couldn't have been more than 48 hours before.

Yet the timing of events still told Parker that Paul must have been murdered back on the 5th. As did one piece of the physical evidence. There was no cash with Paul's body—in fact even his own wallet had been emptied—but two items present did catch Parker's attention. One was an odd piece of leather, which he couldn't place immediately, while the other was a packet of checks that were part of his delivery. Parker reasoned that if Paul had meant to steal the money and run off, and then somehow ran afoul of possible accomplices or some other criminals, he certainly wouldn't have kept those checks in his possession for more than a week. Just as important as why they were there along with the body, meanwhile, was why they were thoroughly wet. Moisture from the ground seemed an unlikely explanation, particularly as the checks had been sealed in a nearly waterproof pouch. Nothing short of being completely submerged in water for a prolonged period could have managed to seep through it.

This smaller problem offered a possible solution to the larger conundrum of dates, when joined to local knowledge drawn from Parker's decades in the area, living, working and often hunting, himself. Profiles of Parker usually summed up his life outside of work as family, the Mount Holly Elks Club, and hunting, and he may even have hunted ducks in the very woods where he was now pursuing bigger game. At any rate he knew the area well enough to propose a remarkable theory. Parker suggested that a man, or more likely two men, intercepted Paul between the bank in Camden and the ferry he meant to take to Philadelphia. They probably offered Paul a ride to the terminal; most likely he knew the men and accepted. They then robbed him and killed him on October 5, and dumped the body in a creek near the shallow grave. Several days later, they realized the risk represented by the approach of duck hunting season and attempted (though unsuccessfully) to prevent the body's discovery by returning to move it out of the creek and into a nearby grave; the ground in between bore at least the suggestion of something heavy dragged from one to the other. As for the body's mysterious preservation, Detective Parker had a theory explaining that as well.

He knew that upstream from the grave the creek passed next to a tannery, which in 1920 probably just discharged waste chemicals right into the water.

If local environmental protections were still primitive, though, forensic chemistry had come a long way since Vidocq a century earlier. Parker could call on modern scientific laboratories, and did so, sending in a sample of water from the creek as well as one of moisture wrung from Paul's clothing. In both cases the analysis found high levels of tannic acid. Certainly enough to preserve a body soaked with that water over a period of days. Once presented with Parker's theory, as well as the lab reports, even the medical examiners agreed that it was plausible, and indeed impressive. It was a piece of deduction that developed into a literal textbook case, in fact, studied for decades afterward.

It was not yet a closed case. But with Parker's conclusions drawn from the forest grave added to Doran's earlier findings, it was close, and offered enough new possibilities for the two detectives to finish the job. One "Lollipop Inn" regular looked especially promising. Aside from his recreational habits and a name that had been notorious in American crime once before, Frank James was a duck hunter, owned a car, and while he could fully account for his time in more recent days, had no alibi for Parker's revised estimate for the time of the murder. What was more, Parker had not been idle while waiting for test results on the water samples, but had visited automobile dealerships with the piece of leather he suspected might be part of a car interior. A Ford salesman was able to confirm that it was from one of their models—such as the Ford that James owned. A search of the car revealed tears closely matching the leather fragment, as well as cracks in the windshield and, possibly even more suspicious, a pristine back seat, probably recently installed.

All of which looked bad for James, but might not convict him, let alone jar loose the identities of likely accomplices. So far the mounting evidence hadn't shaken James, who attempted to explain away the damage to his car as related to one of the wild parties in which he and his circle indulged. It was just the kind of salacious material that private detectives, or at least the most successful ones, could refuse to go near, but men like Parker and Doran had little choice and Parker proceeded to turn it to his advantage. After witnesses identified James Shuck as one of two men seen, along with the owner, in Frank James's Ford around the time of Paul's disappearance, Parker focused his efforts on Shuck, who seemed like he might fold more easily than James if only the right leverage were applied. After weeks of searching, Parker discovered a source of leverage through a woman named Mary. Shuck, it appeared, had dated Mary for nearly a year without letting on that just like the rest of his "swinging" friends he was not the single he had represented himself as. Parker, all casual insouciance, asked several easy routine questions before "accidentally" disillusioning Mary about her suitor. As her attitude to Shuck suddenly and visibly changed for the worse, Parker proceeded to things he really hoped to learn about, like the man's finances. Mary readily provided answers including an unexplained recent windfall. With Mary's information reinforcing all of Parker's other evidence, Shuck finally broke down when grilled by the detective and acknowledged the crime, blaming everything on James, who returned the favor. Both men were eventually sent to the electric chair, and "The Case of the Pickled Corpse" was complete.

If Burlington County's first detective ever struggled with the role in his early years, it found no lasting place in his eventual legend. By the 1920s Parker had found his stride, and was already nearly an institution. He had reliably checked crime and mystery in the pine country for more than a quarter century, and it may well have seemed like he had done so and would go on doing so, forever. In appearance, the moustached, prematurely bald Parker with his pipe and disregard for fashionable dress must have seemed little different as one decade gave way to another; mass produced automobiles, world war, Prohibition, women's suffrage, jazz music, a stock market boom and eventual collapse all transformed society, but through it all there was Detective Parker. He gradually became Chief Parker as other detectives joined him, but essentially he was the same old "Ellis" whom some people had known since their childhood. His world was still home, crime scenes, and his office on the second floor of the county courthouse, as well as his unofficial second office at the Mount Holly Elks Club. Either one was appropriate for Parker's unassuming, casual style. What newspapers described as "the busiest office in Burlington County" and a one-man office "of last resort" was usually cluttered with papers, and accented by a spittoon and burlap sack rumored to contain a few bones from a rare unsolved murder years before.

Newspapers liked featuring Parker, who was an interesting, amiable character as well as a remarkable criminal investigator. They celebrated him, at least locally, as "Ellis H. Parker, Burlington County detective chief and solver of many murder mysteries" and "The most famous detective in the East." Parker certainly enjoyed this attention and the tribute it represented, yet he was highly cautious about compromising an investigation, and as usual found a novel solution for the paradox. Reflecting years afterward, journalist Charles Hansbury recalled in the *Mount Holly Herald* how Parker preferred to be vague and evasive about a case until he was ready to present a dazzling, completed solution all in one go. Despite this, "Ellis H. Parker was the newspaper man's friend."

In every case that he investigated Parker found something of interest to tell the newspaper boys. [...] He might send the gang chasing far up into Pennsylvania to find a Dutch cook who he had "revealed" was a suspect in a famous murder case. He might send them into South Jersey looking for a woman in the case. But at the same time he might be shadowing the real murderer—with enough "on" the man to send him to state prison—and the newspaper boys got the real story when he was ready to release it.

No newspaper man ever resented these wild-goose chases that Ellis loved to give them. They knew that he was helping them, as few other police officials had, to find a story while he "covered up" facts that if told at that time might ruin his investigation.

All of which must suggest a quaint, perhaps even worrying coziness, from a modern perspective. But to all appearances Parker was a consistently clean, honest lawman, even if he seemed a throwback to an earlier era of detection in other ways. When Prohibition began, more than a few Americans became lawbreakers, including many of those charged with upholding the law; some rumors accused Parker of profiting by bootlegging but none proved substantive. A few years later Parker was officially suspended for a brief time following a scandal over rumrunning in the area, but it's likely that the move was little more than belated public relations management in response to events that embarrassed every law enforcement official in the county. Parker may have been somewhat negligent about pressing investigations into "rum traffic" and other violations of a law that much of the country was flouting. But the real source of scandal was more likely "the fact that when the men [arrested in a major action by state troopers] were released on comparatively small bail the next day, most of them disappeared after leaving fictitious names and addresses," per a *New York Times* write-up. Parker had been publicly skeptical about the relatively new state police force. But even if he had been of an astonishingly spiteful mind, the local justice system's handling of their prisoners was hardly under his authority. Accusations of corruption, meanwhile, are difficult to attach to a man who had no habits more lavish than quail hunting. It's very unlikely that Parker ever profited from bootlegging or otherwise abused his office, and the fact that a few rumors and one brief suspension constituted the only blemishes over the course of decades is convincing evidence of his integrity.

On the whole, Parker earned the respect and trust of colleagues, journalists, and the community at large, and received it. It's a significant irony that what might have constituted the one "skeleton in his closet," other than the old bones beside his desk, was plainly documented as part of what became another celebrated job. In solving the 1924 murder of circus owner "Honest" John Brunen, Parker displayed his usual skilled observation and deduction. From just the footprints outside Brunen's home, he built up a general idea of two men involved in the crime, and through other clues he identified Brunen's co-owner Harry Mohr and his crony Charles Powell as a likely match. As with Frank James, however, Mohr refused to be bluffed into a confession, and just as in the "Pickled Corpse" case Parker decided an accomplice might talk more readily. Except Powell lived in Camden, outside of Parker's Burlington County jurisdiction, and when some time passed and Powell failed to make any journeys across the county line the technicality looked like a serious obstacle. Or would have, had Parker paid it any notice; instead, as he casually described it afterward, he turned to "kidnapping."

Other cases, including that of Frank James, suggest that Parker enjoyed a good relationship with the Camden police. But, whatever his reason, he declined to contact them. Instead he simply turned up outside Powell's home with a couple of men, one day, and tried to seize him. Camden's police got involved anyway, once Mrs. Powell understandably called them, though it did her husband little good. They took Parker and his men into custody along with Powell, but then generously decided to overlook the uncharacteristically crude stunt and let Parker proceed to question Powell. He did so, and Powell swiftly confessed to committing the murder on orders from Mohr (after three previous failed attempts that must have left him a nervous wreck before Parker even asked a single question). Both men were convicted and the press claimed the case another triumph for "the old fox;" unlike William Burns, who employed similar tactics in his investigation of the *Los Angeles Times* bombing 15 years before, Parker didn't face charges or even any significant criticism for the incident. The case of "Honest" John Brunen became a staple in stories of Parker's legend, in fact, and more than a decade would pass before something caused some people to see it in a considerably different light.

The press remained admirers of Ellis Parker and so, too, did law enforcement, in spite of his botched end-run around the Camden police. In 1922, neighboring Ocean County had borrowed Burlington County's chief detective for help solving a murder, and a few years later Parker was still in demand, consulting on a double homicide in New Brunswick, New Jersey. Even the army once requested Parker's aid solving a daunting mystery quite accurately remembered as "The Case with 175 Suspects;" Detective Parker questioned every single member of the murdered sergeant's company and found his man once again. In *Master Detective*, Reisinger observes that neither Parker's own few missteps nor the ups and downs of society seemed to dampen interest in him. Through it all,

> Ellis Parker's business was still going strong. Crime knew no Depression. Parker's reputation insured that in addition to whatever lawbreaking he handled in Burlington County, he had a constant stream of requests for his assistance in dealing with mayhem elsewhere.

In 1930, Parker fielded another such request from Ocean County, on a murder investigation that also involved the armed forces again. Working out who killed the two sailors near Lakehurst Naval Station was a particularly complex challenge, ultimately encompassing ballistics evidence, details of the naval station's inventory records, a secret love affair and a plot involving no fewer than four men plus one victim's wife.

For plain baffling stranger-than-fiction mystery, however, it's likely that no investigation in Parker's four-decades-plus career topped the case of Robert Brewer. Other crimes Parker solved appeared more frequently in lists of his most famous cases. And many had novel features such as the murder of the "Left-Sided Man," or "The Case of the Pickled Corpse." But if the story of Robert Brewer's murder never acquired an official title, it still deserves a prominent place in any history of Detective Parker's most remarkable feats of logic.

Perhaps the most confounding feature of the case, particularly for the man trying to solve it, was that initially it couldn't have looked any more open-and-shut. Brewer was badly injured but still alive when a friend discovered him in his smashed up boarding house room. He held on for a few days after being rushed to a hospital, and even regained consciousness long enough to sit up and speak briefly. At which point he accused one Newton Ashby, a known bootlegger, of bashing a bottle over his head. The fatal injury to which Brewer eventually succumbed was actually a gunshot wound to the head, but the victim's own identification of Ashby as his assailant still seemed conclusive. Police duly arrested him. But then Ellis Parker began to discover the simple case's unnerving characteristic of becoming more and more complicated the closer he studied it. Ashby claimed total ignorance of the matter and had a good alibi backing him up. Meanwhile, everything else Parker learned about the crime seemed to indicate not only that Ashby hadn't done it, but that no one could have, at all.

Brewer was well known as a drunk, with a habit of hoarding up the little money he earned as a farmhand for intense sprees, so robbery might have been a motive, particularly given that someone had torn apart his room. But other evidence made this theory seem absurd. Extensive blood stains indicated that Brewer must have been shot in his bed, and that's where he was found. A glass of gin with his fingerprints, however, simply wouldn't fit with any scenario

Parker could imagine. Brewer obviously couldn't have gotten it out after an intruder arrived and shot him. If he had been up drinking when the killer arrived, though, the evidence of the blood stains all over his bed made no sense. And while a person might theoretically leave a drink unfinished, given Brewer's reputation Parker thought it quite unlikely that he would have, at least while still coordinated enough to make it into bed. So, Parker and his detectives brainstormed over the problem, trying to think of some alternate explanation. One of his men suggested that perhaps someone had ransacked the room while Brewer was out, and then a second man killed Brewer after his return. But the requirement that, rather than notifying someone, Brewer had quietly remained home drinking gin, potentially for some time, made the idea a long shot at best. Parker thought that things just might make more sense if Brewer had shot himself for some reason, except that doctors found the bullet that killed him in a location which ruled that out. Plus, searching the room had turned up another .32-caliber bullet and several cartridges of them, but no gun. Every piece of evidence seemed only to reinforce the impossibility of the crime.

Parker didn't give up, however. He had interviewed 175 suspects to find a murderer once, and brought another man to justice after spending 15 years in contact with authorities in all parts of the world to find him. The detective who was not above a deadpan joke at his own expense might have said that he was simply too stubborn to know how to quit, never mind when. So he kept looking for some further evidence that might explain the mystery, even if he couldn't imagine how. Gradually, perseverance revealed a few more clues. Searches of the farm that employed Brewer uncovered a stash of money, likely his, in a sack of flour. When initially questioned, Ashby had noted that Brewer had a habit of hiding his money from himself as much as from anyone else, so that he couldn't spend it all while on a tear; that would seem to account for the absence of any money in his room, but otherwise didn't really help.

Requestioning Brewer's friend Lawyer, who initially found him, yielded better results. While it may well have been no more than stubborn persistence, Parker asked repeatedly about the unexplained points of the case and eventually Lawyer admitted a bit more than he had said before about one of them.

He had found a .32-caliber gun in the room when he discovered Brewer, and taken it with him because it was his own gun, which he'd loaned his friend earlier. Afterward he was rightly leery of mentioning this, but Parker was probably too excited to issue even a token scolding.

He could see an explanation, at last. Brewer had gotten drunk the night of the shooting. Drunk enough that his plan to hide his savings from himself worked, and in fact worked too well: he became obsessed with finding it, tore apart his own room and, failing to find any money, concluded that his entire savings was gone. In despair, so complete that he didn't even finish the gin he had poured, he got in bed and attempted to end his own life. By some miracle he didn't die at once, and thus his friend Lawyer found him clinging to life and called for an ambulance, right after picking up the gun Brewer wasn't likely to need any longer. Meanwhile Brewer, his faculties undoubtedly affected by a bullet to the head, made a nonsensical and impossible accusation about Newton Ashby before expiring. It explained everything, Parker realized, except the placement of the bullet on the X-ray, and here perhaps experience reminded the detective that sometimes medical observations can be wrong. Even in this case, an initial X-ray had missed the bullet entirely. By the time the bullet was finally discovered it might well have shifted somewhat, particularly because Brewer himself had even sat up in bed during his brief rally. Like the hero of fiction he was now and then compared with, Parker had eliminated the impossible and just enough remained that, however improbable, it was undoubtedly the solution. The investigation of Ernest Brewer's death was closed, as a suicide.

After most of four decades as a detective, Parker's career lacked only a crowning achievement. He was respected and admired in the community he policed, and sought out for his insight, not only throughout New Jersey, but even occasionally further afield as in the quest for fugitive San Franciscan George Coumas. The local press faithfully chronicled his words and deeds, and in the early 1930s, historian and author Fletcher Pratt even featured his career in a book with the now awkward title of *The Cunning Mulatto and Other Cases of Ellis Parker, American Detective*. All of this constituted an impressive and just tribute to an investigator who not only found solutions to hundreds of crimes, but also to several genuinely remarkable mysteries.

And yet, whatever their own inherent merits, none of Parker's achievements had by itself equaled the legendary status earned by his record as a whole. He had never taken on a mystery that truly captured the national imagination. Few detectives had, even among the very greatest. And possibly Parker was content with the work, the life and the fame he had, just as Eugène Vidocq had savored his own pioneering detective career despite its lack of any one villain or crime that could claim its own place in history. Vidocq never actually had such a crime to tempt him, however, and that proved one especially significant difference out of all those that separated the two sleuths.

In his day, Ellis Parker enjoyed modest fame, certainly more than most detectives before or since. But no detective in history approached the celebrity that America and the world showered onto a young man from Detroit named Charles A. Lindbergh. After his historic transatlantic flight, Lindbergh was honored with medals, parades, banquets, a postage stamp, and most of all with news stories beyond count. Unfortunately for "Lucky Lindy," fame and fortune have their drawbacks. Not least among them the interest of people eager to acquire one or the other for themselves, and willing to commit harm to get it. The kidnapping of Charles Lindbergh, Jr., from his family's home on March 1, 1932, was likely motivated by fortune, if a series of ransom notes demanding $50,000 (or greater sums) are a reliable indication. But if the crime was committed in hopes of discreetly acquired fortune, it achieved much more success in the exact opposite: staggering, and likely unwanted, nationwide fame.

For criminal infamy the Lindbergh kidnapping was very nearly a "perfect storm." Charles Lindbergh was a national hero, the excitement of his 1927 transatlantic flight still fresh five years later. The photogenic All-American Midwestern boy was widely admired. And the attack on such a national hero, through his defenseless, angel-faced 20-month-old child, produced a shock surpassing even that of the abduction and murder of Saville Kent from a similar bucolic country estate in England, 72 years earlier. The location of the Lindberghs' Hopewell, New Jersey home less than 50 miles from the nation's largest media market served to amplify every twist and turn, as more than a dozen messages arrived by one means or another over the following weeks. When a truck driver discovered the infant on May 12, mutilated and most likely dead for two months, the affair's compelling hold on the nation was complete. Confused, anxious fascination hardened into a determined crusade for answers and vengeance.

Plenty of crusaders were eager to answer the call. Most of them were shut out, or else confined to peripheral roles while New Jersey's State Police claimed primacy. A scramble among municipal, state, and national agencies ultimately reached all the way to the White House, but in this case the buck did not stop there; Washington had its own federal Bureau of Investigation, eager to prove itself, but it had no federal law on kidnapping. Ultimate authority over who would work the case and how thus rested with New Jersey's governor, A. Harry Moore. Governor Moore made the safe, reasonable choice to keep the investigation local and under his authority, but assign it to a relatively large organization with considerable manpower. The state police might not be brilliant, but they could take charge of the chaotic situation and proceed in a professional and reassuringly thorough manner.

Behind the scenes, though, Moore quietly hedged his bets, as, curiously enough, did his eventual successor, Harold Hoffman. Officially entrusting the management of the high profile case, and all of the various forces clamoring to play a role, to the state police was a sound decision. Yet the Garden State had a tempting alternative to hand in its brilliant, veteran county detective Ellis Parker. Meanwhile, after a few days of keeping his peace, Parker was no longer acting shy about promoting his own views of the case. Or about criticizing the official investigation, which he saw as a misguided, overmanned, overly noisy mess. He was convinced that he could do better, and when he indirectly petitioned the governor, Moore responded with a letter encouraging Parker to work on the case.

It was not a formal commission, however, and even when Parker obtained one a few days later, he effectively remained on the outside of matters. New Jersey's Department of Motor Vehicles had a loose authority to investigate a crime like the Lindbergh Kidnapping, and its boss was one of Parker's many old friends. He was willing to authorize a formal investigation of the crime with the legendary Burlington County sleuth on loan as its chief. Parker readily accepted the offer. But even with the DMV's official backing and Governor Moore's unofficial support behind him, there was little he could hope to do. Evidence was already boxed up and moved, and the crime scene literally trampled. The state police couldn't shut down his parallel inquiries, but they had no obligation to cooperate with them, or motivation for helping someone who was already loudly disparaging their efforts and now trying to upstage them.

At one point Parker contacted J. Edgar Hoover in his efforts to get around these limitations, and the Bureau of Investigation chief met with him personally to hear his thoughts on the case. Like Parker, Hoover cherished a hope of upstaging the state police, but for that reason he was hardly inclined to share what little advantage he possessed in access to its details, and their correspondence went no further. So the case of the century was unfolding right outside Ellis Parker's doorstep, and he was both willing and theoretically authorized to solve it. But without access to witnesses, evidence, or the scene of the crime, even his powers were ineffective. He could do little, really, but hope for a lucky break.

So far as Parker let on, this situation hadn't changed at all more than two years later, when the larger investigation by state and federal personnel finally reported discovery of the elusive answer. It was largely the product of time, and slow, methodical work. In the first weeks after the kidnapping, an agent for the Lindbergh family had paid $50,000 to a figure introduced as "John," who first appeared at Woodlawn Cemetery in New York. "Cemetery John" claimed to represent the kidnappers and accepted the money, then vanished without a trace. Part of the ransom consisted of gold certificates, however, and after patient and persistent investigation of each one that turned up afterward, in September 1932 they finally led police to a New York carpenter named Bruno Hauptmann. Between the gold certificates, and Hauptmann's apparent resemblance to "John" as well as to an early criminal "profile," most authorities felt confident that the mystery was solved.

Ellis Parker
Courtesy of William Fullerton. Reproduced with permission.

New Jersey's attorney general David Wilentz was nonetheless worried about one particular loose end. Ellis Parker had repeatedly criticized the mainstream investigation and still had a ready audience in the press. And his habit of keeping the results of his own inquiries quiet until he could spring a complete, detailed solution was well known. So Wilentz made a point of reaching out to him, personally inviting him to a large conference on the case and offering complete access to all of the state's material, with the hope that Parker would reciprocate and give some warning if he had a surprise in store. Burlington County's chief detective (and the New Jersey DMV's borrowed lead investigator) was gracious in response, assuring Wilentz that he hadn't even "a single lead" and that Hauptmann was unquestionably the right man.

Parker was being not only diplomatic, but disingenuous. He actually had deep doubts about Hauptmann's guilt, just like a small, but resolutely skeptical minority both at the time and ever since. Ellis Parker, however, had one particular additional reason to believe that Hauptmann was the wrong man. Contrary to what he told Wilentz, Parker had figured out the identity of the right man. Or so he at least was convinced. That lucky break he needed had literally walked right through his door, only weeks after the case began, in fact. And after observing his suspicious behavior for more than two years, Parker was certain that the Lindbergh kidnapper was none other than a disreputable lawyer named Paul Wendel.

Nearly every detective is eventually likely to encounter one or two shady characters like Wendel. Men who don't quite cross the line into winding up behind bars and, for reasons of personality or usefulness or both, may instead become liked and trusted acquaintances. Unsurprisingly, more than one of these characters also appeared as side notes in the Lindbergh kidnapping case, drawn irresistibly to its rich opportunities for deal making and scams. Gaston Means, whose association proved so disastrous for William Burns, used the kidnapping as a pretext to relieve one wealthy woman of more than $100,000 before his late patron's Bureau finally got him locked up. Paul Wendel wasn't on quite the same level with Means as a con artist, though not necessarily for want of ambition; Reisinger mentions that Wendel once attempted to sell Al Capone, himself, on a process for distilling alcohol from tar. Soon after the

Lindbergh kidnapping, Parker received several vague, anonymous calls about the case, and he suspected that the voice on the other end, though disguised, was Wendel's. His suspicions grew when Wendel contacted him directly about approaching "underworld contacts" to assist with negotiating for the babe's return. Ultimately, the suggestion led nowhere, but Parker had valid reason to wonder, from then on. After wondering about the Lindbergh mystery and about Paul Wendel's odd interest in it for more than two years, he convinced himself that once again he had the answer that everyone else missed. All he needed was Wendel's confession.

A confession to the kidnapping would have upended everything, no question. Because even as the official investigation had proceeded from a suspect to a conviction to a sentence of death, it had produced no admission of guilt. Parker was unaccustomed to losing, and losing to the New Jersey State Police must have been particularly galling, but the fact that their suspect continued unrelentingly to protest his innocence must have felt like persuasive evidence that he had not in fact lost. Throughout 1935, therefore, he committed himself more and more inescapably to pulling off one final spectacular deductive triumph or else failing, miserably and publicly.

Governor Hoffman continued to doubt Hauptmann's guilt also, and trust Parker's instincts. The governor met with Hauptmann personally, and arranged to allow Parker to interview the condemned man in his cell in April, in flagrant violation of prison rules. Parker focused more and more of his efforts on investigating the case against Hauptmann rather than the crime itself, and in October submitted a formal report to Hoffman. Reisinger describes the report, and what it suggests about its author's deepening obsession, in vivid language:

> To be the product of such an organized mind, the report is strangely uncoordinated, almost rambling... many of the points are based on hearsay, third-hand testimony, or even rumors. In addition, it is probably the only official report a governor ever received sprinkled with grammatical errors and curse words.

Two months later, the press uncovered Hoffman's extraordinary, behind-the-scenes effort against his own government's case. In the face of sudden and intense questions about his counterinvestigation, Parker doubled down on betting his whole reputation on overturning the official verdict, proclaiming "Give me the evidence the state was afraid to use at the trial and I will bring in the murderer." When Hauptmann's last appeals and other legal delaying tactics expired, just over two weeks into 1935, Parker raised the stakes even higher for both himself and Governor Hoffman: at a last minute and undoubtedly tense meeting, Parker assured him that he was close to producing the real kidnapper and a confession to the crime, and needed only a little more time. Trusting Ellis Parker—and in the face of predictable and widespread protest—Hoffman ordered a stay of execution for possibly the most reviled man in America. Detective Parker had risked both his own credibility and that of the governor on one high stakes gamble, in which losing was simply unthinkable. He had to win. Under the circumstances, a seemingly minor additional risk or two must have seemed scarcely worth consideration.

When, a month later, four men abducted Paul Wendel at gunpoint and subjected him to a nightmarish week-long interrogation, Parker's role behind it all is therefore in some sense all too easy to explain. He was convinced that Wendel was guilty, and that he would confess. And he had to have that confession, to save not only his own name and that of the governor who was risking so much to back him, but also a man he believed was facing execution for a crime he had nothing to do with. Which meant he had to have Paul Wendel to question. But Wendel was steadfastly refusing to venture outside New York, especially to New Jersey where he faced various outstanding warrants for his arrest. It was Charles Powell and Camden all over again, but the same obstacle hadn't thwarted Parker then, and circumventing it in the same way was hardly going to trouble him in a second case with much, much more on the line. So after a few more tense weeks, on Valentine's Day 1936, Parker dispatched his son Ellis, Jr., and three other men to kidnap his kidnapping suspect.

Unfortunately, the confession Parker continually believed Wendel was right on the cusp of delivering seemed no nearer than before. Based on photos of the man this seems unsurprising; given his history, Wendel must have possessed some degree of charm, but the face glaring out from black-and-white newspaper clippings is that of a hard character. Dragged to a basement by mysterious captors who insisted that he was guilty of the Lindbergh kidnapping and needed to confess, Wendel responded both with bafflement and with a resolute refusal to do any such thing. His captors responded by turning up the pressure, and as days went by without any confession from Wendel his interrogation grew increasingly closer to torture. First hunger and thirst, then sleep deprivation. Then "stress positions," and finally raw, unqualified violence. Finally, after two days of occasional beatings, Wendel elected to tell his captors what they wanted him to say. Parker, upon receiving the news, was jubilant; a reporter described how the staid detective suddenly began "jumping up and down for joy."

His joyous reaction, however, was deeply misguided. Wendel was not so hardheaded that he chose to endure imprisonment and abuse when a few words could set him free, but he was not stupid, either. In fact he was an educated lawyer, even if questionable ethics had once gotten him disbarred. The "confession" he made was full of easily disproven details, very likely by intent. Wendel was undoubtedly suspicious of Parker's strange behavior if not yet aware of his real connection to the recent ordeal, in which both father and son had kept out of sight. So the prisoner played along, after being delivered into the custody of his old friend Chief Parker for "help." But once Parker was satisfied with Wendel's "touched-up" confession, and handed him on to authorities in Mercer County, everything finally began to unravel.

The Lindbergh kidnapping has endured as one of the great mysterious crimes. Despite the fact that the case was formally closed, it still inspires arguments by armchair theorists over seeming holes in the official verdict, just like Inspector Jack Whicher's two great mysteries of 19th century England. The legend of the Lindbergh case surpasses both of them, moreover, in scale and scope for re-imagining. Like Victorian London's greatest unsolved case of all, the details are so involved as to produce their own mythology, with people and evidence assigned arcane sounding names, like "Cemetery John," and "Rail 16." The case also lingers as a subject of doubt because, significantly, no one confessed. Unlike Constance Kent, Bruno Hauptmann consistently denied abducting and murdering his alleged infant victim, right up to his own death in the electric chair. Undoubtedly this was one more compelling factor in Parker's determination to prove his own, alternative solution. Nonetheless, if one reliable conclusion can be made about the various suspects and theories that have paraded forth over the course of 80 years, it is that Ellis Parker went disastrously wrong.

The best thing that can be said for Parker's investigation is that he should have been suspicious of Paul Wendel, and he was. For what it's worth, in addition to being of generally dubious character, Wendel does match the profiler's speculative description of the kidnapper, nearly as well as Hauptmann. Beyond this, Parker quickly climbed into a deep hole, and carrying a shovel. The remarkable coincidence of his desperate longing to find the Lindbergh kidnapper and that presumptive kidnapper turning up among his own acquaintances should have warned him he was on the wrong scent, as should the consistent error of his belief that Wendel's confession was certain to burst forth at any moment. When it didn't, Parker began compounding his bad decisions at an alarming rate. Ordering Wendel's kidnapping was not only desperate and misguided but criminal. Dragging him across state lines into New Jersey for what was a completely illegitimate interrogation anyway, thereby violating new federal laws passed in response to the Lindbergh kidnapping itself, was simply senseless. Parker then crossed another kind of line in holding Wendel prisoner and allowing his torture, at best through careful ignorance and at worst through overt orders; given Parker's thoroughly humane record, the former is certainly plausible but still inexcusable.

Wendel himself was hardly inclined to excuse it. In Mercer County he promptly repudiated his confession and pointed out the multiple logical impossibilities in it. He also explained just what outrageous circumstances had ever prompted him to make such a statement. A grand jury investigation followed, and if Parker's then-known behavior was only suspicious rather than incriminating, he had to face questions. He denied everything, thereby burrowing even deeper.

Meanwhile, Wendel's detailed recollections of the house where he was held prisoner led police to it, and then one by one to members of the plot, including Ellis, Jr. On April 23, he and two of the other men actively involved with Wendel's interrogation were indicted on kidnapping and assault. The younger Parker vanished, and his father angrily blustered that "If my son goes to jail, a lot of people are going to go with him!" He was correct that Ellis, Jr., wasn't going to jail alone. In May, police found the fourth member of the kidnap conspiracy, and by June they had conclusive evidence of the identity of its mastermind: Ellis Parker, Senior.

The three years that followed saw the resilient old detective, who had shepherded so many men into confinement over the years, gradually run out of room to maneuver himself. On June 2, 1936, police arrested Parker in front of his beloved Elks Club. After accompanying them to court he was quickly released on bail. The governor, perhaps thinking of how far Parker had gone in order to justify Hoffman's confidence in him (or perhaps just hoping in vain that he might limit the ensuing scandal) then intervened by denying the State of New York's extradition request. Ellis, Jr., immediately turned himself in and made bail as well, joining his father at liberty within the State of New Jersey while various officials, bureaucrats, lawyers and judges fought over their fate.

In June 1937, a jury finally delivered word of that fate after months of political wrangling and a nine-week trial. The jury's verdict: guilty, with a recommendation of leniency. Ellis Parker received a six-year sentence, with three years for his son. Further arguments and wrangling meant that most of three years passed between their initial arrest and final, much delayed arrival at Lewisburg Federal Penitentiary, but Parker was already suffering the consequences of his ruinous decisions. In 1939 *The Philadelphia Record* described a formerly "hulking, self-willed Parker, now a broken old man," ill and relatively gaunt. The considerable expenses of his legal battles had nearly wiped out his family's savings as well, and he pleaded to be exempted from paying for printing the weighty legal record of the case, saying "he was too nearly broke to foot the bill." At last on June 22, 1939, Parker paid one final visit to the Mount Holly Courthouse and his office of 45 years to thank friends and well wishers, whose numbers and devotion both remained considerable. Then he said goodbye, and reported to prison alongside his son.

*

Both Burlington County and Ellis Parker arrived relatively late to the detective game, but Parker's life and career still overlapped with a number of his famous predecessors. For all of his readiness to offer up an opinion, and long association with journalists happy to record it, though, any thoughts Parker may have had about the other prominent names in his field are now gone along with him. Which loss is on the whole unfortunate. In the case of William Burns, it might be considered almost tragic. The similar, disastrous ends to the two great detectives' careers, one following the other just about a decade afterward, suggest as much as anything that history may not repeat but does, as the saying goes, at least rhyme. In his early 60s, Burns let overconfidence and the chance for one last crowning glory tempt him into a series of bad and even criminal decisions, the most damaging involving a shady associate he should have dismissed long before, and eventually found himself arrested, tried, and sentenced to jail along with one of his sons. Ten years later, Ellis Parker did much the same thing.

It's impossible to say what Parker himself thought about the similarities of his own scandal to that of the earlier sleuth, if he saw any connection at all. There were differences, certainly; among other things Parker got carried away with suspicion of Paul Wendel while Burns should have trusted Gaston Means considerably less. Still, the parallels are worth examining, if only for a possible explanation of what went wrong for Ellis Parker. In the early 1930s he was very much a local hero with a national reputation, and by the end of the decade he was disgraced, broken, and serving a federal prison sentence; any detective worth the name would crave some explanation. It's possible that, like Burns, Parker became recklessly overconfident after decades of finding time and time again that his instincts proved right when others doubted. Both sleuths had, after all, made their own rules before and met with accolades rather than jail time. Reisinger pointedly notes the significant absence of any dissenting voices, throughout all of Parker's increasingly worrisome persecution of Wendel, suggesting that "Such was Parker's reputation that everyone thought if they didn't see what Ellis Parker saw, they must be the ones who were wrong."

Parker's reputation was also enough that, at least locally, people continued to remember and wonder at his bizarre self-destruction even decades later. A 1976 *Burlington Times* story by Gary Lindenmuth considered a variety of possible reasons for Parker's desperate acts. Lindenmuth notes the detective's obvious resentment over being excluded from pursuing a real investigation of the kidnapping, and also speculates that Governor Hoffman's support may have been accompanied by overt pressure to salvage the disaster he had accompanied Parker into. But "perhaps the most plausible explanation," at any rate in Lindenmuth's estimate, "comes from the former County Detective Clint Zeller, one of the few surviving county residents who really knew the famous detective well." Zeller affirms Parker's reputation for beating criminals with his brain rather than with fists, and then suggests that in retrospect that great brain may have been under pressure from more than the external sources. Some time before Wendel's abduction, Zeller noted Parker's personality seemed to change in general ways, or so he claimed later, declaring that Parker "was not himself at all." This, and any connection, can be little more than speculation. However, it is entirely true that some years after Ellis Parker made the worst series of decisions of his life, he was diagnosed with an advanced brain tumor.

Even if his judgment was not genuinely, biologically impaired, and even if the worst interpretation of his role in Wendel's ordeal was true, few could argue that Parker did not adequately suffer for his guilt in the remaining years of his life. He endured the dismantling of his reputation and dissolution of his family's finances, sleeplessness and ill health, imprisonment, and finally an aggressive cancer in his very brain. Perhaps the only solace through it all was a deep reservoir of support from family, friends and acquaintances. People remembered his decades of good work and honesty, and counted them for more than one great act of lawbreaking and dishonesty. When word of Parker's cancer got out, people near and far erupted in sympathy and well-wishes, and cried for mercy on the sick old ex-chief; more than 10,000 names endorsed a petition to President Roosevelt for a pardon.

The story of Ellis Parker was denied any such happy ending. Following a stroke days earlier, he died a prisoner, at 3:30 a.m. on February 4, 1940.

The campaign for his pardon was simply, by a narrow margin, too late. Its approval was only a matter of time according to everyone involved, including even the attorney who had prosecuted the Parkers. The *Courier-Post* reported that "Had Parker lived another week, he would have been back in his beloved Mount Holly—a free man with all his civil rights restored." Instead only his remains returned, for a funeral at which more than 4,000 people joined his family, including Ellis, Jr., who received a temporary release and later, in 1947, a pardon likely issued in sympathy for his father.

Parker had only a small legacy, mostly limited to the region in which people knew him personally, especially as years passed by. A year or so after his death, a local paper published the letter of one resident who fondly recalled the legend of Detective Parker and regretted the state of law enforcement in his absence:

> My, how the folks up here in Burlington county wish that Old Ellis was still around and in active service. There would be no wishful thinking about the escaped killer now supposed to be roaming the Burlington pine country. Ellis would have roped and hogtied that gentleman long before this.

Many other people no doubt shared reminiscences of "Old Ellis" for years afterward. Newspapers published occasional features, usually at the anniversary of his death and, as time passed, at increasingly long intervals.

Outside of Burlington County, meanwhile, world war and the busy new world that followed it soon occupied most Americans, and Parker faded from memory entirely. Even in Mount Holly, decades have now gone by and acquaintances of Ellis Parker are few in number and nearly forgotten themselves. His biographer John Reisinger, who toured nearly all of Parker's old haunts on many visits to the Burlington county seat, notes that today its former hero is all but unknown. Like Burns, and Lees, and nearly all of the great investigators he joined in the detective's Valhalla, Parker and his celebrity have passed by with their era.

EPILOGUE:
SHERLOCK HOLMES AND J. EDGAR HOOVER

DYING BEHIND PRISON BARS was a sad, bad end, both for Ellis Parker and for the tradition of real-life renowned detectives that effectively died along with him. It was also an end that may help explain why that tradition died out. It's not entirely coincidence that both Parker and the more prominent William Burns, also described as the last of his kind in various histories of detection, ended their careers in disgrace, censured by the same society that had lionized them for decades. Yet the connection between the last famous detectives' disastrous blunders, and the disappearance of such men around the same time, is in truth both more and less than the obvious cause-and-effect that it may suggest.

The similar endings of those careers, which also marked the end of an era in detection, should in many ways be considered a red herring. The failings of Burns and Parker didn't cause the closure of their era. Re-imagining their stories to end with quiet retirements, or even spectacular victories in place of the disasters they met, instead, wouldn't have changed the larger trends of history or preserved the place of the detective hero outside the realm of fiction. Modernizing urban, industrial societies had marveled at and admired such men for at least a century by the time Parker and Burns came to grief.

304 • BRILLIANT DEDUCTION

Yet the scandals they created can hardly be a major cause for suspending that admiration because scandal and the great detectives were never far apart, from even the earliest days. As far back as Lees, Whicher, and Vidocq himself, the notable detective was regularly a lightning rod for controversy, many times as a result of the very same unconventional methods that made him notable in the first place. Even Burns and Parker were placed on trial in part for things they had already done in earlier days when they were still heroes. They lost that status as heroes at the same time as did individual detectives, in general, not because their conduct led society to change, but because their careers happened to play out as society was already changing, into a place where such conduct simply had no more place.

People celebrated adventurous individual detectives for a time and forgave their more outré antics—at least in their attitude toward that type of character and often toward specific examples—because people needed them. Then, both the approval of such characters and the tradition of real-world detective heroes went away at much the same time, because people no longer needed them. William Hunt gives a good deal of consideration to why that need evaporated, in *Front Page Detective*, and suggests that

> Burns was the last prominent private detective. The need for such secret forces ended with the New Deal government's intervention on behalf of labor. It also ended because [of] widespread developments in police organizations that occurred in the thirties and later.

Labor strife certainly played a large role in the history of America's great private detective firms, but it's difficult to connect with the broader decline of real-life "front page detectives." Their ranks extended well beyond turn-of-the-century American private industry, and even Burns himself won much of his fame while a government employee. The reference to "developments in police organizations," however, offers more promise.

The great pioneers of detection won notice largely because they were pioneers. Vidocq and Pinkerton were unique talents, but that uniqueness was considerably more amazing in contexts with few others even remotely like them at all. Even for Jonathan Whicher, working alongside other Scotland Yard detectives, the distance between being in the profession and being one of its elite was short; twice, he played key roles in sensational investigations more because he was talented and available than because his talents were so impressive that great numbers of his peers deferred to him and stood idle.

Seventy years later, the story was much different. America was a larger and more raw society, and slower to establish official investigative agencies than Britain. But by the early 1930s, when a child's abduction and murder transfixed his own country, Ellis Parker could scarcely get anywhere near the investigation even though the crime occurred almost in his own backyard. For years, his reputation had drawn invitations to consult on cases far and wide, just like the most prominent detectives of the past. But change may take place gradually, only to appear in fits and starts, and so the Lindbergh kidnapping demonstrated; not only investigators but investigative agencies came out of the woodwork, their full extent made suddenly evident by a crime shocking enough for all of them to converge at once. Because of Parker's reputation dating back to the 19th century he was—nearly—permitted special status one last time. Afterward, however, no one was ever likely to achieve the same again. An age in which even the FBI could not get exclusive access to a national headline investigation meant less need of a famous lone detective, and almost no scope for becoming one.

Expanding government alone did not put the great detectives out of business, of course. Throwing numbers at a complex problem such as a mysterious crime does not guarantee a more efficient solution, and may simply get in the way of one. But since the primitive days of isolated local forces of untrained men and old-fashioned customs ill equipped for the challenges of industrial urban nations, law enforcement agencies made far more advances than simply putting more officers on the street. The quality of recruits improved somewhat, probably. Far more significantly, so did the methods they employed. And in this, the phenomenon of the superstar detective can indeed be described as having brought about its own end; if their disappearance from real life really were a mysterious crime, the explanation is arguably a self-inflicted fatality after all. Except the means of suicide were not final, scandalous failures but instead their greatest, early successes.

The detective's moment in the spotlight was no historical accident. Even before Vidocq, equally or even more brilliant individuals must have stumbled into the role of investigator from time to time. But any pre-industrial great detectives must have been mostly chance prodigies, employing natural talent in isolation; the cosmopolitan, urban world of Rome might have approached a beginning at professional investigators as so many novels have speculated, but of course Rome fell, along with most of its advanced infrastructure. The European civilization that succeeded it, along with its offshoots in the New World, ultimately made even greater (hopefully more lasting) progress toward urbanization. And, out of necessity, toward professionalized specialist investigation of crime. The most important implication of this, for the rise and fall of the great detectives, is that organizational progress was inherent in their very existence right from the beginning. Vidocq himself embraced technical innovations eagerly, but his basic idea of a distinct, established office dedicated to solving unexplained crimes was itself the greatest innovation of the field's whole history.

Meanwhile, the fame of the first eminent detective, just like that of those who followed him, helped propagate the concept of a detective profession in a way that earlier attempts had never managed. By the mid-19th century much of the Western world had imported or begun some partial adoption of that profession. Those who did were not always of an equally innovative disposition; Scotland Yard's creation for example was accomplished only in the face of considerable skepticism and reluctance. But the idea of specialist professional investigators was a good one, and it soon took root even in relatively barren soil and grew even when a committed innovator like Vidocq was not there to tend it.

At first, the results were useful, but still limited. An established detective profession did not immediately make the advantages of the profession's best over its average small enough to dismiss. Into the 20th century, a great talent could still achieve fame and fortune in detection through individual brilliance. Yet none of those who did so relied on brilliance, alone. Most of the great detectives embraced technologies and techniques that did the job more effectively—and more efficiently. Those things aided genius, but cumulatively, they also made it less necessary. A Vidocq or a Lees could never entirely teach their unique intuition to others. But the systems and technologies that they and Pinkerton pioneered and adopted could be reproduced. Gradually, they were.

By Ellis Parker's time, both the need and opportunity for the lone brilliant detective to shine had been nearly reduced out of existence. An average detective could consult the same specialists in ballistics or in chemistry that Parker could, and gradually the employment of specialized techniques has become routine enough that the average detective does so. Once, taking account of minor or unusual details involved in a crime could by itself produce noteworthy results. Now, as demonstrated even by mainstream television programs like *CSI*, *Profilers*, or *The Forensic Files*, it's the basic function of people's jobs. The remarkable era that began with professionalization of investigative work was, in the end, finished off by the systemization and bureaucratization of investigative work.

Thus it is entirely fitting that the careers of that old era's last two representatives intersected directly with the perfect illustration of the new: J. Edgar Hoover. Celebrity detective William Burns's former subordinate succeeded him as director of the future FBI, and mulled over correspondence from Ellis Parker regarding the Lindbergh case which both men badly wanted to solve. Hoover went on to introduce America to a much different idea of a champion against crime, however, than either Burns or Parker would have recognized. The Pinkertons, as Murray Kempton has suggested, might by contrast have recognized a good deal of Hoover's approach, and the William Pinkerton of crusty old age might have heartily improved. For the FBI approach to investigation was in general just the sort of professional, businesslike affair that Pinkerton insisted a legitimate detective agency needed to adopt.

Hoover's one obvious legacy carried over from the world of Burns and other great detectives of the pre-FBI era was, meanwhile, little more than a surface resemblance. He kept the idea of a celebrity law enforcer, actively promoting both the FBI and himself as its assertive champion, and met with considerable success for a while, particularly during the Bureau's battle with high profile gangsters during the 1930s. Then Hoover's legend, too, eventually fell out of favor; he remains widely remembered, but more for the kind of dirty tricks and abuses that prompted the worst criticism of his predecessor. The institution of the FBI has continued, though, and without any director since approaching Hoover's celebrity. It's worth noting that even in his heyday, even his own propaganda presented Hoover as something much more like a masterful general, directing his army of subordinates from a remote headquarters, than a romantic hero challenging the enemy personally. Though he preserved an idea of the nation's "top cop" somewhat like the role great detectives had once played, Hoover made no pretense of being Sherlock Holmes. Every investigator to do so with any real success, since, has operated exclusively out of the Baker Street legend's own realm of fiction.

Investigators of great ability still exist today, even outside that fictional realm. The golden age of the real-world detective hero was the result of a temporary moment in history, when the best talents could apply themselves to such work as a full-fledged career for the first time, and expanding mass media dazzled the public with their exploits while such effective work was still rare. There is no reason to assume such talents never investigated crimes before Vidocq, and no reason to assume that they ceased with Ellis Parker. Today's best detectives simply operate in a different world, with neither the same opportunity nor the same need for individual miracle workers. Criminal investigation is better equipped and better organized; crime, meanwhile, is probably better contained and certainly different. As William Pinkerton lamented more than a century ago, the spectacular bank robbery plots, just like the train hold-ups of the Old West, have been relegated to another era and now recur only in fiction. The security arrangements that his firm helped American commerce establish have worked well, and the results are largely positive for honest citizens but fatal for would-be Napoleons of Crime.

Lawbreaking continues, obviously, but it too has become organized and businesslike in any kind of large scale activity; individual initiative is relegated mainly to minor, commonplace crimes, or to summertime movies. Al Capone, perhaps America's most infamous "master villain" of the 20th century, achieved notoriety mainly through running a large (and violent) corporation in an industry that happened to be illegal, rather than through astonishing individual crimes. By that same token, it's a central part of Capone's legend that he was ultimately brought down not through deductive reasoning but through accounting. A popular true-crime story ending with the theme of taxation's inescapability might say many things about the modern world, but one of them must be that real-life crime now overlaps much less with adventure drama.

Even the rare exception demonstrates how much life has changed for the best detectives. During three decades with Scotland Yard, Jack Slipper earned a reputation as a smart, hands-on detective. He also investigated a few genuinely remarkable crimes, including the "Great Train Robbery" of 1963, which was every bit as dramatic as anything from the old American West or modern Hollywood fiction. Yet 103 years after Scotland Yard dispatched Jonathan Whicher alone to solve a sensational headline crime, the police response could hardly have been more different. As Slipper notes in his autobiography, "Within forty-eight hours of the robbery, a special unit was formed with the Flying Squad to deal with the Great Train Robbery, and I was delighted to be one of the six officers picked," adding that this six-man team was, moreover, only responsible for "the London end of the investigation." Just as notably, despite an eventual resounding success in rounding up the robbers, after his failure to bring back the fugitive Ronnie Biggs from Brazil, Slipper faced something like the outcry once directed at Whicher. Yet he never really had anything like Whicher's opportunity for personal glory, to balance against it. Faced with this reality, it's small wonder that most real-world detectives now simply do their jobs and leave fame to their fictional counterparts.

Long ago, fictional detective stories drew much of their inspiration from real-life sleuthing. Over the course of a century or so, the two worlds seem to have moved steadily apart from one another, yet in the end appearances may conceal one further clue to the fading of history's great detectives. Stories about investigators remain tremendously popular in books and films and television programs, and most people can name far more detectives who practice in imagination than practiced in reality. Within their own world, though, those detectives are generally no more famous than their counterparts in ours. Readers and viewers know well the names of Philip Marlowe or Lieutenant Columbo, but occupants of their fictional worlds are no more likely to recognize them than the average person is to know the name of a real private eye or homicide detective.

Notable exceptions, like the heroes of Doyle or Christie, are celebrated in both worlds, but are themselves very much legacies of another age. Audiences have willingly grandfathered them in to our own, but when it comes to detectives operating as contemporary figures it seems that celebrity sleuths have simply gone out of vogue, even in fiction. Very possibly they just seem too out of place in a more cynical, postmodern world; too much like superheroes and yet too much like figures who could really exist. Superheroes have enjoyed a renaissance, in recent years, but always as characters in an obvious fantasy world. The detective slowly pursuing inquiries in an entirely believable urban setting, by contrast, is now too much like a health inspector or insurance agent or other ordinary professional: useful, and sometimes exemplary, but too familiar to plausibly credit with superhuman feats.

Thus, the story of great detectives began with innovation and specialization, and the same forces contributed to its end. Alongside them, though, one other factor may explain why real-life detectives who were celebrated in their day have not only been discontinued but almost completely forgotten: people just no longer believe in them.

ACKNOWLEDGEMENTS

Many people deserve thanks for making *Brilliant Deduction* better or, indeed, for helping it exist at all. First and foremost I would like to thank my editor, Judi Brown, for invaluable contributions toward making a first draft manuscript into a book ready for publication. Thanks are also due to Mark Morelli, Wendi Thumudo and Nick Reiter for their early feedback, as well as to Joan Husmann, a.k.a. Mom.

Wikipedia and those who support it also deserve thanks; even if one always seeks corroboration for their articles, The Free Encyclopedia is an unmatched guide to just the sort of near forgotten people and events I have chosen to examine. David Lindecke and William Fullerton, as well as Alicia Clarke of the Sanford Museum, also provided much appreciated aid in my researches.

Sean Kleefeld and Neil Baumhover earned my gratitude in multiple ways. Both served on my informal "design committee," providing welcome direction while I was feeling my way toward a cover design. Sean was also an important inspiration, as another designer who rudely invaded the other side of the page and published his own book, among other things. Neil has been both a longtime friend and generous patron.

Last but certainly not least, I offer my most heartfelt thanks to all of the authors who have explored this territory before me. Your works were indispensable in creating my own, and I sincerely hope that any who enjoy the latter will be inspired to investigate the former. For their generous direct assistance to me, particular thanks are due William Secrest and Linden Publishing, and John Reisinger.

SELECTED SOURCES AND FURTHER READING

In writing *Brilliant Deduction*, I relied heavily on secondary sources as a result of both practical necessity and the nature of the subject I chose to explore. Documenting the entire lives and careers of nine men through primary research would have required time and resources well beyond my means (and, in one case, a considerably greater fluency in French than the limited memories remaining from four years of high school studies). Meanwhile, given that a central part of my purpose was providing further exposure to a relatively little-examined corner of history, the number of existing studies available for individual subjects was often limited.

Fortunately the majority of those studies were not only informative and helpful, but also well written, enjoyable reading. I consulted a number of additional sources to round out my impression of events and personalities, but in most cases these are acknowledged within the text. Therefore, in place of a detailed end-notes section I have elected to highlight selected sources that interested readers might actually seek out and read. The following list includes all of the main sources for each chapter, as well as resources of lesser importance that may be particularly interesting or accessible to the reader, with internet addresses included for all items freely accessible online. Links to this content will also be posted at www.brilliantdeduction.info, along with further notes about the work and its subjects.

GENERAL BACKGROUND

Among the various surveys of detectives and detection, Ramsland's offers the most satisfying reading, in addition to being the most recent and relatively easy to find.

Block, Eugene. *Famous Detectives*. Garden City, New York: Doubleday, 1967.

Hall, Angus. *The Crime Busters*. London: Futura, 2006.

Ramsland, Katherine. *Beating the Devil's Game: a History of Forensic Science and Criminal Investigation*. New York: The Berkley Publishing Group, 2007.

Thorwald, Jürgen. *The Century of the Detective*. New York: Harcourt, Brace & World, Inc., 1965.

VIDOCQ

Of the Vidocq biographies I consulted for *Brilliant Deduction*, Edwards' is my personal recommendation; Stead's is entirely readable for its age, but relies on older research in addition to being at least as difficult to locate. A new biography by James Morton, titled *The First Detective*, appeared after my own researches but may also interest readers looking for more about Vidocq. As might *The Crimes of Paris*, which offers a broader survey of crime and crime fighting in 19th century Paris but includes a substantial section on Vidocq as well as being very lively, entertaining writing.

Borowitz, Albert. "Which the Justice Which the Thief? The Life and Influence of Eugène-François Vidocq." *Legal Studies Forum* 29.2 (2005): 825-837.

Edwards, Samuel. *The Vidocq Dossier: The Story of the World's First Detective*. Boston: Houghton Mifflin Company, 1977.

Hoobler, Dorothy and Thomas. *The Crimes of Paris: A True Story of Murder, Theft, and Detection*. New York: Little, Brown and Co., 2009.

Horne, Alistair. *Seven Ages of Paris*. New York: Random House, 2002.

Stead, Philip John. *Vidocq: A Biography*. London: Staples Press, 1953.

WHICHER

For more information about Jack Whicher and his most infamous case, there is nothing else to compare with Summerscale's history. Happily, it's a thoughtful, tremendously well written work. Dickens' short stories about the early detectives, all available online, are also well worth a read, offering both entertainment and a brevity missing from the serialized novels that such briefer sketches helped inform.

Brown, Roly. "Glimpses into the 19th Century Broadside Ballad Trade: No. 15: Constance Kent and the Road murder." Musical Traditions Internet Magazine, 2005. ☞ http://www.mustrad.org.uk/articles/bbals_15.htm

Browne, Douglas G. *The Rise of Scotland Yard: A History*. New York: G.P. Putman's Sons, 1956.

Dickens, Charles. "Three 'Detective' Anecdotes." Reprinted Pieces. eBooks @ Adelaide, 2006.
☞ http://ebooks.adelaide.edu.au/d/dickens/charles/d54rp/chapter15.html

———. "The Detective Police." Reprinted Pieces. eBooks @ Adelaide, 2006.
☞ http://ebooks.adelaide.edu.au/d/dickens/charles/d54rp/chapter14.html

Summerscale, Kate. *The Suspicions of Mr. Whicher: A Shocking Murder and the Undoing of a Great Victorian Detective*. New York: Walker Publishing Company, Inc., 2008.

Woodruff, Douglas. *The Tichborne Claimant: A Victorian Mystery*. New York: Farrar, Straus & Cudahy, 1957.

PINKERTONS

All three of my major sources for the chapters on the Pinkertons have their pros and cons. The newer works incorporate more recent research, in addition to being easier to find; Morn's prose is more dry, however, while Mackay seems insistent on proving his subject faultless, and on repeatedly deprecating Horan in the process. Horan's own work is by far the most complete and engaging narrative, in my opinion, though in addition to being long out of print, it sacrifices something to the author's attempt to shoehorn social criticism into what even he often couldn't help turning into a colorful adventure yarn. Horan's and Morn's books cover Allan, his sons, and brief notes about the later agency; Mackay's focuses on Allan alone.

"The Homestead Strike." *American Experience: The Richest Man in the World: Andrew Carnegie*. PBS Online, 1999.
☞ http://www.pbs.org/wgbh/amex/carnegie/peopleevents/pande04.html

Horan, James D. *The Pinkertons: The Detective Dynasty that Made History*. New York: Crown Publishers, Inc., 1967.

Mackay, James. *Allan Pinkerton: The First Private Eye*. New York: John Wiley & Sons, 1996.

McElderry, Michael, et al. *Pinkerton's National Detective Agency: A Register of Its Records in the Library of Congress*. Washington, DC: Manuscript Division, Library of Congress, 2001.
☞ http://lcweb2.loc.gov/service/mss/eadxmlmss/eadpdfmss/2003/ms003007.pdf

Miller, Donald. *City of the Century: The Epic of Chicago and the Making of America*. New York: Touchstone, 1997.

Morn, Frank. *The Eye that Never Sleeps*. Bloomington, Indiana: Indiana University Press, 1982.

Pinkerton, Allan. *The Expressman and the Detective*. New York: Arno Press, 1976.
☞ Also @ http://www.gutenberg.org/ebooks/22155

Weiser, Kathy. *The Pinkerton Detective Agency – Operating for 150 Years*. Legends of America, 2011.
☞ http://www.legendsofamerica.com/we-pinkertons.html

POLLAKY

No detective has traversed such polar extremes of fame and obscurity as Ignatius Pollaky. He still awaits his first real published biography, at this writing; in the meantime the present work is, in all modesty, the closest thing available. That said, much credit must be given to Derek Ross for the Wikipedia article he has pieced together over a number of years, almost singlehandedly. His detailed scholarship and ready discussion of the subject were invaluable in pointing me toward and helping me organize the other sources I consulted, mostly 19th century British newspaper archives. These, thankfully, are scanned and searchable, though unless one's library subscribes to the appropriate archive service one may have to pay a small fee for access; the indispensable *Argus* story noted below is, however, free.

Dickens, Charles. "Small-Beer Chronicles." *All the Year Round*. 20 June 1863: 404-407.
☞ http://www.djo.org.uk/all-the-year-round/volume-ix/page-404.html

Drydon, Vaughan. "Very Odd Fellows — No. 1: Pollaky: The Detective of Genius: A Sherlock Holmes in Real Life." *The Argus* [Melbourne] 9 June 1934, sec: 1:6.
☞ http://nla.gov.au/nla.news-page561331

The Henry Shelton Sanford Papers. Sanford Museum, Sanford, Florida.

Ross, Derek, et al. "Ignatius Paul Pollaky." *Wikipedia, The Free Encyclopedia*. Wikipedia, The Free Encyclopedia, 2012.
☞ http://en.wikipedia.org/wiki/Ignatius_Paul_Pollaky

LEES

All of the following sources for my account of Isaiah Lees are interesting and worth-while reading, though as with Whicher, one work stands far above the others (and a famous literary contemporary's writings offer some amusing firsthand observations, with the added virtue of being available online). Secrest's biography is both a fascinating account of Lees and, with due respect to Doris Muscatine, also a very credible introduction to "Old San Francisco" itself. None of Twain's dispatches from the era rise to quite the level of narrative as Dickens' detective sketches, but occasional flashes of cynical humor reward reading, all the same.

Lapp, Rudolph M. *Archy Lee: A California Fugitive Slave Case*. San Francisco: The Book Club of California, 1969.

Muscatine, Doris. *Old San Francisco: The Biography of a City From Early Days to the Earthquake*. New York: G.P. Putnam's Sons, 1975.

McConnell, Virginia A. *Sympathy for the Devil: the Emmanuel Baptist Murders of Old San Francisco*. Westport, Connecticut: Praeger Publishers, 2001.

Secrest, William B. *Dark and Tangled Threads of Crime: San Francisco's famous police detective Isaiah W. Lees*. Sanger, California: Word Dancer Press, 2004.

Twain, Mark. *Mark Twain quotations: Newspaper & Magazine Writings*. Barbara Schmidt, 1997.
☞ http://twainquotes.com/newspapercollections.html

BURNS

William Burns was complicated, and even chimaerical, and writing on his life and career reflects this. The best single source is probably Hunt's biography, incorporating better scholarship than Caesar's earlier attempt. Hunt's book is also partly a work of social criticism rather than a dedicated biography and, like Horan, he nonetheless fails to buttress his own arguments at times, leaving them slightly awkward and out of place. If one wants the very worst aspects of Burns, factual and rumored, McCartney's brief notes on Burns's role in the "Ohio Gang" cede primacy to no one. For my own part, Caesar's biography is easily the most enjoyable and entertaining work about Burns if one can find it, though as a source for research it should be checked against another source whenever possible.

Caesar, Gene. *The Incredible Detective: The Biography of William J. Burns.* Englewood Cliffs, New Jersey: Prentice-Hall, 1968.

Costello, Peter. *Conan Doyle: Detective.* New York: Carroll & Graf Publishers, Inc., 2006.

Edwards, Owen Dudley. Introduction. *The Valley of Fear.* By Arthur Conan Doyle. New York: Oxford University Press, 1993.

"Great Cases of Detective Burns: The Monroe-head Counterfeit." *McClure's Magazine.* Nov. 1910: 36.

Hunt, William R. *Front Page Detective: William J. Burns and the Detective Profession 1880-1930.* Bowling Green, Ohio: Bowling Green State University Popular Press, 1990.

McCartney, Laton. *The Teapot Dome Scandal: How Big Oil Bought the Harding White House & Tried to Steal the Country.* New York: Random House, 2008.

"William J. Burns." *FBI.* The Federal Bureau of Investigation.
☞ http://www.fbi.gov/about-us/history/directors/burns

PARKER

It's nearly impossible to find *The Cunning Mulatto* and exceedingly unlikely that anyone will reissue it. Fortunately for modern audiences, John Reisinger tracked down a copy, along with the greater part of those traces of Ellis Parker's life that still survive; the resulting biography is a true pleasure to read. Original newspaper accounts of Parker are also frequently quite entertaining, themselves, and many are easily accessible thanks to the web site maintained by Parker's great-grandson, Pat Fullerton. Meanwhile, works on the Lindbergh case could likely fill their own book-length bibliography, but for the bewildered, the site maintained by Patrick Ranfranz offers a very helpful, concise introduction to all of the main players and events.

Reisinger, John. *Master Detective: The Life and Crimes of Ellis Parker, America's Real-Life Sherlock Holmes*. New York: Citadel Press / Kensington Publishing, 2006.

The Ellis H. Parker Tribute Page. William and Patrick Fullerton, 2007.
☞ http://www.patfullerton.com/ellisparkerhome.html

Ranfranz, Pat. "Lindbergh Kidnapping." *Charles Lindberg: An American Aviator*. Pat Ranfranz, 2007.
☞ http://www.charleslindbergh.com/kidnap/index.asp

INDEX

Emperor Norton. *See* Norton I, Emperor
Expressman and the Detective, The 92, 94, 95, 106, 315

F

Farrington gang 189–191, 197, 205
FBI (Federal Bureau of Investigation) 108, 260–264, 266, 270, 291, 292, 294, 305, 307, 308
fictional detectives. *See* detective fiction
Field, Charles Frederick 50, 53, 64, 115, 116, 119, 122, 123, 126, 138
fingerprinting 18, 171, 199, 219, 262, 287
Forni, Jose 148, 149, 177
Frank, Leo 256–258. *See also* Phagan murder case
Furlong, Tom 229, 232

G

Gammon, L.W. 215, 216, 247
Gilbert & Sullivan 112, 131, 142
Gold Rush 146
Greenhow, Rose 99, 120

H

Harding, Warren G. 261, 263, 265
Harpending, Asbury 161
Hauptmann, Bruno 292, 294–296, 298
Hazen, William 2, 231, 232
Hearst, William R. 181, 243–245
Heney, Francis 243–245
Heyneman, Otto 175, 177
Hickox & Spear 164
Hoffman, Harold 291, 295, 296, 299, 301
Holdsworth, Lionel 126, 127
Holmes, H.H. 4, 208
Holmes, Sherlock 2, 4, 7, 37, 39, 77, 137–139, 142, 164, 223, 224, 269, 289, 308
Homestead strike 201–204, 212, 219, 220, 246, 248, 315
Hoover, J. Edgar 108, 109, 292, 307, 308
Horan, James 87, 97, 98, 101, 108, 187, 192, 193, 197, 199, 205, 210, 224, 315, 317
horse racing 134, 204–206, 212
Hunt, William R. 224, 228, 232, 248, 253, 258, 262, 264, 304

I

International Assocation of Chiefs of Police 216, 258
Iowa 102, 188

K

Kearny Street 151, 167, 168, 169
Kehoe, Jack 206, 207
Keller, Otto 277, 278
Kempton, Murray 108, 307
Kent, Constance 43, 44, 55–60, 62, 63, 68, 72, 111, 112, 298, 314
  confession 59, 60, 62–63, 72, 112, 298
  nightdress 57, 58, 60, 111
Kent, Francis Saville 43, 54–58, 60, 61, 63, 111, 290
Ku Klux Klan 258, 262

L

labor unions 106, 201–203, 248, 249, 253, 255, 262, 304
LaFourge, Maria 143–145, 152
land fraud case 240–241, 258
Larches, The 106
Leary, Red 197, 198, 205
Lee, Archy 155, 156, 160, 316
Lees, Isaiah W. 7, 143–183, 191, 195, 197, 208, 211, 214, 242, 243, 272, 275–276, 307
  as chief of police 163, 178–181
Lees, Jane 147, 149, 150, 153, 171, 179
Left-Sided Man case 276–278
Lincoln, Abraham 76, 88, 95–98, 100, 106, 108, 208, 245
Lindbergh, Charles A. 290
Lindbergh kidnapping case 269, 270, 290–295, 297, 298, 305, 307, 317, 318
Lollipop Inn 280, 282
Lomax, John 130–132, 137
London 37, 44–47, 49, 53, 54, 59, 63, 64, 67, 70, 72, 111–114, 116, 118–123, 125, 129, 132, 133, 135, 137–142, 148, 160, 166, 192, 193, 198, 209, 210, 217, 219, 297, 309, 313, 314
Los Angeles Times bombing 247, 248–255, 265, 286

M

Macé, Gustave 7, 170, 177
Maroney, Nathan 92–95, 208
Mayne, Sir Richard 53, 62

ABOUT THE AUTHOR

Matt Kuhns grew up in small-town Iowa, graduating with honors from Iowa State University. In his always eventful career as a graphic designer, he has worked for a private university, a boutique design studio and a craft products retail chain, as well as various nonprofit institutions and several advertising agencies. He currently operates his own independent design practice as Modern Alchemy LLC. He lives in Lakewood, Ohio. This is his first book.

www.ingramcontent.com/pod-product-compliance
Lightning Source LLC
Chambersburg PA
CBHW020604270326
41927CB00005B/167